GREAT AMERICAN GHOST STORIES

Great American Ghost Stories

Hans Holzer

DORSET PRESS · · · New York

This collection published by Dorset Press,
a division of Marboro Books Corporation,
by arrangement with Hans Holzer.
1990 Dorset Press
ISBN 0-88029-556-2

Printed in the United States of America

M 9 8 7 6 5 4 3 2

Contents

Introduction

Contemporary science all too easily brushes aside any notions smacking of life after death because they do not comfortably fit into the framework of twentieth century empiricism. The trend is to view phenomena so that they can be accounted for or confirmed within the limits of our physical world. But truth does not necessarily lie in occurances which are physically and regularly verifiable.

Included in this anthology are what I have found to be the most provocative and entertaining stories from my several books on hauntings and my thorough investigations of them. I find that definite patterns are emerging, patterns which defy the caveats of traditional scientists who rigidly ignore the manifold signs that ghosts in fact are a part of our world.

One finding that becomes obvious in the very first of our accounts is that ghosts are not Halloween pranks. These real ones bear scant resemblance to the "ghosts" to which most of us have been exposed as children, the classic white blob with two eye holes, and a propensity for hollering "booo". Rather, it appears, the world is full or unresolved psychic issues where some poor soul, having left its phsyical body tragically, either unexpectedly, even violently or after long suffering, is unable or unwilling to adjust to the state that follows—a kind of limbo—neither of this world, nor yet the next. For surely there is a next state into which we all must pass before we eventually return to this dimension to continue the eternal cycle of life and death.

When investigating reported hauntings and ghostly disturbances, I find that these other-world beings are not so much intent on frightening us, but rather, Flying-Dutchman-like, want to call attention to their plight in the hope that they may be redeemed through the intervention of an understanding person and sent onward to the next state of existence.

What if the investigation and evaluation of ghostly phenomena occurred not within the narrow limits of conventional science, but with an openness meant to include all the possible answers to unanswered questions? We might find that ghosts and hauntings, while the exception to the norm in passing from one dimension into another, are nevertheless part of human experience, just as are automobile accidents or illnesses. They have a place in the world of the living, though ghosts ar no longer part of it in the literal sense.

Be kind to ghosts, if you happen to run into one or one happens to run into you. There, but for the Grace of God, goes you or someone you know.

Hans Holzer, Ph.D.

New York, Oct. 31, 1989

1

"Ocean-Born" Mary

Among the ghostly legends of the United States, that of "Ocean-Born" Mary and her fascinating house at Henniker, New Hampshire, is probably one of the best known. To the average literate person who has heard about the colorful tale of Mary Wallace, or the New Englander who knows of it because he lives "Down East," it is, of course, a legend—not to be taken too seriously.

I had a vague idea of its substance when I received a note from a lady named Corinne Russell, who together with her husband, David, had bought the Henniker house and wanted me to know that it was still haunted.

That was in October of 1963. It so happens that Halloween is the traditional date on which the ghost of six-foot Mary Wallace is supposed to "return" to her house in a coach drawn by six horses. On many a Halloween, youngsters from all around Henniker have come and sat around the grounds waiting for Mary to ride in. The local press had done its share of Halloween ghost hunting, so much so that the Russells had come to fear that date as one of the major nuisance days of their year.

After all, Halloween visitors do not pay the usual fee to be shown about the house, but they do leave behind them destruction and litter at times. Needless to say, nobody has ever seen Mary ride in her coach on Halloween. Why should she when she lives there *all year round?*

To explain this last statement, I shall have to take you back to the year 1720, when a group of Scottish and Irish immigrants was approaching the New World aboard a ship called the *Wolf*, from Londonderry, Ireland. The ship's captain, Wilson, had just become the father of a daughter, who was actually born at sea. Within sight of land, the ship was boarded by pirates under the command of a buccaneer named Don Pedro. As the pirates removed all valuables from their prize, Don Pedro went below to the captain's cabin. Instead of gold, he found Mrs. Wilson and her newborn baby girl.

"What's her name?" he demanded.

Unafraid, the mother replied that the child had not yet been baptized, having been recently born.

"If you will name her after my mother, Mary," the pirate said, overcome with an emotion few pirates ever allow into their lives, "I will spare everybody aboard this ship."

Joyously, the mother made the bargain, and "Ocean-Born" Mary received her name. Don Pedro ordered his men to hand back what they had already taken from their prisoners, to set them free, and to leave the captured ship. The vicious-looking crew grumbled and withdrew to their own ship.

Minutes later, however, Don Pedro returned alone. He handed Mrs. Wilson a bundle of silk.

"For Mary's wedding gown," he said simply, and left again.

As soon as the pirate ship was out of sight, the *Wolf* continued her voyage for Boston. Thence Captain and Mrs. Wilson went on to their new home in Londonderry, New Hampshire, where they settled down, and where Mary grew up.

"Ocean-Born" Mary

When she was 18, she married a man named Wallace, and over the years they had four sons. However, shortly after the birth of the fourth son, her husband died and Mary found herself a widow.

Meanwhile, Don Pedro—allegedly an Englishman using the Spanish *nom de pirate* to disguise his noble ancestry—had kept in touch with the Wilsons. Despite the hazards of pirate life, he survived to an old age when thoughts of retirement filled his mind. Somehow he managed to acquire a land grant of 6,000 acres in what is now Henniker, New Hampshire, far away from the sea. On this land, Pedro built himself a stately house. He employed his ship's carpenters, as can be seen in the way the beams are joined. Ship's carpenters have a special way of building, and "Ocean-Born" Mary's house, as it later became known, is an example of this.

The house was barely finished when the aging pirate heard of Mary Wallace's loss of her husband, and he asked Mary and her children to come live with him. She accepted his invitation, and soon became his housekeeper.

The house was then in a rather isolated part of New England, and few callers, if any, came to interrupt the long stillness of the many cold winter nights. Mary took up painting and with her own hands created the eagle that can still be seen gracing the house.

The years went by peacefully, until one night someone attacked Don Pedro and killed him. Whether one of his men had come to challenge the pirate captain for part of the booty, or whether the reputation of a retired pirate had put ideas of treasure in the mind of some local thief, we may never know. All we know is that by the time Mary Wallace got out into the grove at the rear of the house, Don Pedro way dying with a pirate cutlass in his chest. He asked her to bury him under the hearthstone in the kitchen, which is in the rear of the house.

Mary herself inherited the house and what went with it, treasure, buried pirate, and all. She herself passed on in 1814, and ever since then the house had been changing hands.

Unfortunately, we cannot interview the earlier owners of the house, but during the 1930s, it belonged to one Louis Roy, retired and disabled and a permanent guest in what used to be his home. He sold the house to the Russells in the early sixties.

During the great hurricane of 1938, Roy claims that Mary Wallace's ghost saved his life 19 times. Trapped outside the house by falling trees, he somehow was able to get back into the house. His very psychic mother, Mrs. Roy, informed him that she had actually seen the tall, stately figure of "Ocean-Born" Mary moving behind him, as if to help him get through. In the 1950s, *Life* told this story in an illustrated article on famous ghost-haunted houses in America. Mrs. Roy claimed she had seen the ghost of Mary time and time again, but since she herself passed on in 1948, I could not get any details from *her*.

Then there were two state troopers who saw the ghost, but again I could not interview them, as they, too, were also on the other side of the veil.

A number of visitors claimed to have felt "special vibrations" when touching the hearthstone, where Don Pedro allegedly was buried. There was, for instance, Mrs. James Nisula of Londonderry, who visited the house several times. She said that she and her "group" of ghost buffs had "felt the vibrations" around the kitchen. Mrs. David Russell, the owner who contacted me, felt nothing.

I promised to look into the "Ocean-Born" Mary haunting the first chance I got. Halloween or about that time would be all right with me, and I wouldn't wait around for any coach!

"There is a lady medium I think you should know," Mrs. Russell said when I spoke of bringing a psychic with me. "She saw Mary the very first time she came here."

My curiosity aroused, I communicated with the lady. She

4

asked that I not use her married name, although she was not so shy several months after our visit to the house, when she gave a two-part interview to a Boston newspaper columnist. (Needless to say, the interview was not authorized by me, since I never allow mediums I work with to talk about their cases for publication. Thus Lorrie shall remain without a family name and anyone wishing to reach this medium will have to do so without my help.)

Lorrie wrote me she would be happy to serve the cause of truth, and I could count on her. There was nothing she wanted in return.

We did not get up to New Hampshire that Halloween. Mr. Russell had to have an operation, the house was unheated in the winter except for Mr. Roy's room, and New England winters are cold enough to freeze any ghost.

Although there was a caretaker at the time to look after the house and Mr. Roy upstairs, the Russells did not stay at the house in the winter, but made their home in nearby Chelmsford, Massachusetts.

I wrote Mrs. Russell postponing the investigation until spring. Mrs. Russell accepted my decision with some disappointment, but she was willing to wait. After all, the ghost at "Ocean-Born" Mary's house is not a malicious type. Mary Wallace just lived there, ever since she died in 1814, and you can't call a lady who likes to hold on to what is hers an intruder.

"We don't want to drive her out," Mrs. Russell repeatedly said to me. "After all, it *is* her house!"

Not many haunted-house owners make statements like that.

But something had happened at the house since our last conversation.

"Our caretaker dropped a space heater all the way down the stairs at the 'Ocean-Born' Mary house, and when it reached the bottom, the kerosene and the flames started to burn the stairs and climb the wall. There was no water in the house, so my husband went out after snow. While I stood there looking at the fire and powerless to do anything about it, the fire went right out all by itself right in front of my eyes; when my husband got back with the snow it was out. It was just as if someone *had smothered it with a blanket.*"

This was in December of 1963. I tried to set a new date, as soon as possible, and February 22 seemed possible. This time I would bring Bob Kennedy of WBZ, Boston and the "Contact" producer Squire Rushnell with me to record my investigation.

Lorrie was willing, asking only that her name not be mentioned.

"I don't want anyone to know about my being different from them," she explained. "When I was young my family used to accuse me of spying because I knew things from the pictures I saw when I touched objects."

Psychometry, I explained, is very common among psychics, and nothing to be ashamed of.

I thought it was time to find out more about Lorrie's experiences at the haunted house.

"I first saw the house in September of 1961," she began. "It was on a misty, humid day, and there was a haze over the fields."

Strange, I thought, I always get my best psychic results when the atmosphere is moist.

Lorrie, who was in her early forties, was Vermont born and raised; she was married and had one daughter, Pauline. She was a tall redhead with sparkling eyes, and, come to think of it, not unlike the accepted picture of the ghostly Mary Wallace. Coincidence?

A friend of Lorrie's had seen the eerie house and suggested she go and see it also. That was all Lorrie knew about it, and she

6

did not really expect anything uncanny to occur. Mr. Roy showed Lorrie and her daughter through the house and nothing startling happened. They left and started to walk down the entrance steps, crossing the garden in front of the house, and had reached the gate when Pauline clutched at her mother's arm and said:

"Mamma, what is that?"

Lorrie turned to look back at the house. In the upstairs window, a woman stood and looked out at them. Lorrie's husband was busy with the family car. Eventually, she called out to him, but as he turned to look, the apparition was gone.

She did not think of it again, and the weeks went by. But the house kept intruding itself into her thoughts more and more. Finally she could not restrain herself any longer, and returned to the house—even though it was 120 miles from her home in Weymouth, Massachusetts.

She confessed her extraordinary experience to the owner, and together they examined the house from top to bottom. She finally returned home.

She promised Roy she would return on All Hallow's Eve to see if the legend of Mary Wallace had any basis of fact. Unfortunately, word of her intentions got out, and when she finally arrived at the house, she had to sneak in the back to avoid the sensation-hungry press outside. During the days between her second visit and Halloween, the urge to go to Henniker kept getting stronger, as if someone were possessing her.

By that time the Russells were negotiating to buy the house, and Lorrie came up with them. Nothing happened to her that Halloween night. Perhaps she was torn between fear and a desire to fight the influence that had brought her out to Henniker to begin with.

Mediums, to be successful, must learn to relax and not allow their own notions to rule them. All through the following winter and summer, Lorrie fought the desire to return to "Ocean-

Born" Mary's house. To no avail. She returned time and time again, sometimes alone and sometimes with a friend.

Things got out of hand one summer night when she was home alone.

Exhausted from her last visit—the visits always left her an emotional wreck—she went to bed around 9:30 P.M.

"What happened that night?" I interjected. She seemed shaken even now.

"At 11 P.M., Mr. Holzer," Lorrie replied, "I found myself driving on the expressway, wearing my pajamas and robe, with no shoes or slippers, or money, or even a handkerchief. I was ten miles from my home and heading for Henniker. Terrified, I turned around and returned home, only to find my house ablaze with light, the doors open as I had left them, and the garage lights on. I must have left in an awful hurry."

"Have you found out why you are being pulled back to that house?"

She shook her head.

"No idea. But I've been back twice, even after that. I just can't seem to stay away from that house."

I persuaded her that perhaps there was a job to be done in that house, and the ghost wanted her to do it.

We did not go to Henniker in February, because of bad weather. We tried to set a date in May, 1964. The people from WBZ decided Henniker was too far away from Boston and dropped out of the planning.

Summer came around, and I went to Europe instead of Henniker. However, the prospect of a visit in the fall was very much in my mind.

It seemed as if someone were keeping me away from the house very much in the same way someone was pulling Lorrie toward it!

Come October, and we were really on our way, at last.

"Ocean-Born" Mary

Owen Lake, a public relations man who dabbles in psychic matters, introduced himself as "a friend" of mine and told Lorrie he'd come along, too. I had never met the gentleman, but in the end he could not make it anyway. So just four of us—my wife Catherine and I, Lorrie, and her nice, even-tempered husband, who had volunteered to drive us up to New Hampshire—started out from Boston. It was close to Halloween, all right, only two days before. If Mary Wallace were out haunting the countryside in her coach, we might very well run into her. The coach is out of old Irish folktales; it appears in numerous ghost stories of the Ould Sod. I'm sure that in the telling and retelling of the tale of Mary and her pirate, the coach got added.

The countryside is beautiful in a New England fall. As we rolled toward the New Hampshire state line, I asked Lorrie some more questions.

"When you first saw the ghost of 'Ocean-Born' Mary at the window of the house, Lorrie," I said, "what did she look like?"

"A lovely lady in her thirties, with auburn-colored hair, smiling rather intensely and thoughtfully. She stayed there for maybe three minutes, and then suddenly, *she just wasn't there.*"

"What about her dress?"

"It was a white dress."

Lorrie never saw an apparition of Mary again, but whenever she touched anything in the Henniker house, she received an impression of what the house was like when Mary had it, and she had felt her near the big fireplace several times.

Did she ever get an impression of what it was Mary wanted?

"She was a quick-tempered woman; I sensed that very strongly," Lorrie replied. "I have been to the house maybe twenty times altogether, and still don't know why. She just keeps pulling me there."

Lorrie had always felt the ghost's presence on these visits.

"One day I was walking among the bushes in the back of the house. I was wearing shorts, but I never got a scratch on my legs, because I kept feeling heavy skirts covering my legs. I could feel the brambles pulling at this invisible skirt I had on. I felt enveloped by something, or someone."

Mrs. Roy, the former owner's mother, had told of seeing the apparition many times, Lorrie stated.

"As a matter of fact, I have sensed her ghost in the house, too, but it is not a friendly wraith like Mary is."

Had she ever encountered this other ghost?

"Yes, my arm was grabbed one time by a malevolent entity," Lorrie said emphatically. "It was two years ago, and I was standing in what is now the living room, and my arm was taken by the elbow and pulled.

"I snatched my arm back, because I felt she was not friendly."

"What were you doing at the time that she might have objected to?"

"I really don't know."

Did she know of anyone else who had had an uncanny experience at the house?

"A strange thing happened to Mrs. Roy," Lorrie said. "A woman came to the house and said to her, 'What do you mean, the *rest* of the house?' The woman replied, 'Well, I was here yesterday, and a tall woman let me in and showed me half of the house.' But, of course, there was nobody at the house that day."

What about the two state troopers? Could she elaborate on their experience?

"They met her walking down the road that leads to the house. She was wearing a Colonial-type costume, and they found that odd. Later they realized they had seen a ghost, especially as no one of her description lived in the house at the time."

Rudi D., Lorrie's husband, was a hospital technician. He

was with her on two or three occasions when she visited the house. Did he ever feel anything special?

"The only thing unusual I ever felt at the house was that I wanted to get out of there fast," he said.

"The very first time we went up," Lorrie added," something kept pulling me toward it, but my husband insisted we go back. There was an argument about our continuing the trip, when suddenly the door of the car flew open of its own volition. Somehow we decided to continue on to the house."

An hour later, we drove up a thickly overgrown hill and along a winding road at the end of which the "Ocean-Born" Mary house stood in solitary stateliness, a rectangular building of gray stone and brown trim, very well preserved.

We parked the car and walked across the garden that sets the house well back from the road. There was peace and autumn in the air. We were made welcome by Corinne Russell, her husband David, and two relatives who happened to be with them that day. Entering the main door beneath a magnificent early American eagle, we admired the fine wooden staircase leading to the upstairs—the staircase on which the mysterious fire had taken place—and then entered the room to the left of it, where the family had assembled around an old New England stove.

During the three years the Russells had lived at the house, nothing uncanny had happened to Mrs. Russell, except for the incident with the fire. David Russell, a man almost typical of the shrewd New England Yankee who weighs his every word, was willing to tell me about *his* experiences, however.

"The first night I ever slept in what we call the Lafayette room, upstairs, there was quite a thundershower on, and my dog and I were upstairs. I always keep my dog with me, on account of the boys coming around to do damage to the property.

"Just as I lay down in bed, I heard very heavy footsteps. They sounded to me to be in the two rooms which we had just

11

restored, on the same floor. I was quite annoyed, almost fright-ened, and I went into the rooms, but there was nobody there or anywhere else in the house."

"Interesting," I said. "Was there more?"

"Now this happened only last summer. A few weeks later, when I was in that same room, I was getting undressed when I suddenly heard somebody pound on my door. I said to myself, "Oh, it's only the house settling," and I got into bed. A few min-utes later, the door knob turned back and forth. I jumped out of bed, opened the door, and there was absolutely nobody there. The only other people in the house at the time were the invalid Mr. Roy, locked in his room, and my wife downstairs."

What about visual experiences?

"No, but I went to the cellar not long ago with my dog, about four in the afternoon, or rather tried to—this dog never leaves me, but on this particular occasion, something kept her from going with me into the cellar. Her hair stood up and she would not budge."

The Lafayette room, by the way, is the very room in which the pirate, Don Pedro, is supposed to have lived. The Russells did nothing to change the house structurally, only restored it as it had been and generally cleaned it up.

I now turned to Florence Harmon, an elderly neighbor of the Russells, who had some recollections about the house. Mrs. Harmon recalls the house when she herself was very young, long before the Russells came to live in it.

"Years later, I returned to the house and Mrs. Roy asked me whether I could help her locate 'the treasure' since I was reputed to be psychic."

Was there really a treasure?

"If there was, I think it was found," Mrs. Harmon said. "At the time Mrs. Roy talked to me, she also pointed out that there were two elm trees on the grounds—the only two elm trees around. They looked like some sort of markers to her. But before the Roys had the house, a Mrs. Morrow lived here. I know this from my uncle, who was a stone mason, and who built a vault for her."

I didn't think Mrs. Harmon had added anything material to my knowledge of the treasure, so I thanked her and turned my attention to the other large room, on the right hand side of the staircase. Nicely furnished with period pieces, it boasted a fireplace flanked by sofas, and had a rectangular piano in the corner. The high windows were curtained on the sides, and one could see the New England landscape through them.

We seated ourselves around the fireplace and hoped that Mary would honor us with a visit. Earlier I had inspected the entire house, the hearthstone under which Don Pedro allegedly lay buried, and the small bedrooms upstairs where David Russell had heard the footsteps. Each of us had stood at the window in the corridor upstairs and stared out of it, very much the way the ghost must have done when she was observed by Lorrie and her daughter.

And now it was Mary's turn.

"This was her room," Lorrie explained, "and I do feel her presence." But she refused to go into trance, afraid to "let go." Communication would have to be via clairvoyance, with Lorrie as the interpreter. This was not what I had hoped for. Nevertheless we would try to evaluate whatever material we could obtain.

"Sheet and quill," Lorrie said now, and a piece of paper was handed her along with a pencil. Holding it on her lap, Lorrie was poised to write, if Mary wanted to use her hand, so to speak. The pencil suddenly jumped from Lorrie's hand with considerable force.

"Proper quill," the ghost demanded.

I explained about the shape of quills these days, and handed Lorrie my own pencil.

"Look lady," Lorrie explained to the ghost. "I'll show you it writes. I'll write my name."

And she wrote in her own, smallish, rounded hand, "Lorrie."

There was a moment of silence. Evidently, the ghost was thinking it over. Then Lorrie's hand, seemingly not under her own control, wrote with a great deal of flourish "Mary Wallace." The "M" and "W" had curves and ornamentation typical of eighteenth-century calligraphy. It was not at all like Lorrie's own handwriting.

"Tell her to write some more. The quill is working," I commanded.

Lorrie seemed to be upset by something the ghost told her.

"No," she said. "I can't do that. No."

"What does she want?" I asked.

"She wants me to sleep, but I won't do it."

Trance, I thought—even the ghost demands it. It would have been so interesting to have Mary speak directly to us through Lorrie's entranced lips. You can lead a medium to the ghost, but you can't make her go under if she's scared.

Lorrie instead told the ghost to tell *her*, or to write through her. But no trance, thank you. Evidently, the ghost did not like to be told how to communicate. We waited. Then I suggested that Lorrie be very relaxed and it would be "like sleep" so the ghost could talk to us directly.

"She's very much like me, but not so well trimmed," the ghost said of Lorrie. Had she picked her to carry her message because of the physical resemblance, I wondered.

"She's waiting for Young John," Lorrie now said. Not young John. The stress was on young. Perhaps it was one name—Young-john.

"It happened in the north pasture," Mary said through

14

"Ocean-Born" Mary

Lorrie now. "He killed Warren Langerford. The Frazier boys found the last bone."

I asked why it concerned her. Was she involved? But there was no reply.

Then the ghost of Mary introduced someone else standing next to her.

"Mrs. Roy is with her, because she killed her daughter," Lorrie said, hesitatingly, and added, on her own, "but I don't believe she did." Later we found out that the ghost was perhaps not lying, but of course nobody had any proof of such a crime—if it were indeed a crime.

"Why do you stay on in this house?" I asked.

"This house is my house, h-o-u-s-e!" "Ocean-Born" Mary reminded me.

"Do you realize you are what is commonly called dead?" I demanded. As so often with ghosts, the question brought on resistance to face reality. Mary seemed insulted and withdrew.

I addressed the ghost openly, offering to help her, and at the same time explaining her present position to her. This was her chance to speak up.

"She's very capricious," Lorrie said. "When you said you'd bring her peace, she started to laugh."

But Mary was gone, for the present anyway.

We waited, and tried again a little later. This time Lorrie said she heard a voice telling her to come back tonight.

"We can't," I decided. "If she wants to be helped, it will have to be now."

Philip Babb, the pirate's real name (as I discovered later), allegedly had built a secret passage under the house. The Russells were still looking for it. There were indeed discrepancies in the thickness of some of the walls, and there were a number of secret holes that didn't lead anywhere. But no passage. Had the pirate taken his secrets to his grave?

15

I found our experience at Henniker singularly unsatisfactory since no real evidence had been forthcoming from the ghost herself. No doubt another visit would have to be made, but I didn't mind that at all. "Ocean-Born" Mary's place was a place one can easily visit time and again. The rural charm of the place and the timeless atmosphere of the old house made it a first-rate tourist attraction. Thousands of people came to the house every year.

We returned to New York and I thought no more about it until I received a letter from James Caron, who had heard me discuss the house on the "Contact" program in Boston. He had been to the house in quest of pirate lore and found it very much haunted.

James Caron was in the garage business at Bridgewater, Massachusetts. He had a high school and trade school education, and was married, with two children. Searching for stories of buried treasure and pirates was a hobby of his, and he sometimes lectured on it. He had met Gus Roy about six years before. Roy complained that his deceased mother was trying to contact him for some reason. Her picture kept falling off the wall where it was hung, and he constantly felt "a presence." Would Mr. Caron know of a good medium?

In August of 1959, James Caron brought a spiritualist named Paul Amsdent to the "Ocean-Born" Mary house. Present at the ensuing séance were Harold Peters, a furniture salesman; Hugh Blanchard, a lawyer; Ernest Walbourne, a fireman, and brother-in-law of Caron; Gus Roy; and Mr. Caron himself. Tape recording the séance, Caron had trouble with his equipment. Strange sounds kept intruding. Unfortunately, there was among those present someone with hostility toward psychic work, and Gus Roy's mother did not manifest. However, something else did happen.

"There appear to be people buried somewhere around or

in the house," the medium Amsdent said, "enclosed by a stone wall of some sort."

I thought of the hearthstone and of Mrs. Harmon's vault. Coincidence?

Mr. Caron used metal detectors all over the place to satisfy Gus Roy that there was no "pirate treasure" buried in or near the house.

A little later, James Caron visited the house again. This time he was accompanied by Mrs. Caron and Mr. and Mrs. Walbourne. Both ladies were frightened by the sound of a heavy door opening and closing with no one around and no air current in the house.

Mrs. Caron had a strong urge to go to the attic, but Mr. Caron stopped her. Ernest Walbourne, a skeptic, was alone in the so-called "death" room upstairs, looking at some pictures stacked in a corner. Suddenly, he clearly heard a female voice telling him to get out of the house. He looked around, but there was nobody upstairs. Frightened, he left the house at once and later required medication for a nervous condition!

Again, things quieted down as far as "Ocean-Born" Mary was concerned, until I saw a lengthy story—two parts, in fact—in the *Boston Record-American*, in which my erstwhile medium Lorrie had let her hair down to columnist Harold Banks.

It seemed that Lorrie could not forget Henniker, after all. With publicist Owen Lake, she returned to the house in November, 1964, bringing with her some oil of wintergreen, which she claimed Mary Wallace asked her to bring along.

Two weeks later, the report went on, Lorrie felt Mary Wallace in her home in Weymouth near Boston. Lorrie was afraid that Mary Wallace might "get into my body and use it for whatever purpose she wants to. I might wake up some day and *be* Mary Wallace."

That's the danger of being a medium without proper safeguards. They tend to identify with a personality that has come through them. Especially when they read all there is in print about them.

I decided to take someone to the house who knew nothing about it, someone who was not likely to succumb to the wiles of amateur "ESP experts," inquisitive columnists and such, someone who would do exactly what I required of her: Sybil Leek, famed British psychic.

It was a glorious day late in spring when we arrived at "Ocean-Born" Mary's house in a Volkswagen station wagon driven by two alert young students from Goddard College in Vermont: Jerry Weener and Jay Lawrence. They had come to Boston to fetch us and take us all the way up to their campus, where I was to address the students and faculty. I proposed that they drive us by way of Henniker, and the two young students of parapsychology agreed enthusiastically. It was their first experience with an actual séance and they brought with them a lively dose of curiosity.

Sybil Leek brought with her something else: "Mr. Sasha," a healthy four-foot boa constrictor someone had given her for a pet. At first I thought she was kidding when she spoke with tender care of her snake, coiled peacefully in his little basket. But practical Sybil, author of some nine books, saw still another possibility in "Life with Sasha" and for that reason kept the snake on with her. On the way to Henniker, the car had a flat tire and we took this opportunity to get acquainted with Sasha, as Sybil gave him a run around the New Hampshire countryside.

Although I have always had a deep-seated dislike for anything reptilian, snakes, serpents, and other slitherers, terrestrial or maritime, I must confess that I found this critter less repulsive than I had thought he would be. At any rate, "Mr. Sasha" was collected once more and carefully replaced in his basket and the journey continued to Henniker, where the Russells were expecting us with great anticipation.

"Ocean-Born" Mary

After a delightful buffet luncheon—"Mr. Sasha" had his the week before, as snakes are slow digesters—we proceeded to the large room upstairs to the right of the entrance door, commonly called the Lafayette room, and Sybil took the chair near the fireplace. The rest of us—the Russells, a minister friend of theirs, two neighbors, my wife Catherine and I, and our two student friends—gathered around her in a circle.

It was early afternoon. The sun was bright and clear. It didn't seem like it would be a good day for ghosts. Still, we had come to have a talk with the elusive Mary Wallace in her own domain, and if I knew Sybil, she would not disappoint us. Sybil is a very powerful medium, and something *always* happens.

Sybil knew nothing about the house since I had told our hosts not to discuss it with her before the trance session. I asked her if she had any clairvoyant impressions about the house.

"My main impressions were outside," Sybil replied, "near where the irises are. I was drawn to that spot and felt very strange. There is something outside this house which means more than things inside!"

"What about inside the house? What do you feel here?"

"The most impressive room I think is the loom room," Sybil said, and I thought, that's where Ernest Walbourne heard the voice telling him to get out, in the area that's also called the "death" room.

"They don't want us here . . . there is a conflict between two people . . . somebody wants something he can't have . . ."

Presently, Sybil was in trance. There was a moment of silence as I waited anxiously for the ghost of Mary Wallace to manifest itself through Sybil. The first words coming from the lips of the entranced medium were almost unintelligible.

Gradually, the voice became clearer and I had her repeat the words until I could be sure of them.

19

"Say-mon go to the lion's head," she said now. "To the lion's head. Be careful"

"Why should I be careful?"

"In case he catches you."

"Who are you?"

"Mary Degan."

"What are you doing here?"

"Waiting. Someone fetch me."

She said "*Witing*" with a strong cockney accent, and suddenly I realized that the "*say-mon*" was probably a seaman.

"Whose house is this?" I inquired.

"Daniel Burn's." (Perhaps it was "Birch.")

"What year is this?"

"1798."

"Who built this house?"

"Burn . . ."

"How did you get here?"

"All the time, come and go . . . to hide . . . I have to wait. He wants the money. Burn. Daniel Burn."

I began to wonder what had happened to Mary Wallace. Who was this new member of the ghostly cast? Sybil knew nothing whatever of a pirate or a pirate treasure connected by legend to this house. Yet her very first trance words concerned *a seaman and money.*

Did Mary Degan have someone else with her, I hinted. Maybe this was only the first act and the lady of the house was being coy in time for a second act appearance.

But the ghost insisted that she was Mary Degan and that she lived here, "with the old idiot."

"Who was the old idiot?" I demanded.

"Mary," the Degan girl replied.

"What is Mary's family name?"

"Birch," she replied without hesitation.

"Ocean-Born" Mary

I looked at Mrs. Russell, who shook her head. Nobody knew of Mary Wallace by any other name. Had she had another husband we did not know about?

Was there anyone else with her, I asked.

"Mary Birch, Daniel, and Jonathan," she replied.

"Who is Jonathan?"

"Jonathan Harrison Flood," the ghostly girl said.

A week or so later, I checked with my good friend Robert Nesmith, expert in pirate lore. Was there a pirate by that name? There had been, but his date is given as 1610, far too early for our man. But then Flood was a very common name. Also, this Flood might have used another name as his *nom de pirate* and Flood might have been his real, civilian name.

"What are they doing in this house?" I demanded.

"They come to look for their money," Sybil in trance replied. "The old idiot took it."

"What sort of money was it?"

"Dutch money," came the reply. "Very long ago."

"Who brought the money to this house?"

"Mary. Not me."

"Whose money was it?"

"Johnny's."

"How did he get it?"

"Very funny . . . he helped himself . . . so we did."

"What profession did he have?"

"Went down to the sea. Had a lot of funny business. Then he got caught, you know. So they did him in."

"Who did him in?"

"The runners. In the bay."

"What year was that?"

"Ninety-nine."

"What happened to the money after that?"

"She hid it. Outside. Near the lion's head."

21

"Where is the lion's head?"

"You go down past the little rocks, in the middle of the rocks, a little bit like a lion's head."

"If I left the house by the front entrance, which way would I turn?"

"The right, down past the little rock on the right. Through the trees, down the little . . ."

"How far from the house?"

"Three minutes."

"Is it under the rock?"

"Lion's head."

"How far below?"

"As big as a boy."

"What will I find there?"

"The gold. Dutch gold."

"Anything else?"

"No, unless she put it there."

"Why did she put it there?"

"Because he came back for it."

"What did she do?"

"She said it was hers. Then he went away. Then they caught him, and good thing, too. He never came back and she went off, too."

"When did she leave here?"

"Eighteen three."

"What was she like? Describe her."

"Round, not as big as me, dumpy thing, she thought she owned everything."

"How was Jonathan related to Daniel?"

"Daniel stayed here when Johnny went away and then they would divide the money, but they didn't because of Mary. She took it."

"Did you see the money?"

"Ocean-Born" Mary

"I got some money. Gold. It says 1747."

"Is anyone buried in this ground?"

"Sometimes they brought them back here when they got killed down by the river."

"Who is buried in the house?"

"I think Johnny."

I now told Mary Degan to fetch me the other Mary, the lady of the house. But the girl demurred. The other Mary did not like to talk to strangers.

"What do *you* look like?" I asked. I still was not sure if Mary Wallace was not masquerading as her own servant girl to fool us.

"Skinny and tall."

"What do you wear?"

"A gray dress."

"What is your favorite spot in this house?"

"The little loom room. Peaceful."

"Do you always stay there?"

"No." The voice was proud now. "I go where I want."

"Whose house is this?" Perhaps I could trap her if she was indeed Mary Wallace.

"Mary Birch."

"Has she got a husband?"

"They come and go. There's always company here—that's why I go to the loom room."

I tried to send her away, but she wouldn't go.

"Nobody speaks to me," she complained. "Johnny . . . she won't let him speak to me. Nobody is going to send me away."

"Is there a sea captain in this house?" I asked.

She almost shouted the reply.

"*Johnny!*"

"Where is he from?"

"Johnny is from the island."

She then explained that the trouble with Johnny and Mary was about the sea. Especially about the money the captain had.

"Will the money be found?" I asked.

"Not until I let it."

I asked Mary Degan to find me Mary Wallace. No dice. The lady wanted to be coaxed. Did she want some presents, I asked. That hit a happier note.

"Brandy . . . some clothes," she said. "She needs some hair . . . hasn't got much hair."

"Ask her if she could do with some oil of wintergreen," I said, sending up a trial balloon.

"She's got a bad back," the ghost said, and I could tell from the surprised expression on Mrs. Russell's face that Mary Wallace had indeed had a bad back.

"She makes it . . . people bring her things . . . rub her back . . . back's bad . . . she won't let you get the money . . . not yet . . . may want to build another house, in the garden . . . in case she needs it . . . sell it . . . she knows she is not what she used to be because her back's bad . . . she'll never go. Not now."

I assured her that the Russells wanted her to stay as long as she liked. After all, it was her house, too.

"Where is Johnny's body buried?" I now asked.

"Johnny's body," she murmured, "is under the fireplace."

Nobody had told Sybil about the persistent rumors that the old pirate lay under the hearthstone.

"Don't tell anyone," she whispered.

"How deep?"

"Had to be deep."

"Who put him there?"

"I shan't tell you."

"Did you bury anything with him?"

"I shan't tell. He is no trouble now. Poor Johnny."

"Ocean-Born" Mary

"How did Johnny meet Mary?"

"I think they met on a ship."

"Ocean-Born" Mary, I thought. Sybil did not even know the name of the house, much less the story of how it got that name.

"All right," I said. "Did Mary have any children?"

"Four . . . in the garden. You can never tell with her."

"Did anyone kill anyone in this house at any time?"

"Johnny was killed, you know. Near the money. The runners chased him and he was very sick, we thought he was dead, and then he came here. I think she pushed him when he hurt his leg. We both brought him back and put him under the fireplace. I didn't think he was dead."

"But you buried him anyway?" I said.

"She did," the ghost servant replied. "Better gone, she said. He's only come back for the money."

"Then Mary and Johnny weren't exactly friendly?"

"They were once."

"What changed things?"

"The money. She took his money. The money he fought for. Fighting money."

Suddenly, the tone of voice of the servant girl changed.

"I want to go outside," she begged. "She watches me. I can go out because her back is bad today. Can't get up, you see. So I can go out."

I promised to help her.

Suspiciously, she asked, "What do you want?"

"Go outside. You are free to go," I intoned.

"Sit on the rocks," the voice said. "If she calls out? She can get very angry."

"I will protect you," I promised.

"She says there are other places under the floor . . ." the girl ghost added, suddenly.

"Any secret passages?" I asked.

"Yes. Near the old nursery. First floor. Up the stairs, the loom room, the right hand wall. You can get out in the smoke room!"

Mr. Russell had told me of his suspicions that on structural evidence alone there was a hidden passage behind the smoke room. How would Sybil know this? Nobody had discussed it with her or showed her the spot.

I waited for more. But she did not know of any other passages, except one leading to the rear of the house.

"What about the well?"

"She did not like that either, because she thought *he* put his money there."

"Did he?"

"Perhaps he did. She used to put money in one place, he into another, and I think he put some money into the smoke room. He was always around there. Always watching each other. Watch me, too. Back of the house used to be where he could hide. People always looking for Johnny. Runners."

"Who was Mr. Birch?"

"Johnny had a lot to do with his house, but he was away a lot and so there was always some man here while he was away."

"Who paid for the house originally?"

"I think Johnny."

"Why did he want this house?"

"When he got enough money, he would come here and stay forever. He could not stay long ever, went back to the sea, and she came."

I tried another tack.

"Who was Don Pedro?" That was the name given the pirate in the popular tale.

She had heard the name, but could not place it.

"What about Mary Wallace?"

"Ocean-Born" Mary

"Mary Wallace was Mary *Birch*," the ghost said, as if correcting me. "She had several names."

"Why?"

"Because she had several husbands."

Logical enough, if true.

"Wallace lived here a little while, I think," she added.

"Who was first, Wallace or Birch?"

"Birch. Mary Wallace, Mary Birch, is good enough."

Did the name Philip Babb mean anything to her? That allegedly was the pirate's real name.

"She had a little boy named Philip," the ghost said, and I thought, why not? After all, they had named Mary for the pirate's mother, why not reciprocate and name *her* son for the old man? Especially with all that loot around.

"If I don't go now, she'll wake up," the girl said. "Philip Babb, Philip Babb, he was somewhere in the back room. That was his room. I remember him."

How did Philip get on with Johnny? I wanted to know if they were one and the same person or not.

"Not so good," the ghost said. "Johnny did not like men here, you know."

I promised to watch out for Mary, and sent the girl on her way.

I then brought Sybil out of her trance.

A few moments later, we decided to start our treasure hunt in the garden, following the instructions given us by Mary Degan, girl ghost.

Sybil was told nothing more than to go outside and let her intuition lead her toward any spot she thought important. The rest of us followed her like spectators at the National Open Golf Tournament.

We did not have to walk far. About twenty yards from the house, near some beautiful iris in bloom, we located the three stones. The one in the middle looked indeed somewhat like a lion's head, when viewed at a distance. I asked the others in the group to look at it. There was no doubt about it. If there was a lion's head on the grounds, this was it. What lay underneath? What indeed was underneath the hearthstone in the house itself?

The Russells promised to get a mine detector to examine the areas involved. If there was metal in the ground, the instrument would show it. Meanwhile, the lore about "Ocean-Born" Mary had been enriched by the presence in the nether world of Mary Degan, servant girl, and the intriguing picture of two pirates—Johnny and Philip Babb. Much of this is very difficult to trace. But the fact is that Sybil Leek, who came to Henniker a total stranger, was able, in trance, to tell about a man at sea, a Mary, a pirate treasure, hidden passages, a child named Philip, four children of Mary, and the presence of a ghost in the loom room upstairs. All of this had been checked.

Why should not the rest be true also? Including, perhaps, the elusive treasure?

Only time will tell.

2

The Ghosts
of Stamford Hill

"**M**r. Holzer," the voice on the phone said pleasantly, "I've read your book and that's why I'm calling. We've got a ghost in our house."

Far from astonished, I took paper and pencil and, not unlike a grocery-store clerk taking down a telephone order, started to put down the details of the report.

Robert Cowan is a gentleman with a very balanced approach to life. He is an artist who works for one of the leading advertising agencies in New York City and his interests range widely from art to music, theater, history and what have you. But not to ghosts, at least not until he and his actress-wife, Dorothy, moved into the 1780 House in Stamford Hill. The house is thus named for the simplest of all reasons: it was built in that year.

Mr. Cowan explained that he thought I'd be glad to have a look at his house, although the Cowans were not unduly worried about the presence of a non-rent-paying guest at their house. It was a bit disconcerting at times, but more than that, curiosity as to what the ghost wanted, and who the spectre was, had prompted Bob Cowan to seek the help of The Ghost Hunter.

I said, "Mr. Cowan, would you mind putting your experiences in writing, so I can have them for my files?"

I like to have written reports (in the first person, if possible) so that later I can refer back to them if similar cases should pop up, as they often do.

"Not at all," Bob Cowan said, "I'll be glad to write it down for you."

The next morning I received his report, along with a brief history of the 1780 House.

Here is a brief account of the experiences my wife and I have had while living in this house during the past nine and a half years. I'll start with myself because my experiences are quite simple.

From time to time (once a week or so) during most of the time we've lived here I have noticed unidentifiable movements out of the corner of my eye . . . day or night. Most often, I've noticed this while sitting in our parlor and what I see moving seems to be in the living room. At other times, and only late at night when I am the only one awake, I hear beautiful but unidentified music seemingly played by a full orchestra, as though a radio were on in another part of the house.

The only place I recall hearing this is in an upstairs bedroom and just after I'd gone to bed. Once I actually got up, opened the bedroom door to ascertain if it was perhaps music from a radio accidently left on, but it wasn't.

Finally, quite often I've heard a variety of knocks and crashes that do not have any logical source within the structural setup of the house. A very loud smash occurred two weeks ago. You'd have thought a door had fallen off its hinges upstairs but, as usual, there was nothing out of order.

My wife, Dorothy, had two very vivid experiences about

five years ago. One was in the kitchen, or rather outside of a kitchen window. She was standing at the sink in the evening and happened to glance out the window when she saw a face glaring in at her. It was a dark face but not a Negro, perhaps Indian; it was very hateful and fierce.

At first she thought it was a distorted reflection in the glass but in looking closer, it was a face glaring directly at her. All she could make out was a face only and as she recalls it, *it seemed translucent.* It didn't disappear, *she did!*

On a summer afternoon my wife was taking a nap in a back bedroom and was between being awake and being asleep when she heard the sounds of men's voices and the sound of working on the grounds—rakes, and garden tools—right outside the window. She tried to arouse herself to see who they could be, but she couldn't get up.

At that time, and up to that time we had only hired a single man to come in and work on the lawn and flower beds. It wasn't until at least a year later that we hired a crew that came in and worked once a week and we've often wondered if this was an experience of precognition. My wife has always had an uneasy feeling about the outside of the back of the house and still sometimes hears men's voices outside and will look out all the windows without seeing anyone.

She also has shared my experiences of seeing "things" out of the corner of her eye and also hearing quite lovely music at night. She hasn't paid attention to household noises because a long time ago I told her "all old houses have odd structural noises" . . . which is true enough.

Prior to our living here the house was lived in for about 25 years by the Clayton Rich family, a family of five. Mr. Rich died towards the end of their stay here. By the time we bought it, the three children were all married and had moved away.

For perhaps one year prior to that a Mrs. David Cowles lived here. She's responsible for most of the restoration along with a Mr. Fredrick Kinble.

Up until 1927 or 1928, the house was in the Weed family ever since 1780. The last of the line were two sisters who hated each other and only communicated with each other through the husband of one of the sisters. They had divided the house and used two different doors, one used the regular front door into the stair hall and the other used the "coffin door" into the parlor.

Mr. Cowan added that they were selling the house—not because of ghosts, but because they wanted to move to the city again. I assured him that we'd be coming up as soon as possible.

Before we could make arrangements to do so, I had another note from the Cowans. On February 9, 1964, Bob Cowan wrote that they heard a singing voice quite clearly downstairs, and music again.

It wasn't until the following week, however, that my wife and I went to Stamford Hill. The Cowans offered to have supper ready for us that Sunday evening, and to pick us up at the station, since nobody could find the house at night who did not know the way.

It was around six in the evening when our New Haven train pulled in. Bob Cowan wore the Scottish beret he had said he would wear in order to be recognized by us at once. The house stood at the end of a winding road which ran for about ten minutes through woodland and past shady lanes. An American eagle over the door, and the date 1780 stood out quite clearly despite the dusk which had started to settle on the land. The house has three levels, and the Cowans used for their dining room the large room next to the kitchen in what might be called the cellar or ground level.

They had adorned it with eighteenth-century American antiques in a most winning manner, and the fireplace added a warmth to the room that seemed miles removed from bustling New York.

On the next level were the living room and next to that a kind of sitting room. The fireplace in each of these rooms was connected one to the other. Beyond the corridor there was the master bedroom and Bob's rather colorful den. Upstairs were two guest rooms, and there was a small attic accessible only through a hole in the ceiling and by ladder. Built during the American Revolution, the house stands on a wooded slope, which is responsible for its original name of Woodpecker Ridge Farm.

Many years ago, after the restoration of the house was completed, Harold Donaldson Eberlin, an English furniture and garden expert, wrote about it:

> With its rock-ribbed ridges, its boulder-strewn pastures and its sharply broken contours like the choppy surface of a wind-blown sea, the topographical conditions have inevitably affected the domestic architecture. To mention only two particulars, the dwellings of the region have had to accommodate themselves to many an abrupt hillside site and the employment of some of the omnipresent granite boulders. Part of the individuality of the house at Woodpecker Ridge Farm lies in the way it satisfies these conditions without being a type house.
>
> Before communal existence, the country all thereabouts bore the pleasantly descriptive name of Woodpecker Ridge, and Woodpecker Ridge Farm was so called in order to keep alive the memory of this early name. Tradition says that the acres now comprised within the boundaries of Woodpecker Ridge Farm once formed part of the private hunting ground of *the old Indian chief Ponus.*
>
> Old Ponus may, perhaps, appear a trifle mythical and shadowy, as such long-gone chieftains are wont to be. Very sub-

stantial and real, however, was Augustus Weed, who built the house in 1780. And the said Augustus was something of a personage.

War clouds were still hanging thick over the face of the land when he had the foundation laid and the structure framed. Nevertheless, confident and forward-looking, he not only reared a staunch and tidy abode, indicative of the spirit of the countryside, but he seems to have put into it some of his own robust and independent personality as well.

It is said that Augustus was such a notable farmer and took such justifiable pride in the condition of his fields that he was not afraid to make a standing offer of one dollar reward for every daisy that anyone could find in his hay.

About 1825 the house experienced a measure of remodeling in accordance with the notions prevalent at the time. Nothing very extensive or ostentatious was attempted, but visible traces of the work then undertaken remain in the neo-Greek details that occur both outside and indoors.

It is not unlikely that the "lie-on-your-stomach" windows of the attic story date from this time and point to either a raising of the original roof or else some alteration of its pitch. These "lie-on-your-stomach" windows—so called because they were low down in the wall and had their sills very near the level of the floor so that you had almost to lie on your stomach to look out of them—were a favorite device of the *néo-Grec* era for lighting attic rooms. And it is remarkable how much light they actually do give, and what a pleasant light it is.

The recent remodeling that brought Woodpecker Farmhouse to its present state of comeliness and comfort impaired none of the individual character the place had acquired through the generations that had passed since hardy Augustus Weed first took up his abode there. It needs no searching scrutiny to discern the eighteenth-century features impressed on the structure at the beginning—the stout timbers of the framing, the sturdy beams and joists, the wide floor boards, and the generous fireplaces. Neither is close examination required to discover the marks of the 1825 rejuvenation.

The fashions of columns, pilasters, mantelpieces and other features speak plainly and proclaim their origin.

The aspect of the garden, too, discloses the same sympathetic understanding of the environment peculiarly suitable to the sort of house for which it affords the natural setting. The ancient well cover, the lilac bushes, the sweetbriers, the August lilies and the other denizens of an old farmhouse dooryard have been allowed to keep their long-accustomed places.

In return for this recognition of their prescriptive rights, they lend no small part to the air of self-possessed assurance and mellow contentment that pervades the whole place.

After a most pleasant dinner downstairs, Catherine and I joined the Cowans in the large living room upstairs. We sat down quietly and hoped we would hear something along musical lines.

As the quietness of the countryside slowly settled over us, I could indeed distinguish faraway, indistinct musical sounds, as if someone were playing a radio underwater or at great distance. A check revealed no nearby house or parked car whose radio could be responsible for this.

After a while we got up and looked about the room itself. We were standing about quietly admiring the furniture, when both my wife and I, and of course the Cowans, clearly heard footsteps overhead.

They were firm and strong and could not be mistaken for anything else, such as a squirrel in the attic or other innocuous noise. Nor was it an old house settling.

"Did you hear that?" I said, almost superfluously.

"We all heard it," my wife said and looked at me.

"What am I waiting for?" I replied, and faster than you can say Ghost Hunter, I was up the stairs and into the room above our heads, where the steps had been heard. The room lay in total darkness. I turned the switch. There was no one about. Nobody else was in the house at the time, and all windows were closed. We decided to assemble upstairs in the smaller room next to the one in which I had heard the steps. The reason was that Mrs. Cowan had experienced a most unusual phenomenon in that particular room.

"It was like lightning," she said, "a bright light suddenly come and gone."

I looked the room over carefully. The windows were arranged in such a manner that a reflection from passing cars was out of the question. Both windows, far apart and on different walls, opened into the dark countryside away from the only road.

Catherine and I sat down on the couch, and the Cowans took chairs. We sat quietly for perhaps twenty minutes, without lights except a small amount of light filtering in from the stairwell. It was very dark, certainly dark enough for sleep and there was not light enough to write by.

As I was gazing towards the back wall of the little room and wondered about the footsteps I had just heard so clearly, I saw a blinding flash of light, white light, in the corner facing me. It came on and disappeared very quickly, so quickly in fact that my wife, whose head had been turned in another direction at the moment, missed it. But Dorothy Cowan saw it and exclaimed, "There it is again. Exactly as I saw it."

Despite the brevity I was able to observe that the light cast a shadow on the opposite wall, so it could not very well have been a hallucination.

I decided it would be best to bring Mrs. Meyers to the house, and we went back to New York soon after. While we were preparing our return visit with Mrs. Meyers as our medium, I received an urgent call from Bob Cowan.

"Since seeing you and Cathy at our house, we've had some additional activity that you'll be interested in. Dottie and I have both heard knocking about the house but none of it in direct answer to questions that we've tried to ask. On Saturday, the twenty-ninth of February, I was taking a nap back in my studio when I was awakened by the sound of footsteps in the room above me . . . the same room we all sat in on the previous Sunday.

"The most interesting event was on the evening of Thursday, February 27. I was driving home from the railroad station alone. Dottie was still in New York. As I approached the house, I noticed that there was a light on in the main floor bedroom and also a light on up in the sewing room on the top floor, a room Dottie also uses for rehearsal. I thought Dottie had left the lights on. I drove past the house and down to the garage, put the car away and then walked back to the house and noticed that the light in the top floor was now off.

"I entered the house and noticed that the dogs were calm (wild enough at seeing me, but in no way indicating that there was anyone else in the house). I went upstairs and found that the light in the bedroom was also off. I checked the entire house and there was absolutely no sign that anyone had just been there . . . and there hadn't been, I'm sure."

On Sunday, March 15, we arrived at the 1780 House, again at dusk. A delicious meal awaited us in the downstairs room, then we repaired to the upstairs part of the house.

We seated ourselves in the large living room where the music had been heard, and where we had been standing at the time we heard the uncanny footsteps overhead.

"I sense a woman in a white dress," Ethel said suddenly. "She's got dark hair and a high forehead. Rather a small woman."

"I was looking through the attic earlier," Bob Cowan said thoughtfully, "and look what I found—a waistcoat that would fit a rather smallish woman or girl."

The piece of clothing he showed us seemed rather musty.

There were a number of articles up there in the attic that must have belonged to an earlier owner of the house—much earlier.

A moment later, Ethel Meyers showed the characteristic signs of onsetting trance. We doused the lights until only one back light was on.

At first, only inarticulate sounds came from the medium's lips. "You can speak," I said, to encourage her, "you're among friends." The sounds now turned into crying.

"What is your name?" I asked, as I always do on such occasions. There was laughter—whether girlish or mad was hard to tell.

Suddenly, she started to sing in a high-pitched voice.

"You can speak, you can speak," I kept assuring the entity. Finally she seemed to have settled down somewhat in control of the medium.

"Happy to speak with you," she mumbled faintly.

"What is your name?"

I had to ask it several times before I could catch the answer clearly.

"Lucy."

"Tell me, Lucy, do you live here?"

"God be with you."

"Do you life in this house?"

"My house."

"What year is this?"

The entity hesitated a moment, then turned towards Dorothy and said, "I like you."

I continued to question her.

"How old are you?"

"Old lady."

"How old?"

"God be with you."

The conversation had been friendly, but when I asked her,

"What is your husband's name?" the ghost drew back as if I had spoken a horrible word.

"What did you say?" she almost shouted, her voice trembling with emotion. "I have no husband—God bless you—what were you saying?" she repeated, then started to cry again. "Husband, husband," she kept saying it as if it was a thought she could not bear.

"You did not have a husband, then?"

"Yes, I did."

"Your name again?"

"Lucy . . . fair day . . . where is he? The fair day . . . the pretty one, he said to me look in the pool and you will see my face."

"Who is he?" I repeated.

But the ghost paid no heed to me. She was evidently caught up in her own memories.

"I heard a voice, Lucy, Lucy—fair one—alack—they took him out—they laid him cold in the ground. . . ."

"What year was that?" I wanted to know.

"Year, year?" she repeated. "Now, *now!*"

"Who rules this country now?"

"Why, he who seized it."

"Who rules?"

"They carried him out. . . . The Savior of our country. General Washington."

"When did he die?"

"Just now."

I tried to question her further, but she returned to her thoughts of her husband.

"I want to stay here—I wait at the pool—look, he is there!" She was growing excited again.

"I want to stay here now, always, forever—rest in peace—he is there always with me."

"How long ago did you die?" I asked, almost casually. The reaction was somewhat hostile.

"I have not died—never—All Saints!"

I asked her to join her loved one by calling for him and thus be set free of this house. But the ghost would have none of it.

"Gainsay what I have spoke—"

"How did you come to this house?" I now asked.

"Father—I am born here."

"Was it your father's house?"

"Yes."

"What was his name?" I asked, but the restless spirit of Lucy was slipping away now, and Albert, the medium's control, took over. His crisp, clear voice told us that the time had come to release Ethel.

"What about this woman, Lucy?" I inquired. Sometimes the control will give additional details.

"He was not her husband . . . he was killed before she married him," Albert said.

No wonder my question about a husband threw Lucy into an uproar of emotions.

In a little while, Ethel Meyers was back to her old self, and as usual, did not remember anything of what had come through her entranced lips.

Shortly after this my wife and I went to Europe.

As soon as we returned, I called Bob Cowan. How were things up in Stamford Hill? Quiet? Not very.

"Last June," Bob recalled, "Dottie and I were at home with a friend, a lady hair dresser, who happens to be psychic. We were playing around with the ouija board, more in amusement than seriously. Suddenly, the Sunday afternoon quiet was disrupted by heavy footsteps coming up the steps outside the house. Quickly, we hid the ouija board, for we did not want a potential buyer of the house to see us in this unusual pursuit. We were sure someone was coming up to see the house. But the steps stopped abruptly when they reached the front door. I opened, and there was no one outside."

"Hard to sell a house that way," I commented. "Anything else?"

"Yes, in July we had a house guest, a very balanced person, not given to imagining things. There was a sudden crash upstairs, and when I rushed up the stairs to the sewing room, there was this bolt of material that had been standing in a corner, lying in the middle of the room as if thrown there by unseen hands! Margaret, our house guest, also heard someone humming a tune in the bathroom, although there was no one in there at the time. Then in November, when just the two of us were in the house, someone knocked at the door downstairs. Again we looked, but there was nobody outside. One evening when I was in the 'ship' room and Dottie in the bedroom, we heard footfalls coming down the staircase.

"Since neither of us was causing them and the door was closed, only a ghost could have been walking down those stairs."

"But the most frightening experience of all," Dorothy Cowan broke in, "was when I was sleeping downstairs and, waking up, wanted to go to the bathroom without turning on the lights, so as not to wake Bob. Groping my way back to bed, I suddenly found myself up on the next floor in the blue room, which is pretty tricky walking in the dark. I had the feeling someone was forcing me to follow them into that particular room."

I had heard enough, and on December 15, we took Ethel Johnson Meyers to the house for another go at the restless ones within its confines. Soon we were all seated in the ship room on the first floor, and Ethel started to drift into trance.

"There is a baby's coffin here," she murmured. "Like a newborn infant's."

The old grandfather clock in back of us kept ticking away loudly.

"I hear someone call Maggie," Ethel said, "Margaret."

"Do you see anyone?"

"A woman, about five foot two, in a long dress, with a big bustle in the back. Hair down, parted in the middle, and braided on both sides. There is another young woman . . . Laurie . . . very pretty face, but so sad . . . she's looking at you, Hans. . . ."

"What is it she wants?" I asked quietly.

"A youngish man with brown hair, curly, wearing a white blouse, taken in at the wrists, and over it a tan waistcoat, but no coat over it . . ."

I asked what he wanted and why he was here. This seemed to agitate the medium somewhat.

"Bottom of the well," she mumbled, "stones at bottom of the well."

Bob Cowan changed seats, moving away from the coffin door to the opposite side of the room. He complained of feeling cold at the former spot, although neither door nor window was open to cause such a sensation.

"Somebody had a stick over his shoulder," the medium said now, "older man wearing dark trousers, heavy stockings. His hair is gray and kind of longish; he's got that stick."

I asked her to find out why.

"'Take him away,'" Ethel replied. "He says, 'Take him away!'"

"But he was innocent, he went to the well. Who is down the well? Him who I drove into the well, him . . . I mistook . . ."

Ethel was now fully entranced and the old man seemed to be speaking through her.

"What is your name?" I asked.

42

"She was agrievin'," the voice replied, "she were grievin' I did that."

"What is your name?"

"Ain't no business to you."

"How can I help you?"

"They're all here . . . accusin' me . . . I see her always by the well."

"Did someone die in this well?" Outside, barely twenty yards away, was the well, now cold and silent in the night air.

"Him who I mistook. I find peace, I find him, I put him together again."

"What year was that?"

"No matter to you now . . . I do not forgive myself . . . I wronged, I wronged . . . I see always her face look on me."

"Are you in this house now?" I asked.

"Where else can I be and talk with thee?" the ghost shot back.

"This isn't your house any more," I said quietly.

"Oh, yes it is," the ghost replied firmly. "The young man stays here only to look upon me and mock me. It will not be other than mine. I care only for that flesh that I could put again on the bone and I will restore him to the bloom of life and the rich love of her who suffered through my own misdemeanor."

"Is your daughter buried here?" I asked, to change the subject. Quietly, the ghostly voice said "Yes."

But he refused to say where he himself was laid to final—or not so final—rest.

At this point the ghost realized that he was not in his own body, and as I explained the procedure to him, he gradually became calmer. At first, he thought he was in his own body and could use it to restore to life the one he had slain. I kept asking who he was. Finally, in a soft whisper, came the reply, "Samuel."

"And Laurie?"

"My daughter. . . . oh, he is here, the man I wronged . . . Margaret, Margaret!" He seemed greatly agitated with fear now.

The big clock started to strike. The ghost somehow felt it meant him.

"The judgement, the judgement . . . Laurie. . . . they smile at me. I have killed. He has taken my hand! He whom I have hurt."

But the excitement proved too much for Samuel. Suddenly, he was gone, and after a brief interval, an entirely different personality inhabited Ethel's body. It was Laurie.

"Please forgive him," she pleaded, "I have forgiven him."

The voice was sweet and girlish.

"Who is Samuel?"

"My grandfather."

"What is your family name?"

"Laurie Ho-Ho- . . . if I could only get that name."

But she couldn't.

Neither could she give me the name of her beloved, killed by her grandfather. It was a name she was not allowed to mention around the house, so she had difficulty remembering now, she explained.

"What is your mother's name?" I asked.

"Margaret."

"What year were you born?"

Hesitatingly, the voice said, "Seven-teen-fifty-six."

"What year is this now?"

"Seventeen seventy-four. We laid him to rest in seventeen seventy-four."

"In the church?"

"No, Grandfather could not bear it. We laid him to rest on the hill to the north. We dug with our fingers all night.

"Don't tell Grandpa where we put it."

"How far from here is it?"

44

"No more than a straight fly of the lark."

"Is the grave marked?"

"Oh, no."

"What happened to your father?"

"No longer home, gone."

I explained to Laurie that the house would soon change hands, and that she must not interfere with this. The Cowans had the feeling that their ghosts were somehow keeping all buyers away, fantastic though this may be at first thought. But then all of psychic research is pretty unusual and who is to say what cannot be?

Laurie promised not to interfere and to accept a new owner of "their" house. She left, asking again that her grandfather be forgiven his sins.

I then asked Albert, Ethel's control, to take over the medium. That done, I queried him regarding the whole matter.

"The father is buried far from here, but most of the others are buried around here," he said, "during the year seventeen seventy-seven . . . grandfather was not brought here until later when there was forgiveness. The body was removed and put in Christian burial."

"Where is the tombstone?" I asked.

"Lying to the west of a white structure," Albert replied in his precise, slightly accented speech, "on these grounds. The tombstone is broken off, close to the earth. The top has been mishandled by vandals. The old man is gone, the young man has taken him by the hand."

"What was the young man's name?"

"She called him Benjamin."

"He was killed in the well?"

"That is right. He has no grave except on the hill."

"Is the old man the one who disturbs this house?"

45

"He is the main one who brings in his rabble, looking for the young man."

"Who is Lucy?" I asked, referring back to the girl who had spoken to us at the last seance in the late spring.

"That is the girl you were talking about, Laurie. Her name is really Lucy. One and the same person."

"She was not actually married to the young man?"

"In her own way, she was. But they would not recognize it. There were differences in religious ideas. . . . But we had better release the medium for now."

I nodded, and within a moment or two, Ethel was back to herself, very much bewildered as to what went on while she was in trance.

"How do you reconcile these dates with the tradition that this house was built in seventeen eighty?" I asked Bob Cowan.

He shook his head.

"It is only a tradition. We have no proof of the actual date."

We went to the upstairs sewing room where the latest manifestations had taken place, and grouped ourselves around the heavy wooden table. Ethel almost immediately fell into trance again. She rarely does twice in one sitting.

The voice reverberating in the near-darkness now was clearly that of a man, and a very dominating voice it was.

"Who are you?" I demanded.

"Sergeant-major. . . ." No name followed. I asked why was he here in this house.

"One has pleasant memories."

"Your name?"

"Sergeant-major Harm."

"First name?"

Instead of giving it, he explained that he once owned the house and was "friend, not foe." I looked at Bob Cowan, who

46

knows all the owners of the property in the old records, and Bob shook his head. No Harm.

"When I please, I come. I do not disturb willingly. But I will go," the new visitor offered, "I will take him with me; you will see him no more. I am at peace with him now. He is at peace with me."

"How did you pass over?" I inquired.

"On the field of battle. On the banks of the Potomac . . . seventeen seventy-six."

"What regiment were you in?" I continued.

"York. . . . Eight. . . . I was a foot soldier . . . eighteenth regiment . . ."

"What Army?"

"Wayne . . . Wayne . . ."

"Who was your commanding general?"

"Broderick."

"Who was the Colonel of your regiment?"

"Wayne, Wayne."

"You were a Sergeant-major?"

"Sergeant-major, eighteenth regiment, foot infantry."

"Where were you stationed?"

"New York."

"Where in New York?"

"Champlain."

"Your regimental commander again?"

"Broderick." Then he added, not without emotion, "I died under fire, first battle of Potomac."

"Where are you buried?"

"Fort Ticonderoga, New York."

I wondered how a soldier fighting on the banks of the Potomac could be buried in upstate New York. But I must confess that the word "Potomac" had come so softly that I could have been mistaken.

"The date of your death?"

"Seventeen seventy-six."

Then he added, as the voice became more and more indistinct, "I will leave now, but I will protect you from those who . . . who are hungry to . . ." The voice trailed off into silence.

A few moments later, Ethel emerged from the trance with a slight headache, but otherwise her old self. As usual, she did not recall anything that had come through her entranced lips.

We returned to New York soon after, hoping that all would remain quiet in the Cowan house, and, more importantly, that there would soon be a new laird of the manor at the 1780 House.

I, too, heard the ghostly music, although I am sure it does not connect with the Colonial ghosts we were able to evoke. The music I heard sounded like a far-off radio, which it wasn't, since there are no houses near enough to be heard from. What I heard for a few moments in the living room sounded like a full symphony orchestra playing the music popular around the turn of this century.

Old houses impregnated with layers upon layers of people's emotions frequently also absorb music and other sounds as part of the atmosphere.

What about the Sergeant-major?

I checked the regimental records. No soldier named Harm, but a number of officers (and men) named Harmon. I rechecked my tapes. The name "Harm" had been given by the ghost very quietly. He could have said Harmon. Or perhaps he was disguising his identity as they sometimes will.

But then I discovered something very interesting. In the Connecticut state papers there is mention of a certain Benjamin Harmon, Jr. Lt., who was with a local regiment in 1776. The murdered young man had been identified as "Benjamin." Suddenly we have another ghost named Harm or Harmon, evidently an older personality. Was he the father of the murdered young man?

The 1780 House is, of course, recorded as dating back to 1780 only. But could not another building have occupied the area? Was the 1780 house an adaptation of a smaller dwelling of which there is no written record?

We can neither prove nor disprove this.

It is true, however, that General "Mad" Anthony Wayne was in charge of the Revolutionary troops in the New York area at the time under discussion.

At any rate, all this is knowledge not usually possessed by a lady voice teacher, which is what Ethel Meyers is when not being a medium.

3

Hungry Lucy

"June Havoc's got a ghost in her townhouse," Gail Benedict said gaily on the telephone. Gail was in public relations, and a devoted ghost-finder even since I had been able to rid her sister's apartment of a poltergeist the year before.

The house in question was 104 years old, stashed away in what New Yorkers call "Hell's Kitchen," the old area in the 40s between Ninth and Tenth Avenues, close to the theater district. Built on the corner of Forty-fourth Street and Ninth Avenue, it had been in the possession of the Rodenberg family until a Mr. Payne bought it. He remodeled it carefully, with a great deal of respect for the old plans. He did nothing to change its quaint Victorian appearance, inside or out.

About three years later, glamorous stage and television star June Havoc bought the house, and rented the upper floors to various tenants. She herself moved into the downstairs apartment, simply because no one else wanted it. It didn't strike her as strange at the time that no tenant had ever renewed the lease on that floor-through downstairs apartment, but now she knows why. It was all because of *Hungry Lucy*.

The morning after Gail's call, June Havoc telephoned me, and a séance was arranged for Friday of that week. I immediately reached British medium Sybil Leek, but I gave no details. I merely invited her to help me get rid of a noisy ghost. Noise was what June Havoc complained about.

"It seems to be a series of *insistent* sounds," she said. "First, they were rather soft. I didn't really notice them three years ago. Then I had the architect who built that balcony in the back come in and asked him to investigate these sounds. He said there was nothing whatever the matter with the house. Then I had the plumber up, because I thought it was the steam pipes. He said it was not that either. Then I had the carpenter in, for it is a very old house, but he couldn't find any structural defects whatever."

"When do you hear these tapping noises?"

"At all times. Lately, they seem to be more insistent. More demanding. We refer to it as 'tap dancing,' for that is exactly what it sounds like."

The wooden floors were in such excellent state that Miss Havoc didn't cover them with carpets. The yellow pine used for the floorboards cannot be replaced today.

June Havoc's maid had heard loud tapping in Miss Havoc's absence, and many of her actor friends had remarked on it.

"It is always in this area," June Havoc pointed out, "and seems to come from underneath the kitchen floor. It has become impossible to sleep a full night's sleep in this room."

The kitchen leads directly into the rear section of the floor-through apartment, to a room used as a bedroom. Consequently, any noise disturbed her sleep.

Underneath Miss Havoc's apartment, there was another floor-through, but the tenants had never reported anything unusual there, nor had the ones on the upper floors. Only Miss Havoc's place was noisy.

Hungry Lucy

We now walked from the front of the apartment into the back half. Suddenly there was a loud tapping sound from underneath the floor as if someone had shot off a machine gun. Catherine and I had arrived earlier than the rest, and there were just the three of us.

"There, you see," June Havoc said. The ghost had greeted us in style.

I stepped forward at once.

"What do you want?" I demanded.

Immediately, the noise stopped.

While we waited for the other participants in the investigation to arrive, June Havoc pointed to the rear wall.

"It has been furred out," she explained. "That is to say, there was another wall against the wall, which made the room smaller. Why, no one knows."

Soon *New York Post* columnist Earl Wilson and Mrs. Wilson, Gail Benedict, and Robert Winter-Berger, also a publicist, arrived, along with a woman from *Life* magazine, notebook in hand. A little later Sybil Leek swept into the room. There was a bit of casual conversation, in which nothing whatever was said about the ghost, and then we seated ourselves in the rear portion of the apartment. Sybil took the chair next to the spot where the noises always originated. June Havoc sat on her right, and I on her left. The lights were very bright since we were filming the entire scene for Miss Havoc's television show.

Soon enough, Sybil began to "go under."

"Hungry," Sybil mumbled faintly.

"Why are you hungry?" I asked.

"No food," the voice said.

The usually calm voice of Sybil Leek was panting in desperation now.

"I want some food, some food!" she cried.

I promised to help her and asked for her name.

"Don't cry. I will help you," I promised.

"Food . . . I want some food . . ." the voice continued to sob.

"Who are you?"

"Lucy Ryan."

"Do you live in this house?"

"No house here."

"How long have you been here?"

"A long time."

"What year is this?"

"Seventeen ninety-two."

"What do you do in this house?"

"No house . . . people . . . fields . . ."

"Why then are you here? What is there here for you?"

The ghost snorted.

"Hm . . . men."

"Who brought you here?"

"Came . . . people sent us away . . . soldiers . . . follow them . . . sent me away. . . ."

"What army? Which regiment?"

"Napier."

"How old are you?"

"Twenty."

"Where were you born?"

"Hawthorne . . . not very far away from here."

I was not sure whether she said "Hawthorne" or "Hawgton," or some similar name.

"What is you father's name?"

Silence.

"Your mother's name?"

Silence.

"Were you baptized?"

"Baptized?"

Hungry Lucy

She didn't remember that either.

I explained that she had passed on. It did not matter.

"Stay here . . . until I get some food . . . meat . . . meat and corn . . ."

"Have you tried to communicate with anyone in this house?"

"Nobody listens."

"How are you trying to make them listen?"

"I make noise because I want food."

"Why do you stay in one area? Why don't you move around freely?"

"Can't. Can't go away. Too many people. Soldiers."

"Where are your parents?"

"Dead."

"What is your mother's name?"

"Mae."

"Her maiden name?"

"Don't know."

"Your father's first name?"

"Terry."

"Were any of your family in the army?"

Ironical laughter punctuated her next words.

"Only . . . me."

"Tell me the names of some of the officers in the army you knew."

"Alfred . . . Wait."

"Any rank?"

"No rank."

"What regiment did you follow?"

"Just this . . . Alfred."

"And he left you?"

"Yes. I went with some other man, then I was hungry and I came here."

55

"Why here?"

"I was sent here."

"By whom?"

"They made me come. Picked me up. Man brought me here. Put me down on the ground."

"Did you die in this spot?"

"Die, die? I'm not dead. *I'm hungry.*"

I then asked her to join her parents, those who loved her, and to leave this spot. She refused. She wanted to walk by the river, she said. I suggested that she was not receiving food and could leave freely. After a while, the ghost seemed to slip away peacefully and Sybil Leek returned to her own body, temporarily vacated so that Lucy could speak through it. As usual, Sybil remembered absolutely nothing of what went on when she was in deep trance. She was crying, but thought her mascara was the cause of it.

Suddenly, the ghost was back. The floorboards were reverberating with the staccato sound of an angry tap, loud, strong, and demanding.

"What do you want?" I asked again, although I knew now what she wanted.

Sybil also extended a helping hand. But the sound stopped as abruptly as it had begun.

A while later, we sat down again. Sybil reported feeling two presences.

"One is a girl, the other is a man. A man with a stick. Or a gun. The girl is stronger. She wants something."

Suddenly, Sybil pointed to the kitchen area.

"What happened in the corner?"

Nobody had told Sybil of the area in which the disturbances had always taken place.

"I feel her behind me now. A youngish girl, not very well dressed, Georgian period. I don't get the man too well."

Hungry Lucy

At this point, we brought into the room a small Victorian wooden table, a gift from Gail Benedict.

Within seconds after Sybil, June Havoc, and I had lightly placed our hands upon it, it started to move, seemingly of its own volition!

Rapidly, it began to tap out a word, using a kind of Morse code. While Earl Wilson was taking notes, we allowed the table to jump hither and yon, tapping out a message.

None of us touched the table top except lightly. There was no question of manipulating the table. The light was very bright, and our hands almost touched, so that any pressure by one of us would have been instantly noticed by the other two. This type of communication is slow, since the table runs through the entire alphabet until it reaches the desired letter, then the next letter, until an entire word has been spelled out.

"L-e-a-v-e," the communicator said, not exactly in a friendly mood.

Evidently she wanted the place to herself and thought *we* were the intruders.

I tried to get some more information about her. But instead of tapping out another word in an orderly fashion, the table became very excited—if that is the word for emotional tables—and practically leapt from beneath our hands. We were required to follow it to keep up the contact, as it careened wildly through the room. When I was speaking, it moved toward me and practically crept onto my lap. When I wasn't speaking, it ran to someone else in the room. Eventually, it became so wild, at times entirely off the floor, that it slipped from our light touch and, as the power was broken, instantly rolled into a corner—just another table with no life of its own.

We repaired to the garden, a few steps down an iron staircase, in the rear of the house.

"Sybil, what do you feel down here?" I asked.

"I had a tremendous urge to come out here. I didn't know there was a garden. Underneath my feet almost is the cause of the disturbance."

We were standing at a spot adjacent to the basement wall and close to the center of the tapping disturbance we had heard.

"Someone may be buried here," Sybil remarked, pointing to a mound of earth underneath our feet. "It's a girl."

"Do you see the wire covering the area behind you?" June Havoc said. "I tried to plant seeds there, and the wire was to protect them—but somehow nothing, nothing will grow there."

"Plant something on this mound," Sybil suggested. "It may well pacify *her*."

We returned to the upstairs apartment, and soon after broke up the "ghost hunting party," as columnist Sheila Graham called it later.

The next morning, I called June Havoc to see how things were. I knew from experience that the ghost would either be totally gone, or totally mad, but not the same as before.

Lucy, I was told, was rather mad. Twice as noisy, she still demanded her pound of flesh. I promised June Havoc that we'd return until the ghost was completely gone.

A few days passed. Things became a little quieter, as if Lucy were hesitating. Then something odd happened the next night. Instead of tapping from her accustomed corner area, Lucy moved away from it and tapped away from above June's bed. She had never been heard from that spot before.

I decided it was time to have a chat with Lucy again. Meanwhile, corroboration of the information we had obtained had come to us quickly. The morning after our first séance, Bob Winter-Berger called. He had been to the New York Public Library and checked on Napier, the officer named by the medium as the man in charge of the soldier's regiment.

The *Dictionary of National Biography* contained the answer.

Hungry Lucy

Colonel George Napier, a British officer, had served on the staff of Governor Sir Henry Clinton. How exciting, I thought. The Clinton mansion once occupied the very ground we were having the séance on. In fact, I had reported on a ghost at Clinton Court, two short blocks to the north, in *Ghost Hunter* and again in *Ghosts I've Met*. As far as I knew, the place was still not entirely free of the uncanny, for reports continued to reach me of strange steps and doors opening by themselves.

Although the mansion itself no longer stands, the carriage house in the rear was now part of Clinton Court, a reconstructed apartment house on West Forty-sixth Street. How could Sybil Leek, only recently arrived from England, have known of these things?

Napier was indeed the man who had charge of a regiment on this very spot, and the years 1781–1782 are given as the time when Napier's family contracted the dreaded yellow fever and died. Sir Henry Clinton forbade his aide to be in touch with them, and the Colonel was shipped off to England, half-dead himself, while his wife and family passed away on the spot that later became Potter's Field.

Many Irish immigrants came to the New World in those years. Perhaps the Ryan girl was one of them, or her parents were. Unfortunately, history does not keep much of a record of camp followers.

On January 15, 1965, precisely at midnight, I placed Sybil Leek into deep trance in my apartment on Riverside Drive. In the past we had succeeded in contacting *former* ghosts once they had been pried loose in an initial séance in the haunted house itself. I had high hopes that Lucy would communicate and I wasn't disappointed.

"Tick, tock, tickety-tock, June's clock stops, June's clock stops," the entranced medium murmured, barely audibly.

"Tickety-tock, June's clock stops, tickety-tock . . ."

"Who are you?" I asked.

"Lucy."

"Lucy, what does this mean?"

"June's clock stops, June's clock stops, frightened June, frightened June," she repeated like a child reciting a poem.

"Why do you want to frighten June?"

"Go away." "Why do you want her to go away?"

"People there . . . too much house . . . too much June . . . too many clocks . . . she sings, dances, she makes a lot of noise . . . I'm hungry, I'm always hungry. You don't do a thing about it . . ."

"Will you go away if I get you some food? Can we come to an agreement?"

"Why?"

"Because I want to help you, help June."

"Ah, same old story."

"You're not happy. Would you like to see Alfred again?"

"Yes . . . he's gone."

"Not very far. I'll get you together with Alfred if you will leave the house."

"Where would I go?"

"Alfred has a house of his own for you."

"Where?"

"Not very far."

"Frightened to go . . . don't know where to go . . . nobody likes me. She makes noises, I make noises. I don't like that clock."

"Where were you born, Lucy?"

"Larches by the Sea . . . Larchmont . . . by the Sea . . . people disturb me."

Again I asked her to go to join her Alfred, to find happiness again. I suggested she call for him by name, which she did, hesitatingly at first, more desperately later.

"No . . . I can't go from here. He said he would come. He said *wait*. Wait . . . here. Wait. Alfred, why don't you come? Too

60

many clocks. Time, time, time . . . noisy creature. Time, time
. . . three o'clock."

"What happened at three o'clock?" I demanded.

"He said he'd come," the ghost replied. "I waited for him."

"Why at three o'clock in the middle of the night?"

"Why do you think? Couldn't get out. Locked in. Not
allowed out at night. I'll wait. He'll come."

"Did you meet any of his friends?"

"Not many . . . what would *I* say?"

"What was Alfred's name?"

"Bailey . . . Alfred said 'Wait, wait . . . I'll go away,' he
said. 'They'll never find me.'"

"Go to him with my love," I said, calmly repeating over
and over the formula used in rescue circle operations to send the
earthbound ghost across the threshold.

As I spoke, Lucy slipped away from us, not violently as she
had come, but more or less resignedly.

I telephoned June Havoc to see what had happened that
night between midnight and 12:30. She had heard Lucy's tapping
precisely then, but nothing more as the night passed—a quiet
night for a change.

Was Lucy on her way to her Alfred?

We would know soon enough.

In the weeks that followed, I made periodic inquiries of
June Havoc. Was the ghost still in evidence? Miss Havoc did not
stay at her townhouse all the time, preferring the quiet charm of
her Connecticut estate. But on the nights when she did sleep in
the house on Forty-fourth Street, she was able to observe that
Lucy Ryan had changed considerably in personality—the ghost
had been freed, yes, but had not yet been driven from the house.
In face, the terrible noise was now all over the house, although
less frequent and less vehement—*as if she were thinking things over.*

I decided we had to finish the job as well as we could and

another séance was arranged for late March, 1965. Present were—in addition to our hostess and chief sufferer—my wife Catherine and myself; Emory Lewis, editor of *Cue* magazine; Barry Farber, WOR commentator; and two friends of June Havoc. We grouped ourselves around a table in the *front room* this time. This soon proved to be a mistake. No Lucy Ryan. No ghost. We repaired to the other room where the original manifestations had taken place, with more luck this time.

Sybil, in trance, told us that the girl had gone, but that Alfred had no intention of leaving. He was waiting for *her* now. I asked for the name of his commanding officer and was told it was Napier. This we knew already. But who was the next in rank?

"Lieutenant William Watkins."

"What about the commanding general?"

He did not know.

He had been born in Hawthorne, just like Lucy, he told Sybil. I had been able to trace this Hawthorne to a place not far away in Westchester County.

There were people all over, Sybil said in trance, and they were falling down. They were ill.

"Send Alfred to join his Lucy," I commanded, and Sybil in a low voice told the stubborn ghost to go.

After an interlude of table tipping, in which several characters from the nether world made their auditory appearance, she returned to trance. Sybil in trance was near the river again, among the sick.

But no Lucy Ryan. Lucy's gone, she said.

"The smell makes me sick," Sybil said, and you could see stark horror in her sensitive face.

"Dirty people, rags, people in uniform too, with dirty trousers. There is a big house across the river."

"Whose house is it?"

"Mr. Dawson's. Doctor Dawson. Dr. James Dawson . . .

Lee Point. Must go there. Feel sick. Rocks and trees, just the house across the river."

"What year is this?"

"Ninety-two."

She then described Dr. Dawson's house as having three windows on the left, two on the right, and five above, and said that it was called Lee Point—Hawthorne. It sounded a little like Hawgton to me, but I can't be sure.

Over the river, she said. She described a "round thing on a post" in front of the house, like a shell. For messages, she thought.

"What is the name of the country we're in?" I asked.

"Vinelands. Vinelands."

I decided to change the subject back to Hungry Lucy. How did she get sick?

"She didn't get any food, and then she got cold, by the river.

". . . Nobody helped them there. Let them die. Buried them in a pit."

"What is the name of the river?"

"Mo . . . Mo-something."

"Do you see anyone else still around?"

"Lots of people with black faces, black shapes."

The plague, I thought, and how little the doctors could do in those days to stem it.

I asked about the man in charge and she said "Napier" and I wondered who would be left in command after Napier left, and the answer this time was, "Clinton . . . old fool. Georgie."

There were a Henry Clinton and a George Clinton, fairly contemporary with each other.

"What happened after that?"

"Napier died."

"Any other officers around?"

"Little Boy Richardson . . . Lieutenant."

"What regiment?"

"Burgoyne."

Sybil, entranced, started to hiss and whistle. "Signals," she murmured. "As the men go away, they whistle."

I decided the time had come to bring Sybil out of trance. She felt none the worse for it, and asked for something to drink. *Hungry*, like Lucy, she wasn't.

We began to evaluate the information just obtained. Dr. James Dawson may very well have lived. The A.M.A. membership directories aren't that old. I found the mention of Lee Point and Hawthorne interesting, inasmuch as the two locations are quite close. Lee, of course, would be Fort Lee, and there is a "point" or promontory in the river at that spot.

The town of Vinelands does exist in New Jersey, but the river beginning with "Mo-" may be the Mohawk. That Burgoyne was a general in the British army during the Revolution is well known.

So there you have it. Sybil Leek knows very little, if anything, about the New Jersey and Westchester countryside, having only recently come to America. Even I, then a New York resident for 27 years, had never heard of Hawthorne before. Yet there it is on the way to Pleasantville, New York.

The proof of the ghostly pudding, however, was not the regimental roster, but the state of affairs at June Havoc's house.

A later report had it that Lucy, Alfred, or whoever was responsible had quieted down considerably.

They were down, but not out.

I tactfully explained to June Havoc that feeling sorry for a hungry ghost makes things tough for a parapsychologist. The emotional pull of a genuine attachment, no matter how unconscious it may be, can provide the energies necessary to prolong the stay of the ghost.

Hungry Lucy

Gradually, as June Havoc—wanting a peaceful house, especially at 3 A.M.—allowed practical sense to outweigh sentimentality, the shades of Hungry Lucy and her soldier-boy faded into the distant past, whence they came.

4

The Peace Conference
That Failed

In this age of peace conferences that go on for years and years
without yielding tangible results—or, if any, only piecemeal
ones, reached after long deliberation—it is a refreshing thought
to remember that a peace conference held on Staten Island
between Lord Howe, the British commander in America, and a
congressional committee consisting of Benjamin Franklin, John
Adams and Edward Rutledge lasted but a single day—September
11, 1776, to be exact.

The position was this: the British were already in command of New York, Long Island and Staten Island, and the Yankees still held New Jersey and Pennsylvania, with Philadelphia as
the seat of the Continental Congress. In view of his tremendous
successes in the war against the colonists, Lord Howe felt that the
suppression of the independence movement was only a matter of
weeks. Wanting to avoid further bloodshed and, incidentally, to
save himself some trouble, he suggested that a peace conference
be held to determine whether an honorable peace could be concluded at that juncture of events.

Congress received his message with mixed emotions, having but lately worked out internal differences of opinion concern-

ing the signing of the Declaration of Independence. A committee was appointed consisting of the aforementioned three men and empowered to investigate the offer. The three legislators went by horse to Perth Amboy, New Jersey, and were met at the New Jersey shore by a barge manned by British soldiers under a safe-conduct pass across the bay. They landed on the Staten Island shore and walked up to Bentley Manor, the residence of Lord Howe. There they were met with politeness and courtesies but also with a display of British might, for there were soldiers in full battle dress lined up along the road.

Later, the flamboyant John Adams told of soldiers "looking fierce as ten furies, and making all the grimaces and gestures and motions of their muskets, with bayonets fixed, which I suppose, military etiquette requires, but which we neither understood nor regarded."

Lord Howe outlined his plan for a settlement, explaining that it was futile for the Americans to carry on the war and that the British were willing to offer peace with honor. Of course, any settlement would involve the colonies' remaining under British rule. The three envoys listened in polite silence, after which Benjamin Franklin informed Lord Howe that the Declaration of Independence had already been signed on July 4, 1776, and that they would never go back under British rule.

The conference broke up, and Lord Howe, still very polite, had the trio conveyed to Amboy in his own barge, under the safe-conduct pass he had granted them. The following day, September 12, 1776, the war of independence entered a new round: the Yankees knew what the British government was willing to offer them in order to obtain peace, and they realized that they might very well win the war with just a little more effort. Far from discouraging them, the failure of the peace conference on Staten Island helped reinforce the Continental Congress in its determination to pursue the war of independence to its very end.

The Peace Conference That Failed

This historical event took place in a manor house over-looking Raritan Bay, and at the time, and for many years afterward, it was considered the most outstanding building on Staten Island. The two-story white building goes back to before 1680 and is a colonial manor built along British lines. It was erected by a certain Christopher Billopp, a somewhat violent and hard-headed sea captain who had served in the British Navy for many years. Apparently, Captain Billopp had friends at court in London, and when the newly appointed Governor Andros came to America in 1674, he obtained a patent as lieutenant of a company of soldiers. In the process he acquired nearly one thousand acres of choice land on Staten Island. But Billopp got into difficulties with his governor and reentered navy service for a while, returning to Staten Island under Governor Thomas Dongan. In 1687 he received a land grant for Bentley Manor, sixteen hundred acres of very choice land, and on this tract he built the present manor house. The Billopp family were fierce Tories and stood with the crown to the last. The Captain's grandson, also named Christopher, who was already born in the manor, lived there till the end of the Revolution, when he moved to New Brunswick, Canada along with many other Tories who could not stay on in the newly independent colonies.

From then on, the manor house had a mixed history of owners and gradually fell into disrepair. Had it not been built so solidly, with the keen eye of a navy man's perception of carpentry, perhaps none of it would stand today. As it was, an association was formed in 1920 to restore the historical landmark to its former glory. This has now been done, and the Conference House, as it is commonly called, is a museum open to the public. It is located in what was once Bentley Manor but today is called Tottenville, and it can easily be reached from New York City via the Staten Island Ferry. The ground floor contains two large rooms and a staircase leading to the upper story, which is also divided into two rooms. In the basement is a kitchen and a vaultlike enclosure. Both basement and attic are of immense proportions. The large room downstairs to the left of the entrance was originally used as a dining room and the room to the right as a parlor. Upstairs, the large room to the left is a bedroom while the one to the right is nowadays used as a Benjamin Franklin museum. In between the two large rooms is a small room, perhaps a child's room at one time. At one time there was also a tunnel from the vault in the basement to the water's edge, which was used as a means of escape during Indian attacks, a frequent occurrence in pre-colonial days. Also, this secret tunnel could be used to obtain supplies by the sea route without being seen by observers on land.

As early as 1962 I was aware of the Conference House and its reputation of being haunted. My initial investigation turned up a lot of hearsay evidence, hardly of a scientific nature, but nevertheless of some historical significance inasmuch as there is usually a grain of truth in all legendary stories. According to the local legends, Captain Billopp had jilted his fiancée, and she had died of a broken heart in the house. As a result, strange noises, including murmurs, sighs, moans, and pleas of an unseen voice, were reported to have been heard in the house as far back as the mid-nineteenth century. According to the old Staten Island newspaper *The Transcript*, the phenomena were heard by a number of workmen during the restoration of the house after it had been taken over as a museum.

My first visit to the Conference House took place in 1962, in the company of Ethel Johnson Meyers and two of her friends, Rose de Simone and Pearl Winder, who had come along for the ride since they were interested in the work Mrs. Meyers and I were doing. Mrs. Meyers, of course, had no idea where we were going or why we were visiting Staten Island. Nevertheless, when we were still about a half hour's ride away from the house, she volunteered her impressions of the place we were going to. When I encouraged her to speak freely, she said that the house she had yet to see was white, that the ground floor was divided into two rooms, and that the east room contained a brown table and eight chairs. She also stated that the room to the west of the entrance was the larger of the two, and that some silverware was on display in that room.

When we arrived at the house, I checked these statements at once; they were entirely correct, except that the number of chairs were seven, not eight as Mrs. Meyers had stated. I questioned the resident curator about this seeming discrepancy. One of the chairs and the silverware had indeed been on display for years but had been removed from the room eight years prior to our visit.

"Butler," Mrs. Meyers mumbled as we entered the house. It turned out that the estate next to Bentley belonged to the Butlers; undoubtedly, members of that family had been in the Conference House many times. As is my custom, I allowed my medium free rein of her intuition. Mrs. Meyers decided to settle on the second story room to the left of the staircase, where she sat down on the floor for want of a chair.

Gradually entering the vibrations of the place, she spoke of a woman named Jane whom she described as being stout, white haired, and dressed in a dark green dress and a fringed shawl. Then the medium looked up at me and, as if she intuitively knew the importance of her statement, simply said, "Howe." This shook me up, since Mrs. Meyers had no knowledge of Lord Howe's connection with the place she was in. I also found interesting Mrs. Meyers's description of a "presence," that is to say, a ghost, whom she described as a big man in a fur hat, being rather fat and wearing a skin coat and high boots, a brass-buckled belt, and black trousers. "I feel boats around him, nets, sailing boats, and I feel a broad foreign accent," Mrs. Meyers stated, adding that she saw him in a four-masted ship of a square-rigger type. At the same time she mentioned the initial T. What better description of the Tory, Captain Billopp, could she have given!

"I feel as if I am being dragged somewhere by Indians," Mrs. Meyers suddenly exclaimed, as I reported in my original account of this case in my first book, *Ghost Hunter.* "There is violence, and somebody dies on a pyre of wood. Two men, one white, one Indian; and on two sticks nearby are their scalps." It seemed to me that what Mrs. Meyers had tuned in on were remnants of emotional turmoil in the pre-colonial days; as I have noted, Indian attacks were quite frequent during the early and middle parts of the eighteenth century.

When we went down into the cellar, Mrs. Meyers assured us that six people had been buried near the front wall during the Revolutionary War and that they were all British soldiers. She also said that eight more were buried somewhere else on the grounds, and she had the impression that the basement has been used as a hospital during an engagement. Later investigation confirmed that members of the Billopp family had been buried on the grounds near the road and that British soldiers might very well have been buried there too, since there were frequent skirmishes around the house from July 1776 to the end of the year. Captain Billopp was twice kidnapped from his own house by armed bands operating from the New Jersey shore.

It was clear to me that Mrs. Meyers was entering various layers of history and giving us bits and pieces of her impressions, not necessarily in the right order but as she received them. The difficulty with trance mediumship is that you cannot direct it the way you want to, that is to say, ferret out just those entities or layers from the past you are interested in. You have to take "pot luck," as it were, hoping that sufficient material of interest will come through the medium.

Once more we returned to the upper part of the house. Suddenly Mrs. Meyers turned white in the face and held on for

The Peace Conference That Failed

dear life to the winding staircase. For a moment she seemed immobilized. Then, coming to life again, she slowly descended the stairs and pointed to a spot near the landing of the second story. "A woman was killed here with a crooked knife!" she said.

Aha, I thought, there is our legend about Captain Billopp and his jilted fiancée. But he didn't kill her; she had died of a broken heart. Mrs. Earley, the custodian, was trying to be helpful, so I questioned her about any murder that might have occurred in the house. "Why, yes," she obliged. "Captain Billopp once flew into a rage and killed a female slave on that very spot on the stairs." As she spoke, I had the impression that the custodian was shuddering just a little herself.

From time to time people had told me of their visits to the Conference House and wondered whether the "ghost in residence" was still active. Finally I asked a young lady I had been working with for some time to try her hand at picking up whatever might be left in the atmosphere of the Conference House. Ingrid Beckman, an artist by profession, knew very little about the house but had access to the short account of my investigation given in *Ghost Hunter*.

I asked Ingrid to go to the house by herself, and on the afternoon of November 25, 1972, she paid it a visit.

In order to avoid tourists, she had arrived at the house about one o'clock. The house was still closed to visitors so she sat down on a bench outside. "I walked around, and even on the outside I felt a presence," Ingrid began her report to me. "I felt as if the place were really alive. Then I went up to the front porch and peeked into the main hallway, and when I looked up the stairs I had a feeling of gloom and foreboding. I had the distinct sensation of a dangerous situation there."

Strangely enough, Ingrid seemed to have been led to that house. Two weeks prior to her visit, she had happened to find herself in Nyack, browsing through some antique shops. There she

73

met a woman who started to talk to her. The woman explained that she was from Staten Island, and when she discovered that Ingrid lived there also, she suggested that Ingrid visit a certain house, once the property of an old sea captain. The house, the lady said, had an interesting tunnel which began behind a fire-place and ran down to the water's edge. Ingrid, always interested in visiting old houses, had promised to look into the matter. This was two weeks before I mentioned a visit to the Conference House to her.

The following weekend, Ingrid was with some friends at her apartment on Staten Island. She took the opportunity of ask-ing whether any of them had ever heard of the house as described by her acquaintance. One of the young men present affirmed that there was such a house, called the Conference House, and that it was haunted by the spirit of a slave who had been killed there. That was on Sunday. The following Monday I telephoned Ingrid with the request to go to the Conference House.

As Ingrid was sitting on the front porch of the house, wait-ing for the door to be opened, she had the distinct feeling that someone was watching her. "I felt as if someone knew I was there," she explained, "and I especially felt this coming from the window above the hallway. It is a crooked window, and I felt that it had some sort of significance. If anyone were looking at me or wanted to get my attention, it would be through that window. But when I went in, as soon as the door had been opened to visitors, the first place I went to was the basement. As I was looking around the basement, I came upon a little archway, as if I had been *directed* to go there."

The spot made her literally jump; she felt that something terrible had occurred near the fireplace, and she experienced heavy chills at the same time; someone had been brutalized at the entrance to the tunnel. Fortunately, she had managed to go there by herself, having discouraged the tourist guide from taking her around. "The tunnel entrance is particularly terrorizing," Ingrid said. "This tunnel caused me chills all the way up to my neck."

Finally tearing herself away from the basement, she went up the stairs, again by herself. Immediately she arrived at the upper landing and went to the bedroom to the left; as she stood in the entranceway, she heard a noise like a knock.

"The hallway upstairs felt terrible," Ingrid explained. "I turned around and looked down the stairs. As I looked, I almost became dizzy. It felt as if someone had been pushed down them or hurt on them." To be sure that she wasn't imagining things or being influenced by what she had read, Ingrid decided to go up and down those stairs several times. Each time, the sensation was the same. On one of her trips up the stairs, she ascertained that the window, which had so attracted her while she was still waiting outside, was indeed just outside the haunted stairwell.

"I got the impression of a slave woman, especially in the upstairs bedroom; I also felt there was a disturbance around the table downstairs, but I don't think the two are connected. I felt the woman was associated with the upstairs bedroom and the stairway and possibly the tunnel entrance; but the feeling in the basement is another episode, I think."

"What period do you think the disturbances go back to?" I asked.

"I'd say the 1700s, going back before the Revolution."

"Do you have the feeling that there is still something there that hasn't been fully resolved?"

"Yes, definitely. I think that is why I had such strong vibrations about it, and I think that is also why I got the information two weeks beforehand."

"Do you think that is is a man or woman who is 'hung up' in there?"

"I think it is a woman, but there may also be a man because the scene at the table had something to do with a man.

He may have been shot, or he may have been abducted from that room—you know, taken through the tunnel."

I suddenly recalled that Captain Billopp was twice abducted by Yankee irregulars from the Jersey shore. Gabriel Disosway, in his 1846 account of the Manor of Bentley, reported that "Colonel Billopp, at the time a warm party man and military leader, was closely watched, and, it is said, was twice taken from his own house by armed bands from 'the Jerseys,' and thus made a prisoner. Amboy is in sight, and upon one of these occasions, he was observed by some Americans, who had stationed themselves with a spy glass in the church steeple of that town. As soon as they saw him enter his abode, they ran to their boats, rapidly crossed the river, and he was soon their captive."

On January 28, 1973, Ingrid made another, spontaneous visit to the Conference House. She had much the same impressions as before, but this time she managed to speak to the caretaker. The lady admitted hearing heavy footsteps upstairs at times, which sounded to her like those of a man wearing heavy boots with spurs attached. Also, on the anniversary of "the murder," the caretaker claims to have seen a man run up the stairs toward a girl waiting on the first landing. "Her story is that the girl was beheaded," Ingrid reported further. "She says that one afternoon last summer, as she was dusting the room on the left of the ground floor, she could put her hand 'right through' a British soldier! This past summer her daughter from South Carolina came to visit and insisted on staying upstairs in the haunted rooms. That night the daughter allegedly heard a man's laughter, followed by a woman's laughter, and then a shriek. According to the caretaker, this happens at regular intervals."

The caretaker's account fascinated me and would have been even more impressive had Ingrid not also overheard her telling some visiting tourists that I had visited the Conference House in the company of Orson Welles, Ethel Meyers, and Sybil Leek.

The Peace Conference That Failed

Quite obviously, the good lady was confusing my mention of these three people in the same book, *Ghost Hunter*, with my relatively simple and short account of my visit to the Conference House. Under the circumstances, we can't be too sure about the footsteps and the woman's shriek in the night. What we can be sure of, however, is the very real, very tangible imprint of Lord Howe's fruitless discussion with Benjamin Franklin, John Adams, and Edward Rutledge. It is a good thing that these three signers of the Declaration of Independence did not stay the night as guests of Lord Howe. Imagine what would have happened if they had met up with the murdered slave girl on the stairs!

5

A Revolutionary Corollary: Patrick Henry, Nathan Hale, et al.

Nathan Hale, as every schoolboy knows, was the American spy hanged by the British. He was captured at Huntington Beach and taken to Brooklyn for trial. How he was captured is a matter of some concern to the people of Huntington, Long Island. The town was originally settled by colonists from Connecticut who were unhappy with the situation in that colony. There were five principal families who accounted for the early settlement of Huntington, and to this day their descendants are the most prominent families in the area. They were the Sammes, the Downings, the Busches, the Pauldings, and the Cooks. During the Revolutionary War, feelings were about equally divided among the town people: some were Revolutionaries and some remained Tories. The consensus of historians is that members of these five prominent families, all of whom were Tories, were responsible for the betrayal of Nathan Hale to the British.

All this was brought to my attention by Mrs. Geraldine P. of Huntington. Mrs. P. grew up in what she considers the oldest house in Huntington, although the Huntington Historical Society claims that theirs is even older. Be that as it may, it was there when the Revolutionary War started. Local legend has it that an act of violence took place on the corner of the street, which was then a crossroads in the middle of a rural area. The house in which Mrs. P. grew up, stands on that street. Mrs. P. suspects that the capture—or, at any rate, the betrayal—of the Revolutionary agent took place on that crossroads. When she tried to investigate the history of her house, she found little cooperation on the part of the local historical society. It was a conspiracy of silence, according to her, as if some people wanted to cover up a certain situation from the past.

The house had had a "strange depressing effect on all its past residents," according to Mrs. P. Her own father, who studied astrology and white magic for many years, has related an incident that occurred several years ago in the house. He awoke in the middle of the night in the master bedroom because he felt unusually cold. He became aware of "something" rushing about the room in wild, frantic circles. Because of his outlook and training, he spoke up, saying, "Can I help you?" But the rushing about became even more frantic. He then asked what was wrong and what could be done. But no communication was possible. When he saw that he could not communicate with the entity, Mrs. P.'s father finally said, "If I can't help you, then go away." There was a snapping sound, and the room suddenly became quiet and warm again, and he went back to sleep. There have been no other recorded incidents at the house in question. But Mrs. P. wonders if some guilty entity wants to manifest, not necessarily Nathan Hale, but perhaps someone connected with his betrayal.

At the corner of 43rd Street and Vanderbilt Avenue, Manhattan, one of the busiest and noisiest spots in all of New York City, there is a small commemorative plaque explaining that Nathan Hale, the Revolutionary spy, was executed on that spot by the British. I doubt that too many New Yorkers are aware of this, or can accurately pinpoint the location of the tragedy. It is even less likely that a foreigner would know about it. When I sug-

A Revolutionary Corollary:

gested to my good friend Sybil Leek that she accompany me to a psychically important spot for an experiment, she readily agreed. Despite the noises and the heavy traffic, the spot being across from Grand Central Station, Sybil bravely stood with me on the street corner and tried to get some sort of psychic impression.

"I get the impression of food and drink," Sybil said. I pointed out that there were restaurants all over the area, but Sybil shook her head. "No, I was thinking more of a place for food and drink, and I don't mean in the present. It is more like an inn, a transit place, and it has some connection with the river. A meeting place, perhaps, some sort of inn. Of course, it is very difficult in this noise and with all these new buildings here."

"If we took down these buildings, what would we see?"

"I think we would see a field and water. I have a strong feeling that there is a connection with water and with the inn. There are people coming and going—I sense a woman, but I don't think she's important. I am not sure . . . unless it would mean foreign. I hear a foreign language. Something like *Verchenen*.* I can't quite get it. It is not German."

"Is there anything you feel about this spot?"

"This spot, yes. I think I want to go back two hundred years at least, it is not very clear, 1769 or 1796. That is the period. The connection with the water puzzles me."

"Do you feel an event of significance here at any time?"

"Yes. It is not strong enough to come through to me completely, but sufficiently *drastic* to make me feel a little nervous."

"In what way is it drastic?"

"Hurtful, violent. There are several people involved in this violence. Something connected with water, papers connected with water, that is part of the trouble."

Sybil then suggested that we go to the right to see if the

---

*Verplanck's Point, on the Hudson River, was a Revolutionary strongpoint at the time.

impressions might be stronger at some distance. We went around the corner and I stopped. Was the impression any stronger?

"No, the impression is the same. Papers, violence. For a name, I have the impression of the letters P.T. Peter. It would be helpful to come here in the middle of the night, I think. I wish I could understand the connection with water, here in the middle of the city."

"Did someone die here?"

Sybil closed her eyes and thought it over for a moment. "Yes, but the death of this person was important at that time and indeed necessary. But there is more to it than just the death of the person. The disturbance involves lots of other things, lots of other people. In fact, two distinct races were involved, because I sense a lack of understanding. I think that this was a political thing, and the papers were important."

"Can you get anything further on the nature of this violence you feel here?"

"Just a disturbed feeling, an upheaval, a general disturbance. I am sorry I can't get much else. Perhaps if we came here at night, when things are quieter."

I suggested we get some tea in one of the nearby restaurants. Over tea, we discussed our little experiment and Sybil suddenly remembered an odd experience she had had when visiting the Hotel Biltmore before. (The plaque in question is mounted on the wall of the hotel.) "I receive many invitations to go to this particular area of New York," Sybil explained, "and when I go I always get the feeling of repulsion to the extent where I may be on my way down and get into a telephone booth and call the people involved and say, 'No, I'll meet you somewhere else.' I don't like this particular area we just left; I find it very depressing. *I feel trapped.*"

I am indebted to R. M. Sandwich of Richmond, Virginia,

A Revolutionary Corollary:

for an intriguing account of an E.S.P. experience he has connected to Patrick Henry. Mr. Sandwich stated that he has had only one E.S.P. experience and that it took place in one of the early estate-homes of Patrick Henry. He admitted that the experience altered his previously dim view of E.S.P. The present owner of the estate has said that Mr. Sandwich has not been the only one to experience strange things in that house.

The estate-home where the incident took place is called Pine Flash and is presently owned by E. E. Verdon, a personal friend of Mr. Sandwich. It is located in Hanover County, about fifteen miles outside of Richmond. The house was given to Patrick Henry by his father-in-law. After Henry had lived in it for a number of years, it burned to the ground and was not rebuilt until fifteen years later. During that time Henry resided in the old cottage, which is directly behind the house, and stayed there until the main house had been rebuilt. This cottage is frequently referred to in the area as the honeymoon cottage of young Patrick Henry. The new house was rebuilt exactly as it had been before the fire. As for the cottage, which is still in excellent condition, it is thought to be the oldest wood frame dwelling in Virginia. It may have been there even before Patrick Henry lived in it.

On the Fourth of July, 1968, the Sandwiches had been invited to try their luck at fishing in a pond on Mr. Verdon's land. Since they would be arriving quite early in the morning, they were told that the oars to the rowboat, which they were to use at the pond, would be found inside the old cottage. They arrived at Pine Flash sometime around six A.M. Mrs. Sandwich started unpacking their fishing gear and food supplies, while Mr. Sandwich decided to inspect the cottage. Although he had been to the place several times before, he had never actually been inside the cottage itself.

Here then is Mr. Sandwich's report.

"I opened the door, walked in, and shut the door tight behind me. Barely a second had passed after I shut the door when a strange feeling sprang over me. It was the kind of feeling you would experience if you were to walk into an extremely cold, damp room. I remember how still everything was, and then I distinctly heard footsteps overhead in the attic. I called out, thinking perhaps there was someone upstairs. No one answered, nothing. At that time I was standing directly in front of an old fireplace. I admit I was scared half to death. The footsteps were louder now and seemed to be coming down the thin staircase toward me. As they passed me, I felt a cold, crisp, odd feeling. I started looking around for something, anything that could have caused all this. It was during this time that I noticed the closed door open very, very slowly. The door stopped when it was half opened, almost beckoning me to take my leave, which I did at great speed! As I went through that open door, I felt the same cold mass of air I had experienced before. Standing outside, I watched the door slam itself, almost in my face! My wife was still unpacking the car and claims she neither saw nor heard anything."

Revolutionary figures have a way of hanging on to places they like in life. Candy Bosselmann of Indiana has had a long history of psychic experiences. She is a budding trance medium and not at all ashamed of her talents. In 1964 she happened to be visiting Ashland, the home of Henry Clay, in Lexington, Kentucky. She had never been to Ashland, so she decided to take a look at it. She and other visitors were shown through the house by an older man, a professional guide, and Candy became somewhat restless listening to his historical ramblings. As the group entered the library and the guide explained the beautiful ash paneling taken from surrounding trees (for which the home is named), she became even more restless. She knew very well that it was the kind of feeling that forewarned her of some sort of psychic event. As she was looking over toward a fireplace, framed by two candelabra, she suddenly saw a very tall, white-haired man in a long black frock coat standing next to it. One elbow rested on the mantel, and his head was in his hand, as if he were pondering something very important.

Miss Bosselmann was not at all emotionally involved with the house. In fact, the guided tour bored her, and she would have preferred to be outside in the stables, since she has a great interest in horses. Her imagination did not conjure up what she saw: she knew in an instant that she was looking at the spirit imprint of Henry Clay.

In 1969 she visited Ashland again, and this time she went into the library deliberately. With her was a friend who wasn't at all psychic. Again, the same restless feeling came over her. But when she was about to go into trance, she decided to get out of the room in a hurry.

Rock Ford, the home of General Edward Hand, is located four miles south of Lancaster, Pennsylvania, and commands a fine view of the Conestoga River. The house is not a restoration but a well-preserved eighteenth-century mansion, with its original floors, railings, shutters, doors, cupboards, panelings, and window glass. Even the original wall painting can be seen. It is a four-story brick mansion in the Georgian style, with the rooms grouped around a center hall in the design popular during the latter part of the eighteenth century. The rooms are furnished with antiquities of the period. thanks to the discovery of an inventory of General Hand's estate which permitted the local historical society to supply authentic articles of daily usage wherever the originals had disappeared from the house.

Perhaps General Edward Hand is not as well known as a hero of the American Revolution as others are, but to the people of the Pennsylvania Dutch country he is an important figure, even though he was of Irish origin rather than German. Trained as a medical doctor at Trinity College, Dublin, he came to America in 1767 with the Eighteenth Royal Irish Regiment of Foote. However, he resigned British service in 1774 and came to Lancaster to practice medicine and surgery. With the fierce love of liberty so many of the Irish possess, Dr. Hand joined the Revolutionaries in July of 1775, becoming a lieutenant colonel in the Pennsylvania Rifle Battalion. He served in the army until 1800, when he was discharged as a major general. Dr. Hand was present at the Battle of Trenton, the Battle of Long Island, the Battle of White Plains, the Battle of Princeton, the campaign against the Iroquois, and the surrender of Cornwallis at Yorktown. He also served on the tribunal which convicted Major John André, the British spy, and later became the army's adjutant general. He was highly regarded by George Washington, who visited him in his home toward the end of the war. When peace came, Hand became a member of the Continental Congress and served in the Assembly of Pennsylvania as representative of his area. He moved into Rock Ford when it was completed in 1793 and died there in September 1802.

Today, hostesses from a local historical society serve as guides for the tourists who come to Rock Ford in increasing numbers. Visitors are taken about the lower floor and basement and are told of General Hand's agricultural experiments, his medical studies, and his association with George Washington. But unless you ask specifically, you are not likely to hear about what happened to the house after General Hand died. To begin with, the General's son committed suicide in the house. Before long the family died out, and eventually the house became a museum since no one wanted to live in it for very long. At one time, immigrants were contacted at the docks and offered free housing if they would live in the mansion. None stayed. There was something about the house that was not as it should be, something that made people fear it and leave it just as quickly as they could.

Mrs. Ruth S. lives in upstate New York. In 1967 a friend showed her a brochure concerning Rock Ford, and the house intrigued her. Since she was traveling in that direction, she decided to pay Rock Ford a visit. With her family, she drove up to the house and parked her car in the rear. At that moment she had an eerie feeling that something wasn't right. Mind you, Mrs. S. had not been to the house before, had no knowledge about it nor any indication that anything unusual had occurred in it. The group of visitors was quite small. In addition to herself and her family, there were two young college boys and one other couple. Even though it was a sunny day, Mrs. S. felt icy cold.

"I felt a presence before we entered the house and before we heard the story from the guide," she explained. "If I were a hostess there, I wouldn't stay there alone for two consecutive minutes." Mrs. S. had been to many old houses and restorations before but had never felt as she did at Rock Ford.

It is not surprising that George Washington should be the subject of a number of psychic accounts. Probably the best known (and most frequently misinterpreted) story concerns General Washington's vision which came to him during the encampment at Valley Forge, when the fortunes of war had gone heavily in favor of the British, and the American army, tattered and badly fed, was just about falling to pieces. If there ever was a need for divine guidance, it was at Valley Forge. Washington was in the habit of meditating in the woods at times and saying his prayers when he was quite alone. On one of those occasions he returned to his quarters more worried than usual. As he busied himself with his papers, he had the feeling of a presence in the room. Looking up, he saw opposite him a singularly beautiful woman. Since he had given orders not to be disturbed, he couldn't understand how she had gotten into the room. Although he questioned her several times, the visitor would not reply. As he looked at the apparition, for that is what it was, the General became more and more entranced with her, unable to make any move. For a while he thought he was dying, for he imagined that the apparition of such unworldly creatures as he was seeing at that moment must accompany the moment of transition.

Finally, he heard a voice, saying, "Son of the Republic, look and learn." At the same time, the visitor extended her arm toward the east, and Washington saw what to him appeared like white vapor at some distance. As the vapor dissipated, he saw the various countries of the world and the oceans that separated them. He then noticed a dark, shadowy angel standing between Europe and America, taking water out of the ocean and sprinkling it over America with one hand and over Europe with the other. When he did this, a cloud rose from the countries thus sprinkled, and the cloud then moved westward until it enveloped America. Sharp flashes of lightning became visible at intervals in the cloud. At the same time, Washington thought he heard the anguished cries of the American people underneath the cloud. Next, the strange visitor showed him a vision of what America would look like in the future, and he saw villages and towns springing up from one coast to the other until the entire land was covered by them.

"Son of the Republic, the end of the century cometh, look and learn," the visitor said. Again Washington was shown a dark cloud approaching America, and he saw the American people fighting one another. A bright angel then appeared wearing a crown on which was written the word Union. This angel bore the American Flag, which he placed between the divided nation, saying, "Remember, you are brethren." At that instant, the inhabitants threw away their weapons and became friends again.

Once more the mysterious voice spoke. "Son of the Republic, look and learn." Now the dark angel put a trumpet to his mouth and sounded three distinct blasts. Then he took water from the ocean and sprinkled it on Europe, Asia, and Africa. As he did so, Washington saw black clouds rise from the countries he had sprinkled. Through the black clouds, Washington could

A Revolutionary Corollary:

see red light and hordes of armed men, marching by land and sailing by sea to America, and he saw these armies devastate the entire country, burn the villages, towns, and cities, and as he listened to the thundering of the cannon, Washington heard the mysterious voice saying again, "Son of the Republic, look and learn."

Once more the dark angel put the trumpet to his mouth and sounded a long and fearful blast. As he did so, a light as of a thousand suns shone down from above him and pierced the dark cloud which had enveloped America. At the same time the angel wearing the word Union on his head descended from the heavens, followed by legions of white spirits. Together with the inhabitants of America, Washington saw them renew the battle and heard the mysterious voice telling him, once again, "Son of the Republic, look and learn."

For the last time, the dark angel dipped water from the ocean and sprinkled it on America; the dark cloud rolled back and left the inhabitants of America victorious. But the vision continued. Once again Washington saw villages, towns, and cities spring up, and he heard the bright angel exclaim, "While the stars remain and the heavens send down dew upon the earth, so long shall the Union last." With that, the scene faded, and Washington beheld once again the mysterious visitor before him. As if she had guessed his question, the apparition then said:

"Son of the Republic, what you have seen is thus interpreted: Three great perils will come upon the Republic. The most fearful is the third, during which the whole world united shall not prevail against her. Let every child of the Republic learn to live for his God, his land, and his Union." With that, the vision disappeared, and Washington was left pondering over his experience.

One can interpret this story in many ways, of course. If it really occurred, and there are a number of accounts of it in existence which lead me believe that there is a basis of fact to this, then we are dealing with a case of prophecy on the part of General Washington. It is a moot question whether the third peril has already come upon us, in the shape of World War II, or whether it is yet to befall us. The light that is stronger than many suns may have ominous meaning in this age of nuclear warfare.

Washington himself is said to have appeared to Senator Calhoun of South Carolina at the beginning of the War between the States. At that time, the question of secession had not been fully decided, and Calhoun, one of the most powerful politicians in the government, was not sure whether he could support the withdrawal of his state from the Union. The question lay heavily on his mind when he went to bed one hot night in Charleston, South Carolina. During the night, he thought he awoke to see the apparition of General George Washington standing by his bedside. The General wore his presidential attire and seemed surrounded by a bright outline, as if some powerful source of light shone behind him. On the senator's desk lay the declaration of secession, which he had not yet signed. With Calhoun's and South Carolina's support, the Confederacy would be well on its way, having closed ranks. Earnestly, the spirit of George Washington pleaded with Senator Calhoun not to sign the declaration. He warned him against the impending perils coming to America as a divided nation; he asked him to reconsider his decision and to work for the preservation of the Union. But Calhoun insisted that the South had to go its own way. When the spirit of Washington saw that nothing could sway Senator Calhoun, he warned him that the very act of his signature would be a black spot on the Constitution of the United States. With that, the vision is said to have vanished.

One can easily explain the experience as a dream, coming as it did at a time when Senator Calhoun was particularly upset over the implications of his actions. On the other hand, there is

A Revolutionary Corollary:

this to consider: Shortly after Calhoun had signed the document taking South Carolina into the Confederacy, a dark spot appeared on his hand, a spot that would not vanish and for which medical authorities had no adequate explanation.

Mrs. Margaret Smith of Orlando, Florida, has had a long history of psychic experiences. She has personally seen the ghostly monks of Beaulieu, England; she has seen the actual lantern of Joe Baldwin, the famous headless ghost of Wilmington, North Carolina; and she takes her "supernatural" experiences in her stride the way other people feel about their musical talents or hobbies. When she was only a young girl, her grandmother took her to visit the von Steuben house in Hackensack, New Jersey. (General F. W. A. von Steuben was a German supporter of the American Revolution who aided General Washington with volunteers who had come over from Europe because of repressions, hoping to find greater freedom in the New World.) The house was old and dusty, the floorboards were creaking, and there was an eerie atmosphere about it. The house had been turned into an historical museum, and there were hostesses to take visitors through.

While her grandmother was chatting with the guide downstairs, the young girl walked up the stairs by herself. In one of the upstairs parlors she saw a man sitting in a chair in the corner. She assumed he was another guide. When she turned around to ask him a question about the room, he was gone. Since she hadn't heard him leave, that seemed rather odd to her, especially as the floorboards would creak with every step. But being young she didn't pay too much attention to this peculiarity. A moment later, however, he reappeared. As soon as she saw him, she asked the question she had on her mind. This time he did not disappear but answered her in a slow, painstaking voice that seemed to come from far away. When he had satisfied her curiosity about the room, he asked her some questions about herself, and finally asked

the one which stuck in her mind for many years afterward—
"What is General Washington doing now about the British?"

Margaret was taken aback at this question. She was young,
but she knew very well that Washington had been dead for many
years. Tactfully, she told him this and added that Harry Truman
was now president and that the year was 1951. At this information, the man looked stunned and sat down again in the chair.
As Margaret watched him in fascinated horror, he faded away.

6

The Vindication
of Aaron Burr

Very few historical figures have suffered as much from their enemies or have been as misunderstood and persistently misrepresented as the onetime Vice-President of the United States, Aaron Burr, whose contributions to American independence are frequently forgotten while his later troubles are made to represent the man.

Burr was a lawyer, a politician who had served in the Revolutionary forces and who later established himself in New York as a candidate of the Democratic-Republican party in the elections of 1796 and 1800. He didn't get elected in 1796, but in 1800 he received exactly as many electoral votes as Thomas Jefferson. When the House of Representatives broke the tie in Jefferson's favor, Burr became Vice-President.

Burr soon realized that Jefferson was his mortal enemy. He found himself isolated from all benefits, such as political patronage, normally accruing to one in his position, and he was left with no political future at the end of his term. Samuel Engle Burr, a descendant of Theodosia Barstow Burr, Aaron's first wife, and the definitive authority on Aaron Burr himself, calls him "the American Phoenix," and truly he was a man who frequently rose from the ashes of a smashed career.

Far from being bitter over the apparent end of his career, Burr resumed his career by becoming an independent candidate for governor of New York. He was defeated, however, by a smear campaign in which both his opponents, the Federalists, and the regular Democratic-Republican party took part.

"Some of the falsehoods and innuendoes contained in this campaign literature," writes Professor Burr in his namesake's biography, "have been repeated as facts down through the years. They have been largely responsible for much of the unwarranted abuse that has heaped upon him since that time."

Aside from Jefferson, his greatest enemies were the members of the Hamilton-Schuyler family, for in 1791 Burr had replaced Alexander Hamilton's father-in-law, General Philip Schuyler, as the senator from New York. Hamilton himself had been Burr's rival from the days of the Revolutionary War, but the political slurs and statements that had helped to defeat Burr in 1804, and that had been attributed to Hamilton, finally led to the famed duel.

In accepting Burr's challenge, Hamilton shared the illegality of the practice. He had dueled with others before, such as Commodore Nicholson, a New York politician, in 1795. His own son, Philip Hamilton, had died in a duel with New York lawyer George Eacker in 1801. Thus neither party came to Weehawken, New Jersey that chilly July morning in 1804 exactly innocent of the rules of the game.

Many versions have been published as to what happened, but to this day the truth is not clear. Both men fired, and Burr's bullet found its mark. Whether or not the wound was fatal is difficult to assess today. The long voyage back by boat, and the primitive status of medicine in 1804 may have been contributing factors to Hamilton's death.

The Vindication of Aaron Burr

That Alexander Hamilton's spirit was not exactly at rest I proved a few years ago when I investigated the house in New York City where he had spent his last hours after the duel. The house belonged to his physician, but it has been torn down to make room for a modern apartment house. Several tenants have seen the fleeting figure of the late Alexander Hamilton appear in the house and hurry out of sight, as if trying to get someplace fast. I wonder if he was trying to set the record straight, a record that saw his opponent Burr charged with *murder* by the State of New Jersey.

Burr could not overcome the popular condemnation of the duel; Hamilton had suddenly become a martyr, and he, the villain. He decided to leave New York for a while and went to eastern Florida, where he became acquainted with the Spanish colonial system, a subject that interested him very much in his later years. Finally he returned to Washington and resumed his duties as the Vice-President of the United States.

In 1805 he became interested in the possibilities of the newly acquired Louisiana Territory, and tried to interest Jefferson in developing the region around the Ouachita River to establish there still another new state.

Jefferson turned him down, and finally Burr organized his own expedition. Everywhere he went in the West he was cordially received. War with Spain was in the air, and Burr felt the United States should prepare for it and, at the right time, expand its frontiers westward.

Since the government had shown him the cold shoulder, Burr decided to recruit a group of adventurous colonists to join him in establishing a new state in Louisiana Territory and await the outbreak of the war he felt was sure to come soon. He purchased four hundred thousand acres of land in the area close to the Spanish-American frontier and planned on establishing there his dream state, to be called Burrsylvania.

In the course of his plans, Burr had worked with one General James Wilkinson, then civil governor of Louisiana Territory and a man he had known since the Revolutionary War. Unfortunately Burr did not know that Wilkinson was actually a double agent, working for both Washington and the Spanish government.

In order to bolster his position with the Jefferson government, Wilkinson suggested to the President that Burr's activities could be considered treasonable. The immediate step taken by Wilkinson was to alter one of Burr's coded letters to him in such a way that Burr's statements could be used against him. He sent the document along with an alarming report of his own to Jefferson in July of 1806.

Meanwhile, unaware of the conspiracy against his expedition, Burr's colonists arrived in the area around Natchez, when a presidential proclamation issued by Jefferson accused him of treason. Despite an acquittal by the territorial government of Mississippi, Washington sent orders to seize him.

Burr, having no intention of becoming an insurrectionist, disbanded the remnants of his colonists and returned east. On the way he was arrested and taken to Richmond for trial. The treason trial itself was larded with paid false witnesses, and even Wilkinson admitted having forged the letter that had served as the basis for the government's case. The verdict was "not guilty," but the public, inflamed against him by the all-powerful Jefferson political machine, kept condemning Aaron Burr.

Under the circumstances, Burr decided to go to Europe. He spent the four years from 1808 to 1812 traveling abroad, eventually returning to New York, where he reopened his law practice with excellent results.

The disappearance at sea the following year of his only daughter Theodosia, to whom he had been extremely close, shattered him; his political ambitions vanished, and he devoted the rest of his life to an increasingly successful legal practice. In 1833 he married for the second time—his first wife, Theodosia's mother, also called Theodosia, having died in 1794. The bride was the widow of a French wine merchant named Stephen Jumel, who had left Betsy Jumel a rich woman indeed. It was a stormy marriage, and ultimately Mrs. Burr sued for divorce. This was granted on the 14th of September 1836, the very day Aaron Burr died. Betsy never considered herself anything but the *widow* of the onetime Vice-President, and she continued to sign all documents as Eliza B. Burr.

Burr had spent his last years in an apartment at Port Richmond, Staten Island, overlooking New York Harbor. His body was laid to rest at Princeton, the president of which for many years had been Burr's late father, the Reverend Aaron Burr.

I had not been familiar with any of this until after the exciting events of June 1967, when I was able to make contact with the person of Aaron Burr through psychic channels.

My first encounter with the name Aaron Burr came in December of 1961. I was then actively investigating various haunted houses in and around New York City as part of a study grant by the Parapsychology Foundation. My reports later grew into a popular book called *Ghost Hunter*.

One day a publicist named Richard Mardus called my attention to a nightclub on West Third Street doing business as the Cafe Bizarre. Mr. Mardus was and is an expert on Greenwich Village history and lore, and he pointed out to me that the club was actually built into remodeled stables that had once formed part of Richmond Hill, Aaron Burr's estate in New York City. At the time of Burr's occupancy this was farmland and pretty far uptown, as New York City went.

But Mardus did not call to give me historical news only: Psychic occurrences had indeed been observed at the Burr stables, and he asked me to look into the matter. I went down to have a look at the edifice. It is located on a busy side street in the night-club belt of New York, where after dark the curious and the tourists gather to spend an evening of informal fun. In the daytime, the street looks ugly and ordinary, but after dark it seems to sparkle with an excitement of its own.

The Cafe Bizarre stood out by its garish decor and posters outside the entrance, but the old building housing it, three stories high, was a typical early nineteenth-century stone building, well preserved and showing no sign of replacement of the original materials.

Inside, the place had been decorated by a nightmarish array of paraphernalia to suggest the bizarre, ranging from store dummy arms to devil's masks, and colorful lights played on this melee of odd objects suspended from the high ceiling. In the rear of the long room was a stage, to the left of which a staircase led up to the loft; another staircase was in back of the stage, since a hayloft had occupied the rear portion of the building. Sawdust covered the floor, and perhaps three dozen assorted tables filled the room.

It was late afternoon and the atmosphere of the place was cold and empty, but the feeling was nevertheless that of the unusual—uncanny, somehow. I was met by a pretty, dark-haired young woman, who turned out to be the owner's wife, Mrs. Renée Allmen. She welcomed me to the Cafe Bizarre and explained that her husband, Rick, was not exactly a believer in such things as the psychic, but that she herself had indeed had unusual experiences here. On my request, she gave me a written statement testifying about her experiences.

In the early morning of July 27, 1961, at 2:20 A.M., she and her husband were locking up for the night. They walked out to their car when Mrs. Allmen remembered that she had forgotten a package inside. Rushing back to the cafe, she unlocked the doors again and entered the deserted building. She turned on the lights and walked toward the kitchen, which is about a third of the way toward the rear of the place. The cafe was quite empty, and yet she had an eerie sensation of not being alone. She hurriedly picked up her package and walked toward the front door again. Glancing backward into the dark recesses of the cafe, she then saw the apparition of a man, staring at her with piercing black eyes. He wore a ruffled shirt of the kind nobody wears in our time, not even in colorful Greenwich Village. He seemed to smile at her, and she called out to him, "Who is it?"

But the figure never moved or reacted.

"What are you doing here?" Renée demanded, all the while looking at the apparition.

There was no answer, and suddenly Renée's courage left her. Running back to the front door, she summoned her husband from the car, and together they returned to the cafe. Again unlocking the door, which Renée had shut behind her when she fled from the specter, they discovered the place to be quite empty. In the usual husbandly fashion, Mr. Allmen tried to pass it off as a case of nerves or tired eyes, but his wife would not buy it. She knew what she had seen, and it haunted her for many years to come.

Actually, she was not the first one to see the gentleman in the white ruffled shirt with the piercing black eyes. One of their waiters also had seen the ghost and promptly quit. The Village was lively enough without psychic phenomena, and how much does a ghost tip?

I looked over the stage and the area to the left near the old stairs to see whether any reflecting surface might be blamed for the ghostly apparition. There was nothing of the sort, nothing to reflect light. Besides, the lights had been off in the rear section, and those in the front were far too low to be seen anywhere but in the immediate vicinity of the door.

Under the circumstances I decided to arrange for a visit

with psychic Ethel Johnson Meyers to probe further into this case. This expedition took place on January 8, 1962, and several observers from the press were also present.

The first thing Mrs. Meyers said, while in trance, was that she saw three people in the place, psychically speaking. In particular she was impressed with an older man with penetrating dark eyes, who was the owner. The year, she felt, was 1804. In addition, she described a previous owner named Samuel Bottomslee, and spoke of some of the family troubles this man had allegedly had in his lifetime. She also mentioned that the house once stood back from the road, when the road passed farther away than it does today. This I found to be correct.

"I'm an Englishman and I have my rights here," the spirit speaking through Mrs. Meyers thundered, as we sat spellbound. Later I found out that the property had belonged to an Englishman before it passed into Burr's hands.

The drama that developed as the medium spoke haltingly did not concern Aaron Burr, but the earlier settlers. Family squabbles involving Samuel's son Alan, and a girl named Catherine, and a description of the building as a stable, where harness was kept, poured from Ethel's lips. From its looks, she could not have known consciously that this was once a stable.

The period covered extended from 1775 to 1804, when another personality seemed to take over, identifying himself as one John Bottomsley. There was some talk about a deed, and I gathered that all was not as it should have been. It seemed that the place had been sold, but that the descendants of Samuel Bottomslee didn't acknowledge this too readily.

Through all this the initials A.B. were given as prominently connected with the spot.

I checked out the facts afterward; Aaron Burr's Richmond Hill estate had included these stables since 1797. Before that the area belonged to various British colonials.

The Vindication of Aaron Burr

When I wrote the account of this séance in my book *Ghost Hunter* in 1963, I thought I had done with it. And I had, except for an occasional glance at the place whenever I passed it, wondering whether the man with the dark, piercing eyes was really Aaron Burr.

Burr's name came to my attention again in 1964 when I investigated the strange psychic phenomena at the Morris-Jumel Mansion in Washington Heights, where Burr had lived during the final years of his life as the second husband of Mme. Betsy Jumel. But the spectral manifestations at the Revolutionary house turned out to be the restless shades of Mme. Jumel herself and that of her late first husband, accusing his wife of having murdered him.

One day in January of 1967 I received a note from a young lady named Alice McDermott. It concerned some strange experiences of hers at the Cafe Bizarre—the kind one doesn't expect at even so oddly decorated a place. Miss McDermott requested an interview, and on February 4 of the same year I talked to her in the presence of a friend.

She had been "down to the Village" for several years as part of her social life—she was now twenty—and visited the Bizarre for the first time in 1964. She had felt strange, but could not quite pinpoint her apprehension.

"I had a feeling there was *something* there, but I let it pass, thinking it must be my imagination. But there was something on the balcony over the stage that seemed to stare down at me—I mean something besides the dummy suspended from the ceiling as part of the decor."

At the time, when Alice was sixteen, she had not yet heard of me or my books, but she had had some ESP experiences involving premonitions and flashes of a psychic nature.

Alice, an only child, works as a secretary in Manhattan.

Her father is a barge officer and her mother an accountant. She is a very pretty blonde with a sharp mind and a will of her own. Persuaded to try to become a nun, she spent three months in a Long Island convent, only to discover that the religious life was not for her. She then returned to New York and took a job as a secretary in a large business firm.

After she left the convent she continued her studies also, especially French. She studied with a teacher in Washington Square, and often passed the Cafe Bizarre on her way. Whenever she did, the old feeling of something uncanny inside came back. She did not enter the place, but walked on hurriedly.

But on one occasion she stopped, and something within her made her say, "Whoever you are in there, you must be lonely!" She did not enter the place despite a strong feeling that "someone wanted to say hello to her" inside. But that same night, she had a vivid dream. A man was standing on the stage, and she could see him clearly. He was of medium height, and wore beige pants and black riding boots. His white shirt with a kind of Peter Pan collar fascinated her because it did not look like the shirts men wear today. It had puffy sleeves. The man also had a goatee, that is, a short beard, and a mustache.

"He didn't look dressed in today's fashion, then?"

"Definitely not, unless he was a new rock 'n' roll star."

But the most remarkable features of this man were his dark, piercing eyes, she explained. He just stood there with his hands on his hips, looking at Alice. She became frightened when the man kept looking at her, and walked outside.

That was the end of this dream experience, but the night before she spoke to me, he reappeared in a dream. This time she was speaking with him in French, and also to an old lady who was with him. The lady wore glasses, had a pointed nose, and had a shawl wrapped around her—"Oh, and a plain gold band on her finger."

The Vindication of Aaron Burr

The lady also wore a Dutch type white cap, Alice reported. I was fascinated, for she had described Betsy Jumel in her old age—yet how could she connect the ghostly owner of Jumel Mansion with her Cafe Bizarre experience? She could not have known the connection, and yet it fit perfectly. Both Burr and Betsy Jumel spoke French fluently, and often made use of that language.

"Would you be able to identify her if I showed you a picture?" I asked.

"If it were she," Alice replied, hesitatingly.

I took out a photograph of a painting hanging at Jumel Mansion, which shows Mme. Jumel in old age.

I did not identify her by name, merely explaining it was a painting of a group of people I wanted her to look at.

"This is the lady," Alice said firmly, "but she is younger looking in the picture than when I saw her."

What was the conversation all about? I wanted to know.

Apparently the spirit of Mme. Jumel was pleading with her on behalf of Burr, who was standing by and watching the scene, to get in touch with *me!* I asked Alice, who wants to be a commercial artist, to draw a picture of what she saw. Later, I compared the portrait with known pictures of Aaron Burr. The eyes, eyebrows, and forehead did indeed resemble the Burr portraits. But the goatee was not known.

After my initial meeting with Alice McDermott, she wrote to me again. The dreams in which Burr appeared to her were getting more and more lively, and she wanted to go on record with the information thus received. According to her, Aaron poured his heart out to the young girl, incredible though this seemed on the face of it.

The gist of it was a request to go to "the white house in the country" and find certain papers in a metal box. "This will prove my innocence. I am not guilty of treason. There is written proof. Written October 18, 1802 or 1803." The message was specific enough, but the papers of course were long since gone.

The white house in the country would be the Jumel Mansion.

I thanked Alice and decided to hold another investigation at the site of the Cafe Bizarre, since the restless spirit of the late Vice-President of the United States had evidently decided to be heard once more.

At the same time I was approached by Mel Bailey of Metromedia Television to produce a documentary about New York haunted houses, and I decided to combine these efforts and investigate the Burr stables in the full glare of television cameras.

On June 12, 1967 I brought Sybil Leek down to the Bizarre, having flown her in from California two days before. Mrs. Leek had no way of knowing what was expected of her, or where she would be taken. Nevertheless, as early as June 1, when I saw her in Hollywood, she had remarked to me spontaneously that she "knew" the place I would take her to on our next expedition— then only a possibility—and she described it in detail. On June 9, after her arrival in New York, she telephoned and again gave me her impressions.

"I sense music and laughter and drumbeat," she began, and what better is there to describe the atmosphere at the Cafe Bizarre these nights? "It is a three-story place, not a house but selling something; two doors opening, go to the right-hand side of the room and something is raised up from the floor, where the drumbeat is."

Entirely correct; the two doors lead into the elongated room, with the raised stage at the end.

"Three people . . . one has a shaped beard, aquiline nose, he is on the raised part of the floor; very dark around the eyes, an elegant man, lean, and there are two other people near him, one of whom has a name starting with a Th. . . ."

In retrospect one must marvel at the accuracy of the description, for surely Sybil Leek had no knowledge of either the place, its connection with Burr, nor the description given by the other witnesses of the man they had seen there.

This was a brief description of her first impressions given to me on the telephone. The following day I received a written account of her nocturnal impressions from Mrs. Leek. This was still two days *before* she set foot onto the premises!

In her statement, Mrs. Leek mentioned that she could not go off to sleep late that night, and fell into a state of semiconsciousness, with a small light burning near her bed. Gradually she became aware of the smell of fire, or rather the peculiar smell when a gun has just been fired. At the same time she felt an acute pain, as if she had been wounded in the left side of the back.

Trying to shake off the impression, Mrs. Leek started to do some work at her typewriter, but the presence persisted. It seemed to her as if a voice was trying to reach her, a voice speaking a foreign language and calling out a name, Theo.

I questioned Mrs. Leek about the foreign language she heard spoken clairvoyantly.

"I had a feeling it was French," she said.

Finally she had drifted into deeper sleep. But by Saturday afternoon the feeling of urgency returned. This time she felt as if someone wanted her to go down to the river, not the area where I live (uptown), but "a long way the other way," which is precisely where the Burr stables were situated.

Finally the big moment had arrived. It was June 12, and the television crews had been at work all morning in and around the Cafe Bizarre to set up cameras and sound equipment so that the investigation could be recorded without either hitch or interruption. We had two cameras taking turns, to eliminate the need for reloading. The central area beneath the "haunted stage" was to be our setting, and the place was reasonably well lit, certainly brighter than it normally is when the customers are there at night.

Everything had been meticulously prepared. My wife Catherine was to drive our white Citroën down to the Bizarre with Sybil at her side. Promptly at 3:00 P.M. the car arrived, Sybil Leek jumped out and was greeted at the outer door by me, while our director, Art Forrest, gave the signal for the cameras to start. "Welcome to the Cafe Bizarre," I intoned and led my psychic friend into the semidark inside. Only the central section was brightly lit.

I asked her to walk about the place and gather impressions at will.

"I'm going to those drums over there," Sybil said firmly, and walked toward the rear stage as if she knew the way.

"Yes—this is the part. I feel cold. Even though I have not been here physically, *I know this place.*"

"What do we have to do here, do you think?" I asked.

"I think we have to relieve somebody, somebody who's waited a long time."

"Where is this feeling strongest?"

"In the rear, where this extra part seems to be put on."

Sybil could not know this, but an addition to the building was made years after the original had been constructed, and it was precisely in that part that we were now standing.

She explained that there was more than one person involved, but one in particular was dominant; that this was something from the past, going back into another century. I then asked her to take a chair, and Mrs. Renée Allmen and my wife Catherine joined us around a small table.

The Vindication of Aaron Burr

This was going to be a séance, and Sybil was in deep trance within a matter of perhaps five minutes, since she and I were well in tune with one another, and it required merely a signal on my part to allow her to "slip out."

At first there was a tossing of the head, the way a person moves when sleep is fitful.

Gradually, the face changed its expression to that of a man, a stern face, perhaps even a suspicious face. The hissing sound emanating from her tightly closed lips gradually changed into something almost audible, but I still could not make it out.

Patiently, as the cameras ground away precious color film, I asked "whoever it might be" to speak louder and to communicate through the instrument of Mrs. Leek.

"Theo!" the voice said now. It wasn't at all like Sybil's own voice.

"Theo . . . I'm lost . . . where am I?" I explained that this was the body of another person and that we were in a house in New York City.

"Where's Theo?" the voice demanded with greater urgency. "Who are you?"

I explained my role as a friend, hoping to establish contact through the psychic services of Mrs. Leek, then in turn asked who the communicator was. Since he had called out for Theo, he was not Theo, as I had first thought.

"Bertram Delmar. I want Theo," came the reply.

"Why do you want Theo?"

"Lost."

Despite extensive search I was not able to prove that Bertram Delmar ever existed or that this was one of the cover names used by Aaron Burr; but it is possible that he did, for Burr was given to the use of code names during his political career and in sensitive correspondence.

What was far more important was the immediate call for

Theo, and the statement that she was "lost." Theodosia Burr was Burr's only daughter and truly the apple of his eye. When she was lost at sea on her way to join him, in 1813, he became a broken man. Nothing in the up-and-down life of the American Phoenix was as hard a blow of fate than the loss of his beloved Theo.

The form "Theo," incidentally, rather than the full name Theodosia, is attested to by the private correspondence between Theodosia and her husband, Joseph Alston, governor of South Carolina. In a rare moment of foreboding, she had hinted that she might soon die. This letter was written six months before her disappearance in a storm at sea and was signed, "Your wife, your fond wife, Theo."

After the séance, I asked Dr. Samuel Engle Burr whether there was any chance that the name Theo might apply to some other woman.

Dr. Burr pointed out that the Christian name Theodosia occurred in modern times only in the Burr family. It was derived from Theodosius Bartow, father of Aaron Burr's first wife and mother of the girl lost at sea. The mother had been Theodosia the elder, after her father, and the Burrs had given their only daughter the same unusual name.

After her mother's passing in 1794, the daughter became her father's official hostess and truly "the woman in the house." More than that, she was his confidante and shared his thoughts a great deal more than many other daughters might have. Even after her marriage to Alston and subsequent move to Carolina, they kept in touch, and her family was really all the family he had. Thus their relationship was a truly close one, and it is not surprising that the first thought, after his "return from the dead," so to speak, would be to cry out for his Theo!

I wasn't satisfied with his identification as "Bertram Delmar," and insisted on his real name. But the communicator brushed my request aside and instead spoke of another matter.

The Vindication of Aaron Burr

"Where's the gun?"

"What gun?"

I recalled Sybil's remark about the smell of a gun having just been fired. I had to know more.

"What are you doing here?"

"Hiding."

"What are you hiding from?"

"You."

Was he mistaking me for someone else?

"I'm a friend," I tried to explain, but the voice interrupted me harshly.

"You're a soldier."

In retrospect one cannot help feeling that the emotionally disturbed personality was reliving the agony of being hunted down by U.S. soldiers prior to his arrest, confusing it, perhaps, in his mind with still another unpleasant episode when he was being hunted, namely, after he had shot Hamilton!

I decided to pry farther into his personal life in order to establish identity more firmly.

"Who is Theo? What is she to you?"

"I have to find her, take her away . . . it is dangerous, the French are looking for me."

"Why would the French be looking for you?" I asked in genuine astonishment. Neither I nor Mrs. Leek had any notion of this French connection at that time.

"Soldiers watch. . . ."

Through later research I learned that Burr had indeed been in France for several years, from 1808 to 1812. At first, his desire to have the Spanish American colonies freed met with approval by the then still revolutionary Bonaparte government. But when Napoleon's brother Joseph Napoleon was installed as King of Spain, and thus also ruler of the overseas territories, the matter became a political horse of another color; now Burr was

109

advocating the overthrow of a French-owned government, and that could no longer be permitted.

Under the circumstances, Burr saw no point in staying in France, and made arrangements to go back to New York. But he soon discovered that the French government wouldn't let him go so easily. "All sorts of technical difficulties were put in his way," writes Dr. Samuel Engle Burr, "both the French and the American officials were in agreement to the effect that the best place for the former Vice-President was within the Empire of France." Eventually, a friendly nobleman very close to Napoleon himself managed to get Burr out. But it is clear that Burr was under surveillance all that time and probably well aware of it!

I continued my questioning of the entity speaking through an entranced Sybil Leek, the entity who had glibly claimed to be a certain Bertram Delmar, but who knew so many things only Aaron Burr would have known.

What year was this, I asked.

"Eighteen ten."

In 1810, Burr had just reached France. The date fit in well with the narrative of soldiers watching him.

"Why are you frightened?" I asked.

"The soldiers, the soldiers. . . ."

"Have you done anything wrong?"

"Who are you?"

"I'm a friend, sent to help you!"

"Traitor! You . . . you betrayed me. . . ."

"Tell me what you are doing, what are you trying to establish here?"

"Traitor!"

Later, as I delved into Burr's history in detail, I thought that this exchange between an angry spirit and a cool interrogator might refer to Burr's anger at General James Wilkinson, who had indeed posed as a friend and then betrayed Burr. Not the "friend"

The Vindication of Aaron Burr

ostensibly helping Burr set up his western colony, but the traitor who later caused soldiers to be sent to arrest him. It certainly fit the situation. One must understand that in the confused mental state a newly contacted spirit personality often finds himself, events in his life take on a jumbled and fragmentary quality, often flashing on the inner mental screen like so many disconnected images from the emotional reel of his life. It is then the job of the psychic researcher to sort it all out.

I asked the communicator to "tell me all about himself" in the hope of finding some other wedge to get him to admit he was Aaron Burr.

"I escaped . . . from the French."

"Where are the French?"

"Here."

This particular "scene" was apparently being re-enacted in his mind, during the period he lived in France.

"Did you escape from any particular French person?" I asked.

"Jacques . . . de la Beau. . . ."

The spelling is mine. It might have been different, but it *sounded* like "de la Beau."

"Who is Jacques de la Beau?"

Clenched teeth, hissing voice—'I'm . . . not . . . telling you. Even . . . if you . . . kill me."

I explained I had come to free him, and what could I do for him?

"Take Theo away . . . leave me . . . I shall die. . . ."

Again I questioned him about his identity. Now he switched his account and insisted he was French, born at a place called Dasney near Bordeaux. Even while this information was coming from the medium's lips, I felt sure it was a way to throw me off his real identity. This is not unusual in some cases. When

111

I investigated the ghost of General Samuel Edward McGowan some years ago, it took several weeks of trance sessions until he abandoned an assumed name and admitted an identity that could later be proven. Even the discarnates have their pride and emotional "hangups," as we say today.

The name Jacques de la Beau puzzled me. After the séance, I looked into the matter and discovered that a certain Jacques Prevost (pronounced pre-voh) had been the first husband of Aaron Burr's first wife, Theodosia. Burr, in fact, raised their two sons as his own, and there was a close link between them and Burr in later years. But despite his French name, Prevost was in the British service.

When Burr lived in New York, he had opened his home to the daughter of a French admiral, from whom she had become separated as a consequence of the French Revolution. This girl, Natalie, became the close companion of Burr's daughter Theodosia, and the two girls considered themselves sisters. Natalie's father was Admiral de Lage de Volade. This name, too, has sounds similar to the "de la Beau" I thought I had understood. It might have been "de la voh" or anything in between the two sounds. Could the confused mind of the communicator have drawn from both Prevost and de Lage de Volade? Both names were of importance in Burr's life.

"Tell me about your wife," I demanded now.

"No. I don't like her."

I insisted, and he, equally stubborn, refused.

"Is she with you?" I finally said.

"Got rid of her," he said, almost with joy in the voice.

"Why?"

"No good to me . . . deceived me . . . married. . . ."

There was real disdain and anger in the voice now.

Clearly, the communicator was speaking of the second

The Vindication of Aaron Burr

Mrs. Burr. The first wife had passed away a long time before the major events in his life occurred. It is perfectly true that Burr "got rid of her" (through two separations and one divorce action), and that she "deceived him," or rather tricked him into marrying her: He thought she was wealthier than she actually was, and their main difficulties were about money. In those days people did not always marry for love, and it was considered less immoral to have married someone for money than to deceive someone into marrying by the prospects of large holdings when they were in fact small. Perhaps today we think differently and even more romantically about such matters; in the 1830s, a woman's financial standing was as negotiable as a bank account.

The more I probed, the more excited the communicator became; the more I insisted on identification, the more cries of "Theo! Theo!" came from the lips of Sybil Leek.

When I had first broached the subject of Theo's relationship to him, he had quickly said she was his sister. I brought this up again, and in sobbing tones he admitted this was not true. But he was not yet ready to give me the full story.

"Let me go," he sobbed.

"Not until you can go in peace," I insisted. "Tell me about yourself. You are proud of yourself, are you not?"

"Yes," the voice came amid heavy sobbing, "the disgrace . . . the disgrace. . . ."

"I will tell the world what you want me to say. I'm here as your spokesman. Use this chance to tell the world your side of the facts!"

There was a moment of hesitation, then the voice, gentler, started up again.

"I . . . loved . . . Theo. . . . I have to . . . find her. . . ."

The most important thought, evidently, was the loss of his

girl. Even his political ambitions took a back seat to his paternal love.

"Is this place we're in part of your property?"

Forlornly, the voice said,

"I had . . . a lot . . . from the river . . . to here."

Later I checked this statement with Mrs. Leroy Campbell, curator of the Morris-Jumel Mansion, and a professional historian who knew the period well.

"Yes, this is true," Mrs. Campbell confirmed, "Burr's property extended from the river and Varick Street eastward." "But the lot from the river to here does not belong to a Bertram Delmar," I said to the communicator. "Why do you wish to fool me with names that do not exist?"

I launched this as a trial balloon. It took off.

"She *calls me* Bertram," the communicator admitted now. "I'm not ashamed of my name."

I nodded. "I'm here to help you right old wrongs, but you must help me do this. I can't do it alone."

"I didn't kill . . . got rid of her. . . ." he added, apparently willing to talk.

"You mean, your wife?"

"Had to."

"Did you kill *anyone?*" I continued the line of discussion.

"Killed . . . to protect . . . not wrong!"

"How did you kill?"

"A rifle. . . ."

Was he perhaps referring to his service in the Revolutionary War? He certainly did some shooting then.

But I decided to return to the "Bertram Delmar" business once more. Constant pressure might yield results.

"Truthfully, will you tell us who you are?"

Deliberately, almost as if he were reading an official communiqué, the voice replied,

The Vindication of Aaron Burr

"I am Bertram Delmar and I shall not say *that* name. . . ."

"You must say 'that name' if you wish to see Theo again." I had put it on the line. Either cooperate with me, or I won't help you. Sometimes this is the only way you can get a recalcitrant spirit to "come across"—when this cooperation is essential both to his welfare and liberation and to the kind of objective proof required in science.

There was a moment of ominous quiet. Then, almost inaudibly, the communicator spoke.

"An awful name . . . *Arnot.*"

After the investigation I played the sound tapes back to make sure of what I had heard so faintly. It was quite clear. "The communicator" had said "*Arnot.*"

My first reaction was, perhaps she is trying to say Aaron Burr and pronounce Aaron with a broad ah. But on checking this out with both Mrs. Campbell and Dr. Burr I found that such a pronunciation was quite impossible. The night after the séance I telephoned Dr. Burr at his Washington home and read the salient points of the transcript to him.

When I came to the puzzling name given by the communicator I asked whether Arnot meant anything inasmuch as I could not find it in the published biographies of Burr. There was a moment of silence on the other end of the line before Dr. Burr spoke.

"Quite so," he began. "It is not really generally known, but Burr did use a French cover name while returning from France to the United States, in order to avoid publicity. *That name was Arnot.*"

But back to the Cafe Bizarre and our investigation.

Having not yet realized the importance of the word Arnot, I continued to insist on proper identification.

"You must cleanse yourself of ancient guilt," I prodded.

"It is awful . . . awful. . . ."

"Is Theo related to you?"

"She's mine."

"Are you related to her?"

"Lovely . . . little one . . . *daughter.*"

Finally, the true relationship had come to light.

"If Theo is your daughter, then you are not 'Bertram.'"

"You tricked me . . . go away . . . or else I'll kill you!"

The voice sounded full of anger again.

"If you're not ashamed of your name, then I want to hear it from your lips."

Again, hesitatingly, the voice said,

"*Arnot.*"

"Many years have gone by. Do you know what year we're in now?"

"Ten. . . ."

"It is not 1810. A hundred fifty years have gone by."

"You're mad."

"You're using the body of a psychic to speak to us. . . ."

The communicator had no use for such outrageous claims.

"I'm not going to listen. . . ."

But I made him listen. I told him to touch the hair, face, ears of the "body" he was using as a channel and to see if it didn't feel strange indeed.

Step by step, the figure of Sybil, very tensed and angry a moment before, relaxed. When the hand found its way to the chin, there was a moment of startled expression:

"No beard. . . ."

I later found that not a single one of the contemporary portraits of Aaron Burr shows him with a chin beard. Nevertheless, Alice McDermott had seen and drawn him with a goatee, and now Sybil Leek, under the control of the alleged Burr, also felt for the beard that was not there any longer.

The Vindication of Aaron Burr

Was there ever a beard?

"Yes," Dr. Burr confirmed, "there was, although this, too, is almost unknown except of course to specialists like myself. On his return from France, in 1812, Burr sported a goatee in the French manner."

By now I had finally gotten through to the person speaking through Sybil Leek, that the year was 1967 and not 1810.

His resistance to me crumbled.

"You're a strange person," he said, "I'm tired."

"Why do you hide behind a fictitious name?"

"People . . . ask . . . too many . . . questions."

"Will you help me clear your name, not Bertram, but your real name?"

"I was betrayed."

"Who is the President of the United States in 1810?" I asked and regretted it immediately. Obviously this could not be an evidential answer. But the communicator wouldn't mention the hated name of the rival.

"And who is Vice-President?" I asked.

"Politics. . . are bad. . . they kill you. . . I would not betray anyone. . . . I was wronged . . . politics . . . are bad. . . ."

How true!

"Did you ever kill anyone?" I demanded.

"Not wrong . . . to kill to . . . preserve. . . . I'm alone."

He hesitated to continue.

"What did you preserve? Why did you have to kill another person?"

"*Another* . . . critical . . . I'm not talking!"

"You must talk. It is necessary for posterity."

"I tried . . . to be . . . *the best*. . . . I'm not a traitor . . . soldiers . . . beat the drum . . . then you die . . . politics!!"

As I later listened to this statement again and again, I

117

understood the significance of it, coming, as it did, from a person who had not yet admitted he was Aaron Burr and through a medium who didn't even know *where* she was at the time.

He killed to *preserve his honor*—the accusations made against him in the campaign of 1804 for the governorship of New York were such that they could not be left unchallenged. Another was indeed *critical* of him, Alexander Hamilton being that person, and the criticisms such that Burr could not let them pass.

He "tried to be the best" also—tried to be President of the United States, got the required number of electoral votes in 1800, but deferred to Jefferson, who also had the same number.

No, he was not a traitor, despite continued inference in some history books that he was. The treason trial of 1807 not only exonerated the former Vice-President of any wrongdoing, but heaped scorn and condemnation on those who had tried him. The soldiers beating the drum prior to an execution *could* have become reality if Burr's enemies had won; the treason incident under which he was seized by soldiers on his return from the West included the death penalty if found guilty. That was the intent of his political enemies, to have this ambitious man removed forever from the political scene.

"Will you tell the world that you are not guilty?" I asked.

"I told them . . . trial . . . I am not a traitor, a murderer. . . ."

I felt it important for him to free himself of such thoughts if he were to be released from his earthbound status.

"I . . . want to die . . ." the voice said, breathing heavily.

"Come, I will help you find Theo," I said, as promised.

But there was still the matter of the name. I felt it would help "clear the atmosphere" if I could get him to admit he was Burr.

I had already gotten a great deal of material, and the

séance would be over in a matter of moments. I decided to gamble on the last minute or two and try to shock this entity into either admitting he was Burr or reacting to the name in some telling fashion.

I had failed in having him speak those words even though he had given us many incidents from the life of Aaron Burr. There was only one more way and I took it. "Tell the truth," I said, "are you Aaron Burr?"

It was as if I had stuck a red hot poker into his face. The medium reeled back, almost upsetting the chair in which she sat. With a roar like a wounded lion, the voice came back at me,

"Go away . . . GO AWAY!! . . . or I'll kill you!"

"You will not kill me," I replied calmly. "You will tell me the truth."

"I will kill you to preserve my honor!!"

"*I'm* here to preserve your honor. I'm your friend."

The voice was like cutting ice.

"You said that once before."

"You are Aaron Burr, and this is part of your place."

"I'M BERTRAM!"

I did not wish to continue the shouting match.

"Very well," I said, "for the world, then, let it be Bertram, if you're not ready to face it that you're Burr."

"I'm Bertram . . ." the entity whispered now.

"Then go from this place and join your Theo. Be Bertram for her."

"Bertram . . . you won't tell?" The voice was pleading.

"Very well." He would soon slip across the veil, I felt, and there were a couple of points I wanted to clear up before. I explained that he would soon be together with his daughter, leaving here after all this time, and I told him again how much time had elapsed since his death.

"I tarried . . . I tarried . . ." he said, pensively.

"What sort of a place did you have?" I asked.

"It was a big place . . . with a big desk . . . famous house. . . ." But he could not recall its name.

Afterward, I checked the statement with Mrs. Campbell, the curator at the Morris-Jumel Mansion. "That desk in the big house," she explained," is right here in our Burr room. It was originally in his law office." But the restless one was no longer interested in talking to me.

"I'm talking to Theo . . ." he said, quietly now, "in the garden. . . . I'm going for a walk with Theo . . . go away."

Within a moment, the personality who had spoken through Sybil Leek for the past hour was gone. Instead, Mrs. Leek returned to her own self, remembering absolutely nothing that had come through her entranced lips.

"Lights are bright," was the first thing she said, and she quickly closed her eyes again.

But a moment later, she awoke fully and complained only that she felt a bit tired.

I wasn't at all surprised that she did.

Almost immediately after I had returned home, I started my corroboration. After discussing the most important points with Dr. Samuel Engle Burr over the telephone, I arranged to have a full transcript of the séance sent to him for his comments.

So many things matched the Burr personality that there could hardly be any doubt that it *was* Burr we had contacted. "I'm not a traitor and a murderer," the ghostly communicator had shouted. "Traitor and murderer" were the epithets thrown at Burr in his own lifetime by his enemies, according to Professor Burr, as quoted by Larry Chamblin in the Allentown *Call-Chronicle.*

Although he is not a direct descendant of Aaron Burr, the Washington educator is related to Theodosia Barstow Burr, the Vice-President's first wife. A much-decorated officer in both world

The Vindication of Aaron Burr

wars, Professor Burr is a recognized educator and the definitive authority on his famous namesake. In consulting him, I was getting the best possible information.

Aaron Burr's interest in Mexico, Professor Burr explained, was that of a liberator from Spanish rule, but there never was any conspiracy against the United States government. "That charge stemmed from a minor incident on an island in Ohio. A laborer among his colonists pointed a rifle at a government man who had come to investigate the expedition."

Suddenly, the words about the rifle and the concern the communicator had shown about it became clear to me: It had led to more serious trouble for Burr.

Even President Wilson concurred with those who felt Aaron Burr had been given a "raw deal" by historical tradition. Many years ago he stood at Burr's grave in Princeton and remarked,

"How misunderstood . . . how maligned!"

It is now 132 years since Burr's burial, and the falsehoods concerning Aaron Burr are still about the land, despite the two excellent books by Dr. Samuel Engle Burr and the discreet but valiant efforts of the Aaron Burr Association which the Washington professor heads.

In piecing together the many evidential bits and pieces of the trance session, it was clear to me that Aaron Burr had at last said his piece. Why had he not pronounced a name he had been justly proud of in his lifetime? He had not hesitated to call repeatedly for Theo, identify her as his daughter, speak of his troubles in France and of his political career—why this insistence to remain the fictitious Bertram Delmar in the face of so much proof that he was indeed Aaron Burr?

All the later years of his life, Burr had encountered hostility, and he had learned to be careful whom he chose as friends, whom he could trust. Gradually, this bitterness became so strong that in his declining years he felt himself to be a lonely, abandoned old man, his only daughter gone forever, and no one to help him carry the heavy burden of his life. Passing across into the non-physical side of life in such a state of mind, and retaining it by that strange quirk of fate that makes some men into ghostly images of their former selves, he would not abandon that one remaining line of defense against his fellow men: his anonymity.

Why should he confide in me, a total stranger, whom he had never met before, a man, moreover, who spoke to him under highly unusual conditions, conditions he himself neither understood nor accepted? It seemed almost natural for Burr's surviving personality to be cautious in admitting his identity.

But his ardent desire to find Theo was stronger than his caution; we therefore were able to converse more or less freely about this part of his life. And so long as he needed not say he was Burr, he felt it safe to speak of his career also, especially when my questions drove him to anger, and thus lessened his critical judgment as to what he could say and what he should withhold from me.

Ghosts are people, too, and they are subject to the same emotional limitations and rules that govern us all.

Mrs. Leek had no way of obtaining the private, specific knowledge and information that had come from her entranced lips in this investigation; I myself had almost none of it until after the séance had ended, and thus could not have furnished her any of the material from my own unconscious mind. And the others present during the séance—my wife, Mrs. Allmen, and the television people—knew even less about all this.

Neither Dr. Burr nor Mrs. Campbell were present at the Cafe Bizarre, and their minds, if they contained any of the Burr information, could not have been tapped by the medium either, if such were indeed possible.

Coincidence cannot be held to account for such rare

pieces of information as Burr's cover name Arnot, the date, the goatee, and the very specific character of the one speaking through Mrs. Leek, and his concern for the clearing of his name from the charges of treason and murder.

That we had indeed contacted the restless and unfree spirit of Aaron Burr at what used to be his stables is now the only physical building still extant that was truly his own, I do not doubt in the least.

The defense rests, and hopefully, so does a happier Aaron Burr, now forever reunited with his beloved daughter Theodosia.

7

A Visit with Alexander Hamilton's Ghost

There stands at Number 27, Jane Street, in New York's picturesque artists' quarters, Greenwich Village, a mostly wooden house dating back to pre-Revolutionary days. In this house Alexander Hamilton was treated in his final moments. Actually, he died a few houses away, at 80 Jane Street, but No. 27 was the home of John Francis, his doctor, who attended him after the fatal duel with Aaron Burr.

However, the Hamilton house no longer exists, and the wreckers are now after the one of his doctor, now occupied by a writer and artist, Jean Karsavina, who has lived there since 1939.

The facts of Hamilton's untimely passing are well known; D.S. Alexander (in his *Political History of the State of New York*) reports that, because of political enmity, "Burr seems to have deliberately determined to kill him." A letter written by Hamilton calling Burr "despicable" and "not to be trusted with the reins of government" found its way into the press, and Burr demanded an explanation. Hamilton declined, and on June 11, 1804, at Weehawken, New Jersey, Burr took careful aim, and his first shot

125

mortally wounded Hamilton. In the boat back to the city, Hamilton regained consciousness, but knew his end was near. He was taken to Dr. Francis' house and treated, but died within a few days at his own home, across the street.

Ever since moving into 27 Jane Street, Miss Karsavina has been aware of footsteps, creaking stairs, and the opening and closing of doors; and even the unexplained flushing of a toilet. On one occasion, she found the toilet chain still swinging, when there was no one around! "I suppose a toilet that flushes *would* be a novelty to someone from the eighteenth century," she is quoted in a brief newspaper account in June of 1957[*]

She also has seen a blurred "shape," without being able to give details of the apparition; her upstairs tenant, however, reports that one night not so long ago, "a man in eighteenth-century clothes, with his hair in a queue" walked into her room, looked at her and walked out again.

Miss Karsavina turned out to be a well-read and charming lady who had accepted the possibility of living with a ghost under the same roof. Mrs. Meyers and I went to see her in March 1960. The medium had no idea where we were going.

At first, Mrs. Meyers, still in waking condition, noticed a "shadow" of a man, old, with a broad face and bulbous nose; a woman with a black shawl whose name she thought was Deborah, and she thought "someone had a case"; she then described an altar of white lilies, a bridal couple, and a small coffin covered with flowers; then a very old woman in a coffin that was richly adorned, with relatives including a young boy and girl looking into the open coffin. She got the name of Mrs. Patterson, and the girl's as Miss Lucy. In another "impression" of the same premises, Mrs. Meyers described "an empty coffin, people weeping, talking, milling around, *and the American Flag atop the coffin;* in the coffin a man's hat, shoes with silver buckles, gold epaulettes. . . ." She then got close to the man and thought his lungs were filling with liquid and he died with a pain in his side.

Lapsing into semitrance at this point, Mrs. Meyers described a party of men in a small boat on the water, then a man wearing white pants and a blue coat with blood spilled over the pants. "Two boats were involved, and it is dusk," she added.

Switching apparently to another period, Mrs. Meyers felt that "something is going on in the cellar, they try to keep attention from what happens downstairs; there is a woman here, being stopped by two men in uniforms with short jackets and round hats with wide brims, and pistols. There is the sound of shrieking, the woman is pushed back violently, men are marching, someone who had been harbored here has to be given up, an old man in a night-shirt and red socks is being dragged out of the house into the snow."

In still another impression, Mrs. Meyers felt herself drawn up toward the rear of the house where "someone died in child-birth"; in fact, this type of death occurred "several times" in this house. Police were involved, too, but this event or chain of events is of a later period than the initial impressions, she felt. The name Henry Oliver or Oliver Henry came to her mind.

After her return to full consciousness, Mrs. Meyers remarked that there was a chilly area near the center of the down-stairs room. There is; I feel it too. Mrs. Meyers "sees" the figure of a slender man, well-formed, over average height, in white trou-sers, black boots, dark blue coat and tails, white lace in front; *he is associated with George Washington and Lafayette*, and their faces appear to her, too; she feels Washington may have been in this house. The man she "sees" is a *general*, she can see his epaulettes. The old woman and the children seen earlier are somehow con-nected with this, too. He died young, and there "was fighting in a boat." Now Mrs. Meyers gets the name "W. Lawrence." She has a warm feeling about the owner of the house; he took in numbers of people, like refugees.

A "General Mills" stored supplies here—shoes, coats, almost like a military post; food is being handed out. The name Bradley is given. Then Mrs. Meyers sees an old man playing a cornet; two men in white trousers are "seen" seated at a long table, bent over papers, with a crystal chandelier above.

After the séance, Miss Karsavina confirmed that the house belonged to Hamilton's physician, and as late as 1825 was owned by a doctor, who happened to be the doctor for the Metropolitan Opera House. The cornet player might have been one of his patients.

In pre-Revolutionary days, the house may have been used as headquarters of an "underground railroad," around 1730, when the police tried to pick up the alleged instigators of the so-called "Slave Plot," evidently being sheltered here.

"Lawrence" may refer to the portrait of Washington by Lawrence which *used* to hang over the fireplace in the house. On the other hand, I found a T. Lawrence, M. D., at 146 Greenwich Street, *Elliot's Improved Directory for New York* (1812); and a "Widow Patterson" is listed by Longworth (1803) at 177 William Street; a William Lawrence, druggist, at 80 John Street. According to Charles Burr Todd's *Story of New York*, two of Hamilton's pallbearers were *Oliver* Wolcott and John L. *Lawrence*. The other names mentioned could not be found. The description of the man in white trousers is of course the perfect image of Hamilton, and the goings-on at the house with its many coffins, and women dying in childbirth, are indeed understandable for a doctor's residence.

It does not seem surprising that Alexander Hamilton's shade should wish to roam about the house of the man who tried, vainly, to save his life.

8

The Fifth Avenue Ghost

S ome cases of haunted houses require but a single visit to obtain information and evidence, others require two or three. But very few cases in the annals of psychic research can equal or better the record set by the case I shall call The Fifth Avenue Ghost. Seventeen sessions, stretching over a period of five months, were needed to complete this most unusual case. I am presenting it here just as it unfolded for us. I am quoting from our transcripts, our records taken during each and every session; and because so much evidence was obtained in this instance that could only be obtained from the person these events actually happened to, it is to my mind a very strong case for the truth about the nature of hauntings.

It isn't very often that one finds a haunted apartment listed in the leading evening paper.

Occasionally, an enterprising real-estate agent will add the epithet "looks haunted" to a cottage in the country to attract the romanticist from the big city.

But the haunted apartment I found listed in the New York

Daily News one day in July 1953 was the real McCoy. Danton Walker, the late Broadway columnist, had this item—

> "One for the books: an explorer, advertising his Fifth Avenue Studio for sub-let, includes among the attractions 'attic dark room with ghost.' . . ."

The enterprising gentleman thus advertising his apartment for rent turned out to be Captain Davis, a celebrated explorer and author of many books, including, here and there, some ghost lore. Captain Davis was no skeptic. To the contrary, I found him sincere and well aware of the existence of physical research. Within hours, I had discussed the case with the *study group* which met weekly at the headquarters of the Association for Research and Enlightenment, the Edgar Cayce Foundation. A team was organized, consisting of Bernard Axelrod, Nelson Welsh, Stanley Goldberg and myself, and, of course, Mrs. Meyers as the medium. Bernard Axelrod and I knew that there was some kind of "ghost" at the Fifth Avenue address, but little more. The medium knew nothing whatever. Two days *after* the initial session, a somewhat fictional piece appeared in the *New York Times* (July 13, 1953) by the late Meyer Berger, who had evidently interviewed the *host*, but not the *ghost*. Mr. Berger quoted Captain Davis as saying there was a green ghost who had hanged himself from the studio gallery, and allegedly sticks an equally green hand out of the attic window now and then.

Captain Davis had no idea who the ghost was. This piece, it must be re-emphasized, appeared two days *after* the initial sitting at the Fifth Avenue house, and its contents were of course unknown to all concerned at the time.

In order to shake hands with the good Captain, we had to climb six flights of stairs to the very top of 226 Fifth Avenue.

The Fifth Avenue Ghost

The building itself is one of those big old town houses popular in the mid-Victorian age, somber, sturdy, and well up to keeping its dark secrets behind its thickset stone walls. Captain Davis volunteered the information that previous tenants had included Richard Harding Davis, actor Richard Mansfield, and a lady magazine editor. Only the lady was still around and, when interviewed, was found to be totally ignorant of the entire ghost tradition, nor had she ever been disturbed. Captain Davis also told of guests in the house having seen the ghost at various times, though he himself had not. His home is one of those fantastic and colorful apartments only an explorer or collector would own—a mixture of comfortable studio and museum, full of excitement and personality, and offering more than a touch of the Unseen. Two wild jungle cats completed the atmospheric picture, somewhat anticlimaxed by the host's tape recorder set up on the floor. The apartment is a kind of duplex, with a gallery or balcony jutting out into the main room. In the middle of this balcony was the window referred to in the *Times* interview. Present were the host, Captain Davis, Mr. and Mrs. Bertram Long, the Countess de Sales, all friends of the host's, and the group of researchers previously mentioned—a total of eight people, and if you wish, two cats. As with most sittings, tape recordings were made of the proceedings from beginning to end, in addition to which written notes were taken.

MEETING A GHOST

Like a well-rehearsed television thriller, the big clock in the tower across the square struck nine, and the lights were doused, except for the one medium-bright electric lamp. This was sufficient light, however, to distinguish the outlines of most of the sitters, and particularly the center of the room around the medium.

A comfortable chair was placed under the gallery, in which the medium took her place; around her, forming a circle, sat the others, with the host operating the recorder and facing the medium. It was very still, and the atmosphere seemed tense. The medium had hardly touched the chair when she grabbed her own neck in the unmistakable manner of someone being choked to death, and nervously told of being "hung by the neck until dead." She then sat in the chair and Bernard Axelrod, an experienced hypnotist, conditioned her into her usual trance condition, which came within a few minutes.

With bated breath, we awaited the arrival of whatever personality might be the "ghost" referred to. We expected some violence and, as will be seen shortly, we got it. This is quite normal with such cases, especially at the first contact. It appears that a "disturbed personality" continuously relives his or her "passing condition," or cause of death, and it is this last agony that so frequently makes ghostly visitations matters of horror. If emotional anxiety is the cause of death, or was present at death, then the "disturbed personality," or entity, will keep reliving that final agony, much like a phonograph needle stuck in the last groove of a record. But here is what happened on that first occasion.

Sitting of July 11th, 1953, at 226 Fifth Avenue

The Medium, now possessed by unknown entity, has difficulty in speaking. Entity breaks into mad laughter full of hatred.

Entity: . . . curry the horse . . . they're coming . . . curry the horse! Where is Mignon? WHERE IS SHE?
Question: We wish to help you. Who is Mignon?

The Fifth Avenue Ghost

Entity: She should be here . . . where is she . . . you've got her! Where is she? Where is the baby?

Question: What baby?

Entity: What did they do with her?

Question: We're your friends.

Entity: (in tears) Oh, an enemy . . . an enemy . . .

Question: What is your name?

Entity: Guychone . . . Guychone. . . . (express pain at the neck; hands feeling around are apparently puzzled by finding a woman's body)

Question: You are using someone else's body. (Entity clutches throat.) Does it hurt you there?

Entity: Not any more . . . it's whole again . . . I can't see . . . All is so different, all is very strange . . . nothing is the same.

I asked how he died. This excited him immediately.

Entity: (hysterical) I didn't do it . . . I tell you I didn't do it, no . . . Mignon, Mignon . . . where is she? They took the baby . . . she put me away . . . they took her. . . . (Why did she put you away?) So no one could find me (Where?) I stay there (meaning upstairs) all the time.

At this point, tapes were changed. *Entity,* asked where he came from, says Charleston, and that he lived in a white house.

Question: Do you find it difficult to use this body?

Entity: WHAT?? WHAT?? I'm HERE . . . I'm here. . . . This is my house . . . what are YOU doing here?

Question: Tell me about the little room upstairs.

Entity: (crying) Can I go . . . away . . . from the room?

At this point, the entity left, and the medium's *control,* Albert, took over her body.

Albert: There is a very strong force here, and it has been a little

133

difficult. This individual here suffered violence at the hands of several people. He was a Confederate and he was given up, hidden here, while they made their escape.

Question: What rank did he hold?

Albert: I believe that he had some rank. It is a little dubious as to what he was.

Question: What was his name?

Albert: It is not as he says. That is an assumed name, that he likes to take. He is not as yet willing to give full particulars. He is a violent soul underneath when he has opportunity to come, but he hasn't done damage to anyone, and we are going to work with him, if possible, from this side.

Question: What about Mignon and the baby?

Albert: Well, they of course are a long time *on this side*, but he never knew that, what became of them. They were separated cruelly. She did *not* do anything to him.

Question: How did he leave this world?

Albert: By violence. (Was he hanged?) Yes. (In the little room?) Yes. (Was it suicide or murder?) He says it was murder.

The *control* then suggests to end the trance, and try for results in "open" sitting. We slowly awaken the medium.

While the medium is resting, sitter Stanley Goldberg remarks that he has the impression that Guychone's father came from Scotland.

Captain Davis observes that at the exact moment of "frequency change" in the medium, that is, when Guychone left and Albert took over, the control light of the recording apparatus suddenly blazed up *of its own accord*, and had to be turned down by him.

A standing circle was then formed by all present, holding hands, and taking the center of the room. Soon the medium started swinging forward and back like a suspended body. She remarked feeling very stiff "from hanging and surprised to find that I'm whole, having been cut open in the middle."

Both Axelrod and I observed a luminescent white and *greenish* glow covering the medium, creating the impression of an older man without hair, with high cheekbones and thin arms. This was during the period when Guychone was speaking through the medium.

The seance ended at twelve-thirty. The medium reported feeling exhausted, with continued discomfort in the throat and stomach.

THE INVESTIGATION CONTINUES

Captain Davis, unfortunately, left on a worldwide trip the same week, and the new tenant was uncooperative. I felt we should continue the investigation. Once you pry a "ghost" loose from his place of unhappy memories, he can sometimes be contacted elsewhere.

Thus, a second sitting took place at the headquarters of the study group, on West 16th Street. This was a small, normally-furnished room free of any particular atmosphere, and throughout this and all following sittings, subdued light was used, bright enough to see all facial expressions quite clearly. There was smoking and occasional talking in low voices, none of which ever disturbed the work. Before the second sitting, Mrs. Meyers remarked that Guychone had "followed her home" from the Fifth Avenue place, and twice appeared to her at night in a kind of "whitish halo," with an expression of frantic appeal in his eyes. Upon her admonition to be patient until the sitting, the apparition had vanished.

Sitting of July 14th, 1953, at 125 West 16th Street

Question: Do you know what year this is?

Guychone: 1873.

Question: No, it is 1953. Eighty years have gone by. You are no longer alive. Do you understand?

Guychone: Eighty years? EIGHTY YEARS? I'm not a hundred-ten years?

Question: No, you're not. You're forever young. Mignon is on your side, too. We have come to help you understand yourself. What happened in 1873?

Guychone: Nobody's goddamn business . . . mine . . . mine!

Question: All right, keep your secret then, but don't you want to see Mignon? Don't you want justice done? (mad, bitter laughter) Don't you believe in God? (more laughter) The fact you are here and are able to speak, doesn't that prove that there is hope for you? What happened in 1873? Remember the house on Fifth Avenue, the room upstairs, the horse to be curried?

Guychone: Riding, riding . . . find her . . . they took her away.

Question: Who took her away?

Guychone: YOU! (threatens to strike interrogator)

Question: No, we're your friends. Where can we find a record of your Army service? Is it true you were on a dangerous mission?

Guychone: Yes.

Question: In what capacity?

Guychone: That is my affair! I do not divulge my secrets. I am a gentleman, and my secrets die with me.

Question: Give us your rank.

Guychone: I was a Colonel.

Question: In what regiment?

Guychone: Two hundred and sixth.

Question: Were you infantry or cavalry?

The Fifth Avenue Ghost

Guychone: Cavalry.

Question: In the War Between the States?

Guychone: Yes.

Question: Where did you make your home before you came to New York?

Guychone: Charleston . . . Elm Street.

Question: What is your family name, Colonel?

Guychone: (crying) As a gentleman, I am yet not ready to give you that information . . . it's no use, I won't name it.

Question: You make it hard for us, but we will abide by your wishes.

Guychone: (relieved) I am very much obliged to you . . . for giving me the information that it is EIGHTY YEARS. Eighty years!

I explain about the house on Fifth Avenue, and that Guychone's "presence" had been felt from time to time. Again, I ask for his name.

(Apparently fumbling for paper, he is given paper and fountain pen; the latter seems to puzzle him at first, but he then writes in the artistic, stylized manner of the mid-Victorian age— "Edouard Guychone."

Question: Is your family of French extraction?

Guychone: Yes.

Question: Are you yourself French or were you born in this country?

Guychone: In this country . . . Charleston.

Question: Do you speak French?

Guychone: No.

Question: Is there anything you want us to do for you? Any unfinished business?

Guychone: Eighty years makes a difference . . . I am a broken man . . . God bless you . . . Mignon . . . it is so dark, so dark. . . .

I explain the reason for his finding himself temporarily in

a woman's body, and how his hatred had brought him back to the house on Fifth Avenue, instead of passing over to the "other side."

Guychone: (calmer) There IS a God?

I ask when was he born.

Guychone: (unsure) 1840 . . . 42 years old. . . .

This was the most dramatic of the sittings. The transcript cannot fully convey the tense situation existing between a violent, hate-inspired and God-denying personality fresh from the abyss of perennial darkness, and an interrogator trying calmly to bring light into a disturbed mind. Toward the end of the session, Guychone understood about God, and began to realize that much time had passed since his personal tragedy had befallen him. Actually, the method of "liberating" a "ghost" is no different from that used by a psychiatrist to free a flesh-and-blood person from obsessions or other personality disturbances. Both deal with the mind.

It became clear to me that many more sessions would be needed to clear up the case, since the entity was reluctant to tell all. This is not the case with most "ghosts," who generally welcome a chance to "spill" emotions pent up for long years of personal hell. Here, however, the return of reason also brought back the critical faculty of reasoning, and evaluating information. We had begun to liberate Guychone's soul, but we had not yet penetrated to his conscience. Much hatred, fear, and pride remained, and had to be removed, before the true personality could emerge.

Sitting of July 21st, 1953

Albert, the medium's control, spoke first.
Question: Have you found any information about his wife and child?
Albert: You understand that this is our moral code, that that which comes from the individual within voluntarily is his sacred devel-

opment. That which he wishes to divulge makes his soul what it should eventually be.

I asked that he describe Guychone's appearance to us.

Albert: At the moment he is little developed from the moment of passing. He is still like his latter moments in life. But his figure was of slight build, tall . . . five feet nine or ten . . . his face is round, narrow at the chin, high at the cheekbones, the nose is rather prominent, the mouth rather wide . . . the forehead high, at the moment of death and for many years previous very little hair. The eyes set close to the nose.

Question: Have you learned his *real* name?

Guychone: It is not his wish as yet. He will tell you, he will develop his soul through his confession. Here he is!

Guychone: (at first grimacing in pain) It is nice to come, but it is hell . . . I have seen the light. It was so dark.

Question: Your name, sir?

Guychone: I was a gentleman . . . my name was defiled. I cannot see it, I cannot hear it, let me take it, when it is going to be right. I have had to pay for it; she has paid her price. I have been so happy. I have moved about. I have learned to right wrongs. I have seen the light.

Question: I am going to open your eyes now. Look at the calendar before you, and tell me what is the date on it? (placing calendar)

Guychone: Nineteen fifty-three. . . . (pointing at the tape recorder in motion) Wagon wheels!

Question: Give us the name of one of your fellow officers in the war. Write it down.

Guychone: I am a poor soul. . . . (writes: Mignon my wife . . . Guychone) Oh, my feet, oh my feet . . . they hurt me so now . . . they bleed . . . I have to always go backwards, backwards. What shall I do with my feet? They had no shoes . . . we walked over burning weed . . . they burned the weed . . . (Who?) The Damn Yankees . . . I wake up, I see the burning weed. . . . (Where? When?) I have to reach out, I have so much to reach for, have patience with me, I can only reach so far—I'll forget. I will tell you everything. . . . (Where?) Georgia! Georgia! (Did you fight under General Lee?) I fell under him. (Did you die under him?) No, no.

Question: Who was with you in the regiment?

Guychone: Johnny Greenly . . . it is like another world . . . Jerome Harvey. (Who was the surgeon?) I did not see him. Horse doctors. (Who was your orderly?) Walter . . . my boy . . . I can't tell the truth, and I try so hard. . . . I will come with the truth when it comes, you see the burning weeds came to me . . . I will think of happier things to tell . . . I'd like to tell you about the house in Charleston, on Elm Street. I think it is 320, I was born in it.

Question: Any others in the family?

Guychone: Two brothers. They died. They were in the war with me. I was the eldest. William, and Paul. (And you're Edward?) Yes. (Your mother?) Mary. (Your father?) Frederick. (Where was he born?) Charleston. (Your mother's maiden name?) Ah . . . ! (Where did you go to college?) William . . . William and . . . a white house with green grass. (When did you graduate?) Fifty-three . . . ONE HUNDRED YEARS. . . . It is hard to get into those corners where I can't think any more.

"I never had my eyes open before, in trance," observed Mrs. Meyers afterwards. "While I could look at you and you looked like yourself, I could almost look through you. That never happened before. I could only see what I focused on.

This machine . . . it seemed the wheels were going much, much *faster* than they are going now."

On July 25th, 1953, a "planchette" session was held at the home of Mrs. Meyers, with herself and the late Mrs. Zoe Britton present, during which Guychone made himself known, and stated that he had a living son, eighty-nine years old, now living in a place called Seymour, West Virginia.

Evidential material begins to pile up

By now we knew we had an unusual case. I went through all the available material on this period (and there is a lot), without turning up anyone named Guychone.

These were extremely hot afternoons, but the quest went on. Rarely has any psychic researcher undertaken a similarly protracted project to hunt down psychic evidence.

Sitting of July 28th, 1953

Finding a St. Michael's medal around my neck, Guychone says it reminds him of a medal of St. Anne, which his "Huguenot mother," Marie Guychone, had given him.

Question: Do you remember the name of your college?
Guychone: Two colleges. St. Anne's in Charleston, South Carolina. . . . Only one thought around another, that's all I had— curry the horses. Why? I know now. I remember. I want to say my mother is here, I saw her, she says God bless you. I understand more now. Thank you. Pray for me.

Sitting of August 4th, 1953

This sitting repeated previous information and consisted in a cat-and-mouse game between Guychone and myself. However, toward the end, Guychone began to speak of his son Gregory, naming him for the first time. He asked us to find him. We asked, "What name does Gregory use?" Guychone casually answered: "I don't know . . . Guychone . . . maybe McGowan. . . ." The name McGowan came very quietly, but sufficiently distinct to be heard by all present. At the time, we were not overwhelmed. Only when research started to yield results did we realize that it was his real name at last. But I was not immediately successful in locating McGowan on the regimental rosters, far from it! I was misled by his statement of having served in the cavalry, and naturally gave the cavalry rosters my special attention, but he wasn't in them. Late in August I went through the city records of Charleston, West Virginia, on a futile search for the Guychone family, assuming still that they were his in-laws. Here I found mention of a "McGowan's Brigade."

Sitting of August 18th, 1953

Question: Please identify yourself, Colonel.

McGowan: Yes . . . Edward . . . I can stay? I can stay?

Question: Why do you want so much to stay? Are you not happy where you are?

McGowan: Oh yes. But I like to talk very much . . . how happy I am.

Question: What was your mother's name?

McGowan: Marie Guychone.

Question: What is your own name?

McGowan: Guychone.

Question: Yes; that is the name you *used*, but you really are . . .?

142

The Fifth Avenue Ghost

McGowan: Edward Mac . . . Mac . . . curry the horses! (excited, is calmed by me) Yes, I see . . . Mac . . . McGowan! I remember more now, but I can only tell what I know . . . it is like a wall . . . I remember a dark night, I was crazy . . . war on one hand, fighting, bullets . . . and then, flying away, chasing, chasing, chasing . . .

Question: What regiment were you with?

McGowan: Six . . . two . . . sometimes horse . . . oh, in that fire. . . .

Question: Who was your commanding general?

McGowan: But—Butler.

He then speaks of his service in two regiments, one of which was the Sixth South Carolina Regiment, and he mentions a stand on a hill, which was hell, with the Damyankees on all sides. He says it was at Chattanooga.

Question: The house on Fifth Avenue, New York . . . do you remember the name of your landlord?

McGowan: A woman . . . Elsie (or L. C.) . . . stout. . . .

Actually, he says, a man collected the rent, which he had trouble paying at times. He knew a man named Pat Duffy in New York. He was the man who worked for his landlady, collecting the rent, coming to his door.

During the interrogation about his landlord, McGowan suddenly returns to his war experiences. "There was a Griffin," he says, referring to an officer he knew.

Sitting of August 25th, 1953

"The Colonel," as we now called him, came through very clearly. He introduced himself by his true name. Asked again about the landlady in New York, he now adds that she was a widow. Again, he speaks of "Griff . . . Griff. . . ." Asked what school he went to, he says "St. Anne's College in Charleston, South Carolina, and also William and Mary College in Virginia, the latter in 1850, 51, 52, 53, 54." What was his birthday? He says "February 10, 1830." Did he write any official letters during the war? He says, "I wrote to General Robert E. Lee." What about? When? "January, 1864. Atlanta. . . . I needed horses, horses, wheels to run the things on." Did you get them? "No." What regiment was he with then? "The Sixth from South Carolina." But wasn't he from West Virginia? Amazed, McGowan says, "No, from South Carolina."

I then inquired about his family in New York.

McGowan explained that his mother did live with him there, and died there, but after his own death "they" went away, including his sister-in-law Gertrude and brother William. Again, he asks that we tell his son Gregory "that his father did *not* do away with himself."

I asked, "Where is there a true picture of you?" McGowan replied, "There is one in the courthouse in Charleston, South Carolina." What kind of a picture? "Etch . . . etch . . . *tintype!*"

All through these sittings it was clear that McGowan's memory was best when "pictures" or scenes were asked for, and worst when precise names or dates were being requested. He was never sure when he gave a figure, but was very sure of his facts when he spoke of situations or relationships. Thus, he gave varying dates for his own birthday, making it clear that he was hazy about it, not even aware of having given discrepant information within a brief period.

But then, if a living person undergoes a severe shock, is he not extremely hazy about such familiar details as his name or address? Yet, most shock victims can *describe* their house, or their loved ones. The human memory, apparently, is more reliable in terms of associations, when under stress, than in terms of factual information, like names and figures.

By now research was in full swing, and it is fortunate for the sake of the Survival View that so much prima-facie evidence was obtained *before* the disclosure of McGowan's true name started the material flowing. Thus, the old and somewhat tiring argument of "mental telepathy" being responsible for some of the information, can only be applied, if at all, to a part of the sittings. No one can read facts in a mind *before* they get into that mind!

The sittings continued in weekly sessions, with Colonel McGowan rapidly becoming our "star" visitor.

Sitting of September 1st, 1953

Question: What was your rank at the end of the war?
McGowan: That was on paper . . . made to serve.
Question: Did you become a general?
McGowan: Naw . . . honors . . . I take empty honors. . . .
Question: When you went to school, what did you study?
McGowan: The law of the land.
Question: What happened at Manassas?
McGowan: Oh . . . defeat. Defeat.
Question: What happened to you personally at Manassas?
McGowan: Ah, cut, cut. Bayonets. Ah. Blood, blood.
Question: What happened at Malvern Hill?
McGowan: Success. We took the house. Low brick building. We wait. They come up and we see right in the mouth of a cannon. 1864. They burned the house around our ears. But we didn't move.
Question: What was under your command at that time?
McGowan: Two divisions.
Question: How many regiments?
McGowan: Four . . . forty . . . (Four?) TEEN!

Question: What did you command?

McGowan: My commander was shot down, I take over. (Who for?) John . . . Major. . . .

Question: Listen, Colonel, your name is not Edward. Is there any other first or middle name you used? (Silence) Did anyone of high rank serve from South Carolina? (My brother William) Anyone else? (Paul)

McGowan: Do you think of Charles McGowan? That was no relation of mine. He was on the waterfront. He was . . . exporter.

Question: Were you at Gettysburg, Colonel? (Yes.) What regiments were under your command then?

McGowan: I had a wound at Gettysburg. I was very torn. (Where did you get the wound?) Atlanta . . . change of rank. Empty honors (About his son Gregory) Seymour . . . many years Lowell, Massachusetts, and then he went back down South, Seymour, South Carolina, and sometimes West Virginia . . . he was in a store, he left and then he came into property, mother also had property, down there near Charleston in West Virginia . . . that is where he is, yes.

Question: You say your father was Frederick? (Yes.) Who was William. (My brother.) Who was Samuel? (Long pause, *stunned*, then: *I wrote that name!*) Why didn't you tell us? (Crying: I didn't want to tell. . . .) Tell us your true rank, too. (I don't care what it was). Please don't evade us. What was your rank? (Brigadier . . . General). Then you are General Samuel McGowan?

McGowan: You made me very unhappy . . . such a name (crying) . . . blood, empty honors. . . .

Question: Who was James Johnson? (My commander.) What happened to him? (Indicates he was shot.) Who took over for Johnson? (I did.) What regiment was it?

McGowan: I don't know the figures . . . I don't know.

Question: Your relative in New York, what was his name?'

The Fifth Avenue Ghost

McGowan: Peter Paul.

Question: What was his profession?

McGowan: A doctor. (Any particular kind of doctor?) Cuts. (What kind?) (McGowan points to face.) (Nose doctor?) (McGowan points to mouth and shakes head.) (Mouth doctor?) (McGowan violently grabs his teeth and shakes them.))Oh, teeth? A dentist) (McGowan nods assent.)

Question: I will name some regiments, tell me if any of them mean anything to you. The 10th . . . the 34th . . . the 14th . . . (McGowan reacts.) The 14th? Does it mean anything to you?

McGowan: I don't know, figures don't mean anything on this side. . . .

Some interesting facts brought out by research

In the sitting of August 18th, McGowan stated his landlord was a woman and that her name was "Elsie" or L. C. *The Hall of Records* of New York City lists the owner of 226 Fifth Avenue as "Isabella S. Clarke, from 1853 to (at least) March 1, 1871." In the same sitting, McGowan stated that Pat Duffy was the man who actually came to collect the rent, working for the landlady. Several days *after* this information was *voluntarily* received from the entity, I found in *Trow's New York Directory for 1869/70:*

Page 195: "Clark, Isabella, wid. Constantine h. (house) 45 Cherry."

Page 309: "Duffy, Patrick, laborer, 45 Cherry."

This could be known only to someone who actually *knew* these people, eighty years ago; it proved our ghost was *there* in 1873!

The sitting of September 1st also proved fruitful.

A "Peter McGowan, dentist, 253 W. 13 St." appears in *Trow's New York City Directory for 1870/71.*

J. F. J. Caldwell, in his *"History of a Brigade of South Carolinians known first as Gregg's, and subsequently as McGowan's Brigade."* (Philadelphia, 1866) reports:

Page 10: "The 14th Regiment South Carolina Volunteers selected for field officers . . . Col. James Jones, *Lt. Col. Samuel McGowan* . . . (1861)."

Page 12: "Colonel Samuel McGowan commands the 14th Regiment."

Page 18: "McGowan arrives from the Chickahominy river (under Lee)."

Page 24: "Conspicuous gallantry in the battle of Malvern Hill."

Page 37: ". . . of the 11 field officers of our brigade, seven were wounded: Col. McGowan, etc. (in the 2nd battle of Manassas)."

Page 53: "Col. Samuel McGowan of the 14th Regiment (at Fredericksburg)."

Page 60: "The 13th and 14th regiments under McGowan. . . ."

Page 61: "Gen. Gregg's death Dec. 14, 1862. McGowan succeeds to command."

Page 66: "Biography: Born Laurens district, S.C. 1820. Graduated 1841 South Carolina College, Law; in Mexican War, then settled as lawyer in Abbeville, S.C. Became a Brig. Gen. January 20, 1863, assists in taking Ft. Sumter April 1861; but lapsing commission as General in State Militia, he becomes Lt. Col. in the Confederate Army, takes part at Bull Run, Manassas Plains, under Gen. Bonham. Then elected Lt. Col. of 14th Regiment, S.C.; Spring 1862, made full Col. *succeeding Col. Jones who was killed.* McGowan is *wounded* in battle of Manassas." Biographer Caldwell, who was McGowan's aide as a lieutenant, says (in 1866) "he still lives."

Page 79. "April 29, 1863, McGowan's *Brigade* gets orders to be ready to march. Gen. McGowan commands the brigade."

Page 80: "Wounded again (Fredericksburg)."

Page 89: "Gen. Lee reviews troops including McGowan's. Brigade now consists of 1st, 12th, 13th, 14th Regiments and Orr's Rifles. Also known as 'McGowan's Sharpshooters.'"

Page 91: "McGowan takes part in battle of Chancellorsville."

Page 96: "Battle of Gettysburg: McGowan commands 13th, 12th, 14th, and 1st."

Page 110: "McGowan near Culpepper Courthouse."

Page 22: "Gen. McGowan returned to us in February (1864). He had not sufficiently recovered from the wound received at Chancellorsville to walk well, but remained with us and discharged all the duties of his office."

Page 125: *About Butler:* "Butler to lead column (against McGowan) from the Eastern coast." Another Butler (Col.) commanded the Confederate 1st Regt. (Battle of Chickamauga)

Page 126sq.: "Battle of Spottsylvania, May 1864."

Page 133: "Gen. Lee and Gen. Hill were there (defeat)."

Page 142: "McGowan wounded by a 'minie ball,' in the right arm, quits field."

But to continue with our sittings, and with McGowan's personal recollections—

Sitting of September 8th, 1953

McGowan: (speaking again of his death) "It was in the forties . . . they killed me on the top floor. They dragged me up, that 'man of color' named Walter. He was a giant of a man. She was a virtuous woman, I tell you she was. But they would not believe it."

I wanted to get his reaction to a name I had found in the records, so I asked, "Have you ever met a McWilliams?"

McGowan: You have the knowledge of the devil with you. *Her* family name.

Question: Did you stay in New York until your passing?

McGowan: 1869, 1873. Back and forth. I have written to Lee, Jackson, James, and Beaufort. 1862–63, March.

Question: What did you do at the end of the war?

McGowan: Back and forth, always on the go. Property was gone, ruined. Plantations burned. I did not work. I could not. Three or four bad years. I quit. My wits, my wits. My uncle. The house burned in Charleston. Sometimes Columbia. (Then, of Mignon, his wife, he says) She died in 1892 . . . Francois Guychone . . . he was so good to little boys, he made excursions in the Bay of Charleston—we sailed in boats. He was my uncle.

Sitting of September 15th, 1953

I asked, what did he look like in his prime.

McGowan: I wasn't too bad to look at, very good brow, face to the long, and at one time I indulged in the whiskers . . . not so long, for the chin . . . colonial . . . I liked to see my chin a good deal, sometimes I cover (indicates mustache). . . .

Question: What can you tell us about the cemetery in Abbeville?

McGowan: There is a monument, the family cemetery . . . nobody cared . . . my father was born the fifth of January. . . . (What was on your tombstone?) Samuel Edward McGowan, born . . . 32? . . . died 1883? 1873? 1–8–7 hard to read so dirty . . . age 40 . . . 41 . . . gray-brown stars . . . battered. . . . I go between the bushes, I look at the monument, it's defaced. . . .

Question: What news did your family give out of your death?

McGowan: Foul play. (What happened to the body?) Cremated

The Fifth Avenue Ghost

I guess, I think in this city. The remains were destroyed: not in the grave, a monument to a memory. . . . (What did they tell the public?) Lost forever . . . I could have been at sea . . . house was destroyed by fire. . . . (Do you mean there is no official record of your death?) No. *Not identical to passing*, they never told the exact month or day . . . I see . . . 1879 . . . very blurred . . . September 4th. . . .

Question: Were you ever injured in an argument?

McGowan: I spent much time on my back because of a wound . . . on my head. (An argument?) Yes. (With whom?) A man. Hand to hand. Rapier. . . . Glen, Glen . . . Ardmore.

Sitting of September 22nd, 1953

"Mother" Marie Guychone spoke briefly in French and was followed by McGowan. He said he was at one time "An Associate Justice" in the city of Columbia.

Here again do I wish to report some more research information bearing on this part of the investigation. Evans, in his *Confederate Military History*, 1899[*] has a picture of the General which became available to us *after* the September 22nd sitting. His biography, on page 414, mentions the fact that "he was associate Justice of the (State) Supreme Court." Curiously, this author also states that McGowan died in "December 1893." Careful scrutiny of two major New York dailies than existing (*Post* and *Times*) brought to light that the author of the *Confederate Military History* made a mistake, albeit an understandable one. A certain Ned McGowan, described as a "notorious character, aged 80" had died in San Francisco on December 9, 1893. This man was also a Confederate hero. (*The New York Times*, XII/9). However, the same source (*The New York Times*, August 13, 1897) reports General

[*]Vol. V., p. 409.

151

McGowan's death as having occurred on the ninth of August, *1897*. The obituary contains the facts already noted in the biography quoted earlier, plus one interesting additional detail, that McGowan *received a cut across the scalp in a duel*.

Another good source, *The Dictionary of American Biography*, says of our subject: "*McGowan, Samuel*. Son of William and Jeannie McGowan, law partner of William H. Parker. Died August 9, 1897 in Abbeville. Buried in Long Cane Cemetery in Abbeville. Born Oct. 9, 1819 in Crosshill section of Laurens district, S. C. *Mother's name was McWilliams*. Law partner of *Perrin* in Abbeville. Representative in State House of South Carolina. Elected to Congress, *but not seated.*"

A Colonel at Gettysburg, by Varina Brown, about her late husband Colonel Brown, contains the following: "In the battle of Jericho Mills, '*Griffin's Division*' of Federals wrought havoc against McGowan's Brigade."

Correspondence with Mrs. William Gaynes, a resident of Abbeville, revealed on October 1st, 1953—"The old general was a *victim of the failing mind* but he was doctored up until the date of his death. He was attended by his cousin *Dr. F. E. Harrison.*"

Eminent & Representative Men of South Carolina by Brant & Fuller (Madison, Wisconsin, 1892) gives this picture:

"Samuel McGowan was born of *Scotch* Irish parents in Laurens County S.C. on October 9th 1819. Graduated with distinction from the South Carolina College in 1841. Read law at Abbeville with T. C. Perrin who offered him a partnership. He entered the service as a private and went to Mexico with the Palmetto Regiment. He was appointed on the general Quartermaster's Staff with the rank of Captain. After the war he returned to Abbeville and resumed the practice of Law with T. C. Perrin. He married Susan Caroline, eldest daughter of Judge David Lewis Wardlaw and they lived in Abbeville until some years after the death of Gen. McGowan in 1897. The home of Gen. McGowan still stands in Abbeville and was sold some time ago to the Baptist Church for 50,000 dollars. . . . After the war he entered law practice with William H. Parker (*1869/1879*) *in Abbeville*. He took an interest in political affairs . . . member of the Convention that met in Columbia in September, 1865. Elected to Congress but not allowed to take his seat. Counted out on the second election two years later. In 1878 he was a member of the State Legislature and in 1879 he was elected Associate Justice of the State Supreme Court.

"General McGowan lived a long and honorable life in Abbeville. He was a contributing member of the Episcopal Church, Trinity, and became a member later in life. At his death the following appeared in the *Abbeville Medium*, edited by Gen. R. R. Hemphill who had served in McGowan's Brigade. 'General Samuel McGowan *died at his home in this city* at 8:35 o'clock last Monday morning August 8th. Full of years and honors he passed away surrounded by his family and friends. He had been in declining health for some time and suffered intense pain, though his final sickness was for a few days only and at the end all was Peace. Impressive services were held in *Trinity Church* Tuesday afternoon, at four o'clock, the procession starting from the residence. At the Church, the procession . . . preceded by Dr. Wm. M. Grier and Bishop Ellison Capers who read the solemn service . . . directly behind the coffin old Daddy Willis Marshall, a colored man who had served him well, bore a laurel wreath. Gen. McGowan was buried at *Long Lane* cemetery and there is a handsome stone on the plot."

Mrs. William Gaynes further reports:

"Gen. McGowan had a 'fine line of profanity' and used it frequently in Court. He was engaged in a duel once with Col. John *Cunningham* and was wounded behind one ear and came near passing out. Col. Cunningham challenged Col. *Perrin who refused* the challenge on the ground that he did not approve of dueling, and Gen. McGowan took up the challenge and the duel took place at Sand Bar Ferry, near Augusta, with McGowan being wounded.

"As far as I know, there was never any difficulty between Mr. McGowan and the old General. His father-in-law, Judge Wardlaw, married *Sarah* Rebecca Allen, and *her* mother was Mary Lucia *Garvey*."

In other words, Judge Wardlaw married *Sarah Garvey*.

Mrs. Gaynes continues: "I have seen him frequently on his way to his law office, for he had to pass right by *our* office. If he ever was out of town for any length of time, Abbeville *did not know it*."

The inscription on Samuel McGowan's tombstone in Long Cane Graveyard reads as follows:

"Samuel McGowan, born Laurens County 9 October 1819. Died in Abbeville 9 August 1897. Go soldier to thy honored rest, thy trust and honor valor bearing. The brave are the tenderest, the loving are the daring."

Side 2: "From humble birth he rose to the highest honor in Civic and military life. A patriot and a leader of men. In peace his country called him, he waited not to her call in war. A man's strength, a woman's tenderness, a child's simplicity were his and his a heart of charity fulfilling the law of love. He did good and not evil all the days of his life and at its end his country his children and his children's children rise up and call him blessed. In Mexican War 1846–1848. A Captain in United States Army. The Confederate War 1861–1865. A Brigadier General C.S.A. Member of the Legislature 1848–50. Elected to Congress 1866. Associate Justice of Supreme Court of South Carolina 1878–1894. A hero in two wars. Seven times wounded. A leader at the Bar, a wise law giver a righteous judge. He rests from his labors and his works do follow him."

MCGOWAN BECOMES A "REGULAR" OF THE WEEKLY SITTINGS.

General McGowan had by now become an always impatient weekly "guest" at our sittings, and he never liked the idea of leaving. Whenever it was suggested that time was running short, McGowan tried to prolong his stay by becoming suddenly very talkative.

Sitting of September 29th, 1953

A prepared list of eight names, all fictitious but one (the sixth is that of Susan Wardlaw, McGowan's wife) is read to him several times. McGowan reacts to two of the nonexistent names, but not to the one of his wife. One of the fictitious names is John D. Sumter, to which McGowan mumbles, "Colonel." Fact is there *was* a Colonel Sumter in the Confederate Army!

McGowan also described in detail the farm where his son Gregory now lives. Asked about the name Guychone, he says it comes from Louisiana; Mignon, on her mother's side, had it. He identifies his hometown newspapers as "Star-Press." ("*Star-Press*, paper, picture, Judge, Columbia, picture in paper. . . .")

Question: Who was Dr. Harrison?
McGowan: Family doctor.
Question: Is your home in Abbeville still standing?
McGowan: It isn't *what it was*. Strange pictures and things. (Anyone live in it?) No. Strange things, guns and cannons.

Sitting of October 14th, 1953

McGowan says he had two daughters. Trying again to read his tombstone, he says, "1887, or is it 97?" As to his birthyear, he reads, "1821. . . . 31?"

Sitting of October 20th, 1953

When the control introduces McGowan, there is for several moments intense panic and fear brought on by a metal necklace worn by the medium. When McGowan is assured that there is no longer any "rope around his neck," he calms down, and excuses himself for his regression.

Question: Who was the Susan you mentioned the last time?
McGowan: The mother of my children.
Question: What was her other name?
McGowan: Cornelia.
Question: Were you elected to Congress?
McGowan: What kind of Congress? (The U. S. Congress.) I lost. Such a business, everybody grabs, everybody steals. . . . Somebody always buys the votes and it's such a mess.
Question: Are Mignon and Susan one and the same person or not?
McGowan: I don't wish to commit myself. (I insist.) They are *not!*
Question: Let us talk about Susan. What profession did your father-in-law follow?
McGowan: Big man . . . in the law.
Question: What was your mother-in-law's first name?
McGowan: Sarah.
Question: Did she have another name?
McGowan: Garfey. . . .
Question: Coffee? Spell it.
McGowan: Not coffee. *Garvey!*

At a sitting on October 28th, 1953, at the home of Mrs.

Meyers, McGowan's alleged grandson, Billy, manifested himself as follows:

"My name is William, I passed in 1949, at Charleston. I'm a grandson of General McGowan. I was born in Abbeville, January 2nd, 1894. Gregory is half-brother, son of the French bitch. He (McGowan) would have married her, but he had a boss, grandfather, who held the purse strings. Susan's father of Dutch blood, hard-headed."

Sitting of October 29th, 1953

McGowan: You must find Gregory. He may be surprised about his father, but I must let him know I wanted for him, and they took for *them* . . . all. And they gave him nothing. Nothing! I had made other plans. (Was there a will?) There was . . . but I had a Judge in the family that made other plans . . . THEY WERE NOT MINE! You must tell Gregory I provided. . . . I tell you only the truth because I was an honest man . . . I did the best for my family, for my people, for those I considered my countrymen, that what you now call posterity . . . I suffer my own sins. . . . For you maybe it means nothing, for me, for those who remember me, pity . . . they are now aware of the truth, only now is my son unaware of the truth. Sir, you are my best friend. And I go into hell for you. I tell you always the truth, Sir, but there are things that would not concern you or anybody. But I will give you those names yet!

Question: I ask again for the name of McGowan's father-in-law.

McGowan: Wida . . . Wider.

THE "GHOST" IS FREED

One of the functions of a "rescue circle" is to make sure a disturbed entity does not return to the scene of his unhappiness. This mission was accomplished here.

Sitting of November 3rd, 1953

McGowan: I see the house where I lived, you know, where you found me. *I go there now, but I am not anymore disturbed.* I found my mother and my father. They could not touch me, but *now,* we touch hands. I live over my life, come back to many things. Herman! He was a good soul, he helped me when I was down in Atlanta. He bathed my feet, my legs were scorched, and he was good to me, and he is over here. I thank him. I thanked him then, but I was the big man, and he was nothing, but now I see he is a fine gentleman, he polished my boots, he put my uniform in order.

Sitting of November 6th, 1953

I was alone with the medium, Mrs. Meyers, at her home, when I had a chance to question McGowan about his apparent murder, and the "conspiracy of silence" concerning it.

McGowan: The Judge protected them, did not report my death. They had devised the kidnapping. I was murdered downstairs, strangled by the kidnapper Walter. He took her (Mignon) all the way to Boston. I wore the uniform of Damyankees (during the war), rode a horse *every night* to Boston. . . no, I made a mistake. I came to my Uncle Peter Paul in New York, I had a letter from Marie Guychone, she was in New York. Begged me to find Mignon and Gregory. I come to New York. I can't find her, she was in Boston then, but I didn't know that until later. Marie Guychone remained with my uncle, and I gave up the chase, and like a thief crawled back to Confederate grounds. That was in 1863. After the war, there was a struggle, property was worthless, finally the Union granted that we withdraw our holdings, and with that I came to New York. My mother and father came also, until rehabilitation was sufficient for their return.

I continued to live with my wife, Susan, and the children,

and I found Mignon. She had escaped, and came to her mother in New York. I made a place for them to live with my uncle and when my wife returned to stay with her father (the Judge), I had Mignon, but she was pregnant and she didn't know it, and there was a black child—there was unpleasantness between us, I didn't know if it were mine and Mignon was black, but it was not so, it was his child (Walter's), and he came for it and for her, he traced her to my house (on Fifth Avenue); my father-in-law (the Judge) was the informer, and he (Walter) strangled me, he was a big man.

And when I was not dead yet, he dragged me up the stairs. Mignon was not present, not guilty. I think . . . it was in January 1874. But I may be mistaken about time. Gregory had two sons, William and Edward. William died on a boat in the English Channel in 1918. Gregory used the name *Fogarty*, not McGowan. The little black boy died, they say. It was just as well for him.

McGowan then left peacefully, promising more information about the time lag between his given date and that officially recorded. I told him the difference was "about twenty years." For the first time, McGowan had stated his story reasonably, although some details of it would be hard to check. No murder or suicide was reported in the newspapers of the period, similar to this case. But of course anyone planning a crime like this might have succeeded in keeping it out of the public eye. We decided to continue our sittings.

Sitting of November 10th, 1953

McGowan talked about the duel he fought, which cost him his hair, due to a wound on the left side, back and top of ;his

159

head. It was over a woman and against a certain Colonel C., something like "Collins," but a longer name. He said that Perry or Perrin *did so* make a stand, as if someone had doubted it!

MORE PROOF TURNS UP!

Leading away from personal subjects, the questioning now proceeded toward matters of general interest about New York at the time of McGowan's residence here. The advantage of this line of questioning is its neutral value for research purposes; and as *no research* was undertaken until after the sittings of November 17th, mental telepathy must be excluded as an alternate explanation!

Sitting of November 17th, 1953

McGowan: You don't have a beard. They called them *milksops* in my days, the beardless boys!

Question: What did they call a man who was a nice dresser and liked ladies?

McGowan: A Beau Brummel.

Question: What did they call a gentleman who dressed too well, too fancifully?

McGowan: A fop.

Question: What was your favorite sport?

McGowan: Billiards (He explains he was good at it, and the balls were *made of cloth.*)

Question: What was the favorite game of your day?

McGowan: They played a *Cricket* kind of game. . . .

Question: Who was mayor of New York?

McGowan: Oh . . . Grace. Grace . . . *Edmond* . . . Grace . . . something like it.

The Fifth Avenue Ghost

William R. Grace was mayor of New York, 1881–1882, and Franklin Edson (not Edmond) followed, 1883–1884. Also, plastic billiard balls as we know them today are a comparatively recent invention, and billiard balls in the Victorian era were indeed made of cloth. The cricket kind of game must be baseball. Beau Brummel, fop, milksop are all authentic Victorian expressions.

Sitting of November 26th, 1953

I asked the General about trains in New York in his time.

McGowan: They were smoke stacks, up in the air, smoke got in your eyes, they went down to the Globe Building near City Hall. The *Globe* building was near Broadway and Nassau. The train went up to Harlem. It was a *nice* neighborhood. I took many strolls in the park.

Question: Where was the Hotel Waldorf-Astoria?

McGowan: Near Fifth Avenue and 33rd, near my house . . . and the Hotel Prince George. Restaurants were Ye Olde Southern, Hotel Brevoort. You crack my brain, you are worse than that boss in the Big House, Mr. Tammany and Mr. Tweed. (I discussed his house, and he mentioned doing business with—) Somebody named *Costi* . . . I paid $128.50 a month for the entire house. A suite of clothes cost $100.00.

Question: Who lived next door to you?

McGowan: Herman . . . *was a carriage smith.* He had a business where he made carriages. He lived next door, but his business was not there, the shop was on Third Avenue, Third Street, near the river.

Question: Any other neighbors?

McGowan: Corrigan Brown, *a lawyer* . . . lived three houses down. The editor of the *Globe* was White . . . Stone . . . White . . . the editor of the *Globe* was not good friends with

161

the man in the Big House. THey broke his house down when he lived on Fifth Avenue. *He was a neighbor.* Herman the carriage maker made good carriages. I bought one with fringes and two seats, a cabrio. . . .

Question: Did you have a janitor?

McGowan: There was a black boy named Ted, mainly colored servants, we had a gardener, white, named Patrick. He collects the rent, he lives with the Old Crow on Cherry Street. Herman lives next door. He had a long mustache and square beard. He wore a frock coat, a diamond tie pin, and spectacles. I never called him Herman . . . (trying to remember his true name) . . . Gray . . . I never called him Herman. He had a wife named Birdie. His wife had a sister named Finny who lived there too . . . Mrs. Finny . . . she was a young widow with two children . . . she was a good friend to my Susan.

McGowan then reluctantly signs his name as requested.

Research, undertaken *after* the sitting, again excluded mental telepathy. The facts were of a kind not likely to be found in the records, *unless* one were specifically looking for them!

The *New York Globe* building, which McGowan remembers "near Broadway and Nassau," was then (1873) at 7 Spruce Street and apparently also at 162 Nassau Street.[*] The *Globe* is on Spruce, and *Globe and Evening Press* on Nassau, around the corner.

McGowan describes the steam-powered elevated railroad that went from City Hall to Harlem. Steam cars started in 1867 and ran until 1906, according to the New York Historical Society, and there were two lines fitting his description, "Harlem, From

[*] *Trow's New York City Directory for 1872/73,* p. 448 regular section and p. 38 City Register section.

The Fifth Avenue Ghost

Park Row to . . . E. 86th Street" and "Third Avenue, from Ann Street through Park Row to . . . Harlem Bridge."[*]

McGowan was right in describing Harlem as a nice neighborhood in his day. Harlem did not become a low-rent, colored section until the present century.

McGowan also acknowledged at once that he had been to the Waldorf-Astoria, and correctly identified its position at Fifth Avenue and 33rd Street. The Waldorf-Astoria came into being on March 14th, 1893. Consequently, McGowan *was alive then,* and evidently sane, if he could visit such places as the Waldorf, Brevoort, and others.

McGowan refers to a (later) landlord as Costi. In 1895, a real-estate firm by the name of George and John Coster was situated at 173 Fifth Avenue, a few houses down the street from McGowan's place.[**]

As for the carriage smith named Herman, a little later referred to as Herman Gray, there was a carriage maker named William H. Gray from 1872 or earlier, and existing beyond the turn of the century, whose shop was at first at 20 Wooster Street,[***] and who lived at 258 West Fourth Street, until at least 1882. In 1895 he is listed as living at 275 West 94th Street. Not all Trow volumes in between are available, so that residence in McGowan's neighborhood can neither be confirmed nor denied. At one time, Gray's shops were on West Broadway. As for Corrigan Brown, the lawyer neighbor, McGowan's mispronouncing of names almost tripped me up. There was no such lawyer. There was, however, one Edmond Congar Brown, lawyer, listed for the first time as such in 1886, and before that only as a clerk. No home is, unfortunately, listed for his later years.[*] McGowan stated

[*] *Ibid.* City Register, p. 18, under "City Railroads."
[**] *Trow,* 1895/96, p. 550.
[***] *Trow,* 1872/73, City Register, p. 27.

that the editor of the *Globe* was named White-and-something, and that he lived near his (McGowan's) house on Fifth Avenue.

Well, one Horace P. Whitney, editor, business, 128 Fulton Street, home, 287 Fifth Avenue, is listed in Trow.** And 128 Fulton Street is the place of the *Globe's* competitor, the *New York Mercury*, published by Cauldwell and Whitney.***

That McGowan did not die in 1873 seems certain to me, as the above information proves. But if he did not die in 1873, something very traumatic must have been done to him at that time. Or perhaps the murder, if such it was, took place in 1897?

It could well be that General McGowan will take this ultimate secret with him into the Great Land where he now dwells safely forever.

*Trow, 1895/96, p. 174, list his office as 132 Nassau.

**1872, p. 1287, regular section.

***Trow, 1872, City Register section, p. 39.

9

The "Spy House" Ghosts of New Jersey

In June, 1696, one Daniel Seabrook, aged 26 and a planter by profession, took his inheritance of 80 pounds sterling and bought 202 acres of property from his stepfather, Thomas Whitlock. For 250 years this plantation was in the hands of the Seabrook family who worked the land and sailed their ships from the harbor. The "Spy House" is probably one of the finest pieces of Colonial architecture available for inspection in the eastern United States, having been restored meticulously over the years.

The house is built in the old manner, held together with wooden pegs. There are handmade bricks, filled with clay mortar. The house has two stories and is painted white. Every room has its own fireplace as that was the only way in which Colonial houses could be heated.

Today, the house, which is located near Middletown, New Jersey, can easily be reached from New York City. It is being kept by a group headed by curator Gertrude Neidlinger, helped by her historian-brother, Travis Neidlinger, and as a museum it displays not only the furniture of the Colonial period but some of the implements of the whalers who were active in the area well into the nineteenth century. As an historical attraction, it is something that should not be missed by anyone, apart from any ghostly connections.

One of the rooms in the house is dedicated to the period of the Battle of Monmouth. This room, called the spy room by the British for good reasons, as we shall see, has copies of the documents kept among General Washington's private papers in the Library of Congress in Washington, D.C..

In 1778, the English were marching through Middletown, pillaging and burning the village. Along the shoreline the Monmouth militia and the men who were working the whale boats, got together to try to cut down the English shipping. General Washington asked for a patriot from Shoal Harbor, which was the name of the estate where the spy house is located, to help the American side fight the British. The volunteer was a certain Corporal John Stillwell, who was given a telescope and instructions to spy on the British from a hill called Garrett's Hill, not far away, the highest point in the immediate area.

The lines between British and Americans were intertwined and frequently intercut each other, and it was difficult for individuals to avoid crossing them at times. The assignment given Corporal Stillwell was not an easy one, especially as some of his own relatives favored the other side of the war. Still, he was able to send specific messages to the militia who were able to turn these messages into attacks on the British fleet.

At that point, Stillwell observed there were 1,037 vessels in the fleet lying off the New Jersey coastline, at a time when the American forces had no navy at all. But the fishermen and their helpers on shore did well in this phase of the Revolutionary War. John Stillwell's son, Obadiah Stillwell, 17 years old, served as message carrier from his father's observation point to the patriots.

Twenty-three naval battles were fought in the harbor after the battle of Monmouth. The success of the whaleboat operation was a stunning blow to the British fleet and a great embarrassment. Even daylight raids became so bold and successful that in one day two pilot boats were captured upsetting the harbor shipping.

Finally, the British gave the order to find the spy and end the rebel operation. The searching party declared the Seabrook homestead as a spy house, since they knew its owner, Major Seabrook, was a patriot. They did not realize that the real spy was John Stillwell, operating from Garrett's Hill. Nevertheless, they burned the spy house. It was, of course, later restored. Today, descendants of John Stillwell are among the society of friends of the museum, supporting it.

Gertrude Neidlinger turned to me for help with the several ghosts she felt in the house. Considering the history of the house, it is not surprising that there should be ghosts there. Miss Neidlinger, herself, has felt someone in the entrance room whenever she has been alone in the house, especially at night. There is also a lady in white who comes down from the attic, walks along the hall and goes into what is called the blue and white room, and there tucks in the covers of a crib or bed. Then she turns and goes out of sight. Miss Neidlinger was not sure who she was, but thought she might have been the spirit of Mrs. Seabrook, who lived through the Revolutionary War in a particularly dangerous position, having relatives on both sides of the political fence.

In 1976, I brought Ingrid Beckman, my psychic friend, to the spy house, which is technically located in Keansburg, New Jersey, near Middletown. The number on the house is 119, but of course everyone in the area calls it the Spy House. As Ingrid walked about the place, she immediately pointed out its ancient usage as an outpost. While we were investigating the house, we both clearly heard footsteps overhead where there was no one walking. Evidently, the ghosts knew of our arrival.

Without knowing anything about the history of the house, Ingrid commented, "Down here around the fireplace I feel there are people planning strategy, worried about British ships." Then she continued, "This was to mobilize something like the minutemen, farming men who were to fight. This was a strategic point because it was the entry into New York."

I then asked Ingrid to tell me whether she felt any ghosts, any residues of the past still in the house.

When we went upstairs, Ingrid tuned into the past with a bang. "There's a woman here. She ties in with this house and something about spying, some kind of spying went on here." Then she added, "Somebody spied behind the American lines and brought back information."

Upstairs near the window on the first floor landing, Ingrid felt a man watching, waiting for someone to come his way. Ingrid felt there was a man present who had committed an act of treason, a man who gave information back to the British. His name was Samuels. She felt that this man was hanged publicly. The people call him an ex-patriot. This is the entity, Ingrid said, who cannot leave this house out of remorse.

Ingrid also asserted that the house was formerly used as a public house, an inn, when meetings took place here. The curator, Miss Neidlinger, later confirmed this. Also, Ingrid felt that among the families living in the area, most of the members served in the patriot militia, but that there were occasional traitors, such as George Taylor. Colonel George Taylor might have been the man to whom Ingrid was referring. As for the man who was hanged, it would have been Captain Huddy, and he was hanged for having caused the death of a certain Philip White. Captain Joshua Huddy had been unjustly accused of having caused the death of the patriot Philip White and despite his innocence, was lynched by the patriots. Again, Ingrid had touched on something very real from history.

But the ghostly lady and the man who was hanged and the man who stared out the window onto the bay are not the only

The "Spy House Ghosts"

ghosts at the spy house. On the Fourth of July, 1975, a group of local boys were in the house in the blue and white room upstairs. Suddenly, the sewing machine door opened by itself and the pedals worked themselves without benefit of human feet. One of the boys looked up, and in the mirror in the bureau across the room, he could see a face with a long beard.

Another boy looked down the hall and there he saw a figure with a tall black hat and a long beard and sort of very full trousers as they were worn in an earlier age. That was enough for them and they ran from the house and never went back again.

One of the ladies who assists the curator, Agnes Lyons, refuses to do any typing in the upstairs room because the papers simply will not stand still. A draft seems to go by all the time and blow the papers to the floor even though the windows are closed. A Mrs. Lillian Boyer also saw the man with the beard standing at the top of the stairs, wearing a black hat and dressed in the period of the later 1700s. He had very large eyes, and seemed to be a man in his forties. He just stood there looking at her and she of course wouldn't pass him. Then he seemed to flash some sort of light back and forth, a brilliant light like a flashlight. And there were footsteps all over the house at the same time. She could even hear the man breathe, yet he was a ghost!

If you want to visit the spy house, address yourself to Gertrude Neidlinger, Curator, at the Spy House, postal address, Port Monmouth, New Jersey 07758. She's a gracious lady and I'm sure will make you welcome.

10

The Metuchen Ghost

One day last spring, while the snow was still on the ground and the chill in the air, my good friend Bernard Axelrod, with whom I have shared many a ghostly experience, called to say that he knew of a haunted house in New Jersey, and was I still interested.

I was, and Bernard disclosed that in the little town of Metuchen, there were a number of structures dating back to Colonial days. A few streets down from where he and his family live in a modern, up-to-date brick building, there stands one wooden house in particular which has the reputation of being haunted, Bernard explained. No particulars were known to him beyond that. Ever since the Rockland County Ghost in the late Danton Walker's colonial house had acquainted me with the specters from George Washington's days, I have been eager to enlarge this knowledge. So it was with great anticipation that I gathered a group of helpers to pay a visit to whoever might be haunting the house in Metuchen. Bernard, who is a very persuasive fellow, managed to get permission from the owner of the house, Mr. Kane, an advertising executive. My group included Mrs. Meyers, as medium, and two associates of hers who would operate the tape recorder and take notes, Rosemarie de Simone and Pearl Winder. Miss de Simone is a teacher and Mrs. Winder is the wife of a dentist.

It was midafternoon of March 6, 1960, when we rolled into the sleepy town of Metuchen. Bernard Axelrod was expecting us, and took us across town to the colonial house we were to inspect.

Any mention of the history or background of the house was studiously avoided en route. The owners, Mr. and Mrs. Kane, had a guest, a Mr. David, and the eight of us sat down in a circle in the downstairs living room of the beautifully preserved old house. It is a jewel of a colonial country house, with an upper story, a staircase and very few structural changes. No doubt about it, the Kanes had good taste, and their house reflected it. The furniture was all in the style of the period, which I took to be about the turn of the eighteenth century, perhaps earlier. There were several cats smoothly moving about, which helped me greatly to relax, for I have always felt that no house is wholly bad where there are cats, and conversely, where there are several cats, a house is bound to be wonderfully charming. For the occasion, however, the entire feline menagerie was put out of reach into the kitchen, and the tape recorder turned on as we took our seats in a semi-circle around the fireplace. The light was the subdued light of a late winter afternoon, and the quiet was that of a country house far away from the bustling city. It was a perfect setting for a ghost to have his say.

As Mrs. Meyers eased herself into her comfortable chair, she remarked that certain clairvoyant impressions had come to her almost the instant she set foot into the house.

"I met a woman upstairs—in spirit, that is—with a long face, thick cheeks, perhaps forty years old or more, with ash-brown hair that may once have been blond. Somehow I get the name Mathilda. She wears a dress of striped material down to her knees, then wide plain material to her ankles. She puts out a hand, and I see a heavy wedding band on her finger, *but it has a cut in it,* and she insists on calling my attention to the cut. Then there is a man, with a prominent nose, tan coat and black trousers, standing in the back of the room looking as if he were sorry about something . . . he has very piercing eyes . . . I think she'd like to find something she has lost, and he blames her for it."

We were listening attentively. No one spoke, for that would perhaps give Mrs. Meyers an unconscious lead, something a good researcher will avoid.

"That sounds very interesting," I heard Bernard say, in his usual noncommittal way. "Do you see anything else?"

"Oh, yes," Mrs. Meyers nodded, "quite a bit—for one thing, there are *other* people here who don't belong to *them* at all . . . they come with the place, but in a different period . . . funny, halfway between upstairs and downstairs, I see one or two people *hanging.*"

At this remark, the Kanes exchanged quick glances. Evidently my medium had hit pay dirt. Later, Mr. Kane told us a man committed suicide in the house around 1850 or 1860. He confirmed also that there was once a floor in between the two floors, but that this later addition had since been removed, when the house was restored to its original colonial condition.

Built in 1740, the house had replaced an earlier structure, for objects inscribed "1738" have been unearthed here.

"Legend has always had it that a revolutionary soldier haunts the house," Mr. Kane explained after the seance. "The previous owners told us they did hear *peculiar noises* from time to time, and that they had been told of such goings-on also by the owner who preceded *them.* Perhaps this story has been handed down from owner to owner, but we have never spoken to anyone in our generation who has heard or seen anything unusual about the place."

"What about you and your wife?" I inquired.

"Oh, we were a bit luckier—or unluckier—depending on how you look at it. One day back in 1956, the front door knocker banged away very loudly. My wife, who was all alone in the house at the time, went to see who it was. There was nobody there. It was winter, and deep snow surrounded the house. *There were no tracks in the snow.*"

"How interesting," Bernard said. All this was new to him, too, despite his friendship with the family.

Mr. Kane slowly lit a pipe, blew the smoke toward the low ceiling of the room, and continued.

"The previous owners had a dog. Big, strapping fellow. Just the same, now and again he would hear some strange noises and absolutely panic. In the middle of the night he would jump into bed with them, crazed with fear. But it wasn't just the dog who heard things. They, too, heard the walking—steps of someone walking around the second floor, and in their bedroom, on the south side of the house—at times of the day when they *knew* for sure there was nobody there."

"And after you moved in, did you actually *see* anything?" I asked. Did they have any idea what the ghost looked like?

"Well, yes," Mr. Kane said. "About a year ago, Mrs. Kane was sleeping in the Green Room upstairs. *Three nights in a row, she was awakened in the middle of the night, at the same time, by the feeling of a presence.* Looking up, she noticed a white form standing beside her bed. Thinking it was me, at first, she was not frightened. But when she spoke to it, it just disappeared into air. She is sure it was a man."

Although nothing unusual had occurred since, the uncanny feeling persisted, and when Bernard Axelrod mentioned his interest in ghosts, and offered to have me come to the house with a qualified medium, the offer was gladly accepted. So there we were, with Mrs. Meyers slowly gliding into trance. Gradually, her description of what she saw or heard blended into the personalities themselves, as her own personality vanished temporarily. It was a very gradual transition, and well controlled.

"She is being blamed by him," Mrs. Meyers mumbled. "Now I see a table, she took four mugs, four large mugs, and one small one. Does she mean to say, four older people and a small one? I get a name, Jake, John, no, *Jonathan!* Then there are four Indians, and they want to make peace. *They've done something they should not have*, and they want to make peace." Her visions continued.

"Now instead of the four mugs on the table, there's a whole line of them, fifteen altogether, but I don't see the small mug now. There are many individuals standing around the table, with their backs toward me—then someone is calling and screaming, and someone says 'Off above the knees.'"

I later established through research that during the Revolutionary War the house was right in the middle of many small skirmishes; the injured may well have been brought here for treatment.

Mrs. Meyers continued her narrative with increasing excitement in her voice.

"Now there are other men, all standing there with long-tailed coats, white stockings, and talking. Someone says 'Dan Dayridge' or 'Bainbridge,' I can't make it out clearly; he's someone with one of these three-cornered hats, a white wig, tied black hair, a very thin man with a high, small nose, not particularly young, with a fluffy collar and large eyes. Something took place here in which he was a participant. He is one of the men standing there with those fifteen mugs. It is night, and there are two candles on either side of the table, food on the table—*smells like chicken*—and then there is a paper with red seals and gold ribbon. But something goes wrong with this, and now there are only four mugs on the table . . . I think it means, only four men return. *Not the small one.* This man is one of the four, and somehow the little mug is pushed aside, I see it put away on the shelf. I see now a small boy, he has disappeared, he is gone . . . but always trying to *come back.* The name *Allen . . .* he followed the man, but the Indians got him and he never came back. They're looking for him, trying to find him. . . ."

Mrs. Meyers now seemed totally entranced. Her features assumed the face of a woman in great mental anguish, and her voice quivered; the words came haltingly and with much prodding from me. For all practical purposes, the medium had now been taken over by a troubled spirit. We listened quietly, as the story unfolded.

"*Allen's* coming back one day . . . call him back . . . my son, do you hear him? They put those Indians in the tree, do you hear them as they moan?"

"Who took your boy?" I asked gently.

"They did . . . he went with them, with the men. With his father, *Jon.*"

"What Indians took him?"

"Look there in the tree. They didn't do it. I know they didn't do it."

"Where did they go?"

"To the *river.* My boy, did you hear him?"

Mrs. Meyers could not have possibly known that there was a river not far from the house. I wanted to fix the period of our story, as I always do in such cases, so I interrupted the narrative and asked what day this was. There was a brief pause, as if she were collecting her thoughts. Then the faltering voice was heard again.

"December One. . . ."

December One! The old-fashioned way of saying December First.

"What year is this?" I continued.

The Metuchen Ghost

This time the voice seemed puzzled as to why I would ask such an obvious thing, but she obliged.

"Seventeen . . . seventy . . . six."

"What does your husband do?"

"Jonathan . . .?"

"Does he own property?"

"The field. . . ."

But then the memory of her son returned. "Allen, my son Allen. He is calling me. . . .

"Where was he born?"

"Here."

"What is the name of this town?"

"Bayridge."

Subsequently, I found that the section of Metuchen we were in had been known in colonial times as *Woodbridge*, although it is not inconceivable that there also was a Bayridge.

The woman wanted to pour her heart out now. "Oh, look," she continued, "they didn't do it, they're in the tree . . . those Indians, dead ones. They didn't do it, I can see their souls and they were innocent of this . . . in the cherry tree."

Suddenly she interrupted herself and said—"Where am I? Why am I so sad?"

It isn't uncommon for a newly liberated or newly contacted "ghost" to be confused about his or her own status. Only an emotionally disturbed personality becomes an earthbound "ghost."

I continued the questioning.

Between sobs and cries for her son, Allen, she let the name "Mary Dugan" slip from her lips, or rather the lips of the entranced medium, who now was fully under the unhappy one's control.

"Who is Mary Dugan?" I immediately interrupted.

"He married her, Jonathan."

"Second wife?"

"Yes . . . I am under the tree."

"Where were you born? What was your maiden name?"

"Bayridge . . . Swift . . . my heart is so hurt, so cold, so cold."

"Do you have any other children?"

"Allen . . . Mary Anne . . . Georgia. They're calling me, do you hear them? Allen, he knows I am alone waiting here. He thought he was a *man!*"

"How old was your boy at the time?" I said. The disappearance of her son was the one thing foremost in her mind.

"My boy . . . eleven . . . December One, 1776, is his birthday. That was his birthday all right."

I asked her if Allen had another name, and she said, Peter. Her own maiden name? She could not remember.

"Why don't I know? They threw me out . . . it was Mary took the house."

"What did your husband do?"

"He was a *potter.* He also was paid for harness. His shop . . . the road to the south. Bayridge. In the tree orchard we took from two neighbors."

The neighborhood is known for its clay deposits and potters, but this was as unknown to the medium as it was to me until *after* the seance, when Bernard told us about it.

In *Boyhood Days in Old Metuchen*, a rare work, Dr. David Marshall says: "Just south of Metuchen there are extensive clay banks."

But our visitor had enough of the questioning. Her sorrow returned and suddenly she burst into tears, the medium's tears, to be sure, crying—"I want Allen! Why is it I look for him? I hear him calling me, I hear his step . . . I know he is here . . . why am I searching for him?"

I then explained that Allen was on "her side of the veil," too, that she would be reunited with her boy by merely "standing still" and letting him find her; it was her frantic activity that made it impossible for them to be reunited, but if she were to becalm herself, all would be well.

After a quiet moment of reflection, her sobs became weaker and her voice firmer.

"Can you see your son now?"

"Yes, I see him." And with that, she slipped away quietly.

A moment later, the medium returned to her own body, as it were, and rubbed her sleepy eyes. Fully awakened a moment later, she remembered nothing of the trance. Now *for the first time* did we talk about the house, and its ghostly visitors.

"How much of this can be proved?" I asked impatiently.

Mr. Kane lit another pipe, and then answered me slowly.

"Well, there is quite a lot," he finally said. "For one thing, this house used to be a tavern during revolutionary days, known as the Allen House!"

Bernard Axelrod, a few weeks later, discovered an 1870 history of the town of Metuchen. In it, there was a remark anent the house, which an early map showed at its present site in 1799:

"In the house . . . lived a Mrs. Allen, and on it was a sign 'Allentown Cake and Beer Sold Here.' Between the long Prayer Meetings which according to New England custom were held mornings and afternoons, with half hour or an hour intermission, it was not unusual for the young men to get ginger cake and a glass of beer at this famous restaurant. . . ."

"What about all those Indians she mentioned?" I asked Mr. Kane.

"There were Indians in this region all right," he confirmed.

"Indian arrowheads have been found right here, near the pond in back of the house. Many Indian battles were fought around here, and incidentally, during the War for Independence, both sides came to this house and had their ale in the evening.

179

This was a kind of no-man's land between the Americans and the British. During the day, they would kill each other, but at night, *they ignored each other over a beer at Mrs. Allen's tavern!*"

"How did you get this information?" I asked Mr. Kane.

"There was a local historian, a Mr. Welsh, who owned this house for some thirty years. He also talked of a revolutionary soldier whose ghost was seen plainly 'walking' through the house about a foot off the ground."

Many times have I heard a ghostly apparition described in just such terms. The motion of walking is really unnecessary, it seems, for the spirit form *glides* about a place.

There are interesting accounts in the rare old books about the town of Metuchen in the local library. These stories spoke of battles between the British and Americans, and of "carts loaded with dead bodies, after a battle between British soldiers and Continentals, up around Oak Tree on June 26th, 1777."

No doubt, the Allen House saw many of them brought in along with the wounded and dying.

I was particularly interested in finding proof of Jonathan Allen's existence, and details of his life.

So far I had only ascertained that Mrs. Allen existed. Her husband was my next goal.

After much work, going through old wills and land documents, I discovered a number of Allens in the area. I found the will of his father, Henry, leaving his "son, Jonathan, the land where he lives" on April 4th, 1783.

A 1799 map shows a substantial amount of land marked "Land of Allen," and Jonathan Allen's name occurs in many a document of the period as a witness or seller of land.

The Jonathan Allen I wanted had to be from Middlesex County, in which Metuchen was located. I recalled that he was an able-bodied man, and consequently must have seen some service. Sure enough, in the *Official Register of the Officers and Men*

The Metuchen Ghost

of New Jersey in the Revolutionary War, I found my man—"Allen, Jonathan—Middlesex."

It is good to know that the troubled spirit of Mrs. Allen can now rest close to her son's; and perhaps the other restless one, her husband, will be accused of negligence in the boy's death no more.

11

The Strange Case of the Colonial Soldier

Somerton, Pennsylvania, is now a suburb of Philadelphia, albeit a pretty outlying one. It takes you all of an hour by car from downtown Philadelphia, but when you get there, it's worth it, especially Byberry Road. How the builders of modern chunks of concrete managed to overlook this delightful country lane in the backyard of the big city is beyond my knowledge, but the fact is that we have here a winding, bumpy road, good enough for one car at a time, that goes for several miles without a single high-rise building. Instead, old homes line it in respectable intervals, allowing even a bit of green and open spaces between the dwellings.

One of the most unusual sights along this winding road is a pretty, wooden Colonial house built in 1732, and untouched except for minor alterations, mainly inside the house. That in itself is a rarity, of course, but the owners who lived here since the Revolutionary period evidently were house-proud people who *cared*.

The current tenants are David and Dolores Robinson, whose greatest pleasure is being in that house. They don't advertise the fact they've got an authentic pre-Revolutionary home, but they're not exactly shy about it either; to them, it is a thrill to live as our ancestors did, without the constant urge to "improve" things with shiny new gadgets that frequently don't work, or to tear down some portion of their home just because it looks old or has been used for a long time.

The Robinsons are house-proud, and they have a keen sense of the antiquarian without any formal education in that area. Mr. Robinson works for the telephone company and his wife works for her brother, a photographer, as a retouch artist. Both are in early middle age and they have three children in the pre-teenage group.

Theirs is a happy family without problems or frustrations: They'd like to make a little more money, advance a little faster, get a better car—but that is the normal average American's dream. With the Robinsons lives Mr. Robinson Senior, an elderly gentleman whose main occupation seemed to be watching TV.

I first heard of the Robinsons and their homestead when I appeared on a local radio show in the area, and I was fascinated by the prospect of an apparently untouched house with many layers of history clinging to it that a psychic might be able to sense. I put the house on my mental list of places to visit for possible psychometry experiments.

Finally, in April of 1967, that opportunity arose and a friend of ours, Tom Davis, drove us out to Byberry Road. There is something strange about Philadelphia distances; they grow on you somehow, especially at night. So it was with considerable delay that we finally showed up at the house, but we were made welcome just the same by the owners.

The house could not be missed even in the dark of night. It is the only one of its kind in the area, and sits back a bit from the road. With its graceful white pillars that support the roof of the porch, it is totally different from anything built nowadays or even in Victorian times. From the outside it looks smaller than it really is. There are three stories, and a storage room beneath the rear part of the house, the oldest portion. We entered through the front door and found ourselves in a delightfully appointed living room leading off to the left into the older portion of the house. The house had a mixture of Colonial and Victorian furniture in it, somehow not out of context with the over-all mood of the place, which was one of remoteness from the modern world. Across the narrow hall from the downstairs living room, a staircase led to the next floor, which contained bedrooms and one of the largest bathrooms I ever saw. Considering the Colonial reluctance to bathe to excess, it struck me as incongruous, until I realized later that the house had had some quasi-public usage at one period.

A few steps led from the living room to the rear section, which was the original portion of the house. A large fireplace dominates it. Next to it is a rear staircase also leading to the upper stories, and the low ceiling shows the original wooden beams just as they were in pre-Revolutionary days.

The Robinsons weren't particularly addicted to the psychic even though they're both Irish, but Mrs. Robinson admits to having had ESP experiences all her life. Whether this is her Irishness (with a well-developed sense of imagination, as she puts it) or just a natural ability, it's there for better or worse. When she was fourteen, she was reading in bed one night, and it was very, very late. This was against the rules, so she had made sure the door to her bedroom was shut. Suddenly, the door opened and her brother Paul stood there looking at her reproachfully. He had been dead for eight years. Dolores screamed and went under the covers. Her mother rushed upstairs to see what was the matter. When she arrived, the door was still wide open! Since that time, Mrs. Robinson has often known things before they really happened—such as who would be at the door before she answered it, or just before the telephone rang, who would be calling. Today, this is just a game to her, and neither her husband nor she takes it too seriously.

Both of them are high school graduates, Dolores has had some college training, and her husband has electro-engineering skills which he uses professionally; nevertheless they don't scoff at the possibility that an old house might contain some elements from its violent past.

When they first moved into the house in 1960, Mrs. Robinson felt right at home in it, as if she had always lived there. From the very first, she found it easy to move up and down the stairs even in the dark without the slightest accident or need to orient herself. It was almost as if the house, or someone in it, were guiding her steps.

But soon the Robinsons became acutely aware that the house was *alive*: There were strange noises and creaking boards, which they promptly ascribed to the settling of an old building. But there were also human footsteps that both husband and wife heard, and there were those doors. The doors, in particular, puzzled them. The first time Mrs. Robinson noticed anything unusual about the doors in their house was when she was working late over some photography assignments she had brought home with her. Her husband was out for the evening and the three children were fast asleep upstairs. The children have their bedrooms on the third floor, while the Robinsons sleep on the second floor. Suddenly Mrs. Robinson heard footsteps on the ceiling above her bedroom. Then the door of the stairwell opened, steps reverberated on the stairs, then the door to the second floor opened, and a blast of cold air hit her. Without taking her eyes from her work, Mrs. Robinson said, "Go back to bed!" assuming it was one of her children who had gotten up for some reason. There was no answer.

She looked up, and there was no one there. Annoyed, she rose and walked up the stairs to check her children's rooms. They were indeed fast asleep. Not satisfied and thinking that one of them must be playing tricks on her, she woke them one by one and questioned them. But they had trouble waking up, and it was evident to Mrs. Robinson that she was on a fool's errand; her children had not been down those stairs.

That was the beginning of a long succession of incidents involving the doors in the house. Occasionally, she would watch with fascination when a door opened quite by itself, without any logical cause, such as wind or draft; or to see a door open for her just as she was about to reach for the doorknob. At least, whatever presence there was in the old house, was polite: It opened the door to a lady! But reassuring it was not, for to live with the unseen can be infuriating, too. Many times she would close a door, only to see it stand wide open again a moment later when she knew very well it could not do that *by itself*.

She began to wonder whether there wasn't perhaps a hidden tunnel beneath their back living room. Frequently they would hear a booming sound below the floor, coming from the direction of the cold storage room below. The doors would continually open for her now, even when she was alone in the house and the children could not very well be blamed for playing pranks on her. During the summer of 1966, there were nights when the activities in the house rose to frenzy comparable only with the coming and going of large crowds. On one occasion her daughter Leigh came down the stairs at night wondering who was in the living room. She could hear the noises up to the top floor! That night Mrs. Robinson was awakened six times by footsteps and closing doors.

Around that time also, her father-in-law reported a strange experience in his room on the second floor. He was watching television when his door opened late one night, and a woman came in. He was so startled by this unexpected visitor, and she disappeared again so quickly, he did not observe her too closely, but he thought she had either long black hair or a black veil. There was of course no one of that description in the house at the time.

Then there were those moments when an invisible rocking chair in the living room would rock by itself as if someone were in it.

Just prior to our visit, Mrs. Robinson's patience was being sorely tried. It was the week of April 4, and we had already announced our coming about a week or so afterward. Mrs. Robinson was on the cellar stairs when she heard a clicking sound and looked up. A rotisserie rack was sailing down toward her! Because she had looked up, she was able to duck, and the missile landed on the stairs instead of on her head. But she thought this just too much. Opening doors, well, all right, but rotisserie racks? It was high time we came down to see her.

I carefully went all over the house, examining the walls, floors, and especially the doors. They were for the most part heavy hinged doors, the kind that do not slide easily but require a healthy push before they will move. We looked into the back room and admired the beams, and I must confess I felt very uneasy in that part of the house. Both Catherine and I had an oppressive feeling, as if we were in the presence of something tragic, though unseen, and we could not get out of there fast enough.

I promised the Robinsons to return with a good psychometrist and perhaps have a go at trance, too, if I could get Mrs. Leek to come down with me on her next visit east. The prospect of finding out what it was that made their house so lively, and perhaps even learn more about its colorful past, made the mysterious noises more bearable for the Robinsons, and they promised to be patient and bear with me until I could make the required arrangements.

It was not until June 1967 that the opportunity arose, but finally Mrs. Leek and I were planning to appear on Murray Burnett's radio program together, and when I mentioned what else we intended doing in the area, Murray's eyes lit up and he offered to include himself in the expedition and drive us to and fro.

The Colonial Soldier

The offer was gladly accepted, and after a dinner at one of Murray's favorite places—during which not a word was exchanged about the Robinson house—we were off in search of adventure in his car. "It it's one thing I do well," he intoned, as we shot out onto the expressway, "it's driving an automobile." He did indeed. He drove with verve and so fast we missed the proper exit, and before long we found ourselves at a place called King of Prussia, where even a Prussian would have been lost.

We shrugged our combined shoulders and turned around, trying to retrace our steps. Murray assured me he knew the way and would have us at the Robinson house in no time at all. There was a time problem, for we all had to be back in the studio by eleven so that we could do the radio program that night. But the evening was still young and the Pennsylvania countryside lovely.

It was just as well that it was, for we got to see a good deal of it that evening. There was some confusion between Roosevelt Boulevard and Roosevelt Avenue, and the directions I had faithfully written down were being interpreted by us now the way two of Rommel's Afrika Korps officers must have studied the caravan routes.

"We should have turned off where we didn't," I finally remarked, and Murray nodded grimly. The time was about an hour after our appointed hour. No doubt the Robinsons must be thinking we're lost, I thought. At least I hoped that that's what they would think, not that we had abandoned *the project*.

The neighborhood seemed vaguely familiar now; no doubt it was. We had been through it several times already that same evening. Were the "forces" that kept opening and closing doors at the Robinson homestead preventing our coming so that they could continue to enjoy their anonymity?

When you're lost in Pennsylvania, you're really lost. But now Murray came to a decision. He turned north and we entered an entirely different part of town. It bore no similarity to the direction in which we wanted to go, but at least it was a well-lit section of town. I began to understand Murray's strategy: He was hoping we would run across someone—no, that's an unhappy word—*find* someone who just might know which way Somerton was. We met several motorists who didn't and several others who thought they did but really didn't, as we found out when we tried to follow their directions.

Ultimately, Murray did the smart thing: He hailed the first cop he saw and identified himself, not without pride. Everybody in Philadelphia knew his radio show.

"We're lost, officer," he announced, and explained our predicament.

"It's Mercury retrograding," Sybil mumbled from the back seat. All during our wild ghost chase she had insisted that astro-logically speaking it was not at all surprising that we had gotten lost.

"Beg your pardon?" the officer said, and looked inside.

"Never mind Mercury," Murray said impatiently, "will you please show us the way?"

"I'll do better than that, sir," the policeman beamed back, "I'll personally escort you."

And so it came to pass that we followed a siren-tooting patrol car through the thick and thin of suburban Philadelphia.

Suddenly, the car in front of us halted. Murray proved how skillful a driver he really was. He did not hit anyone when he pulled up short. He merely jumbled us.

"Anything wrong, officer?" Murray asked, a bit nervously. It was half past nine now.

"My boundary," the officer explained. "I've already tele-phoned for my colleague to take you on further."

We sat and waited another ten minutes, then another police car came up and whisked us in practically no time to our destination. When the Robinsons saw the police car escort us to

The Colonial Soldier

their house, they began to wonder what on earth we had been up to. But they were glad to see us, and quickly we entered the house. Sybil was hysterical with laughter by now, and if we had had something to drink en route, the whole odyssey might have been a jolly good party. But now her face froze as she entered the downstairs portion of the house. I watched her change expression, but before I had a chance to question her, she went to the lady's room. On emerging from it she reported that the first word that had impressed itself upon her was a name—"Ross."

She explained that she felt the strongest influence of this person to the right of the fireplace in the oldest part of the house, so I decided we should go to that area and see what else she might pick up.

Although the house itself was started in 1732, the particular section we were in had definitely been dated to 1755 by local historians, all of whom admired the Robinson house as a showcase and example of early American houses.

"Seventeen forty-six is what I get," Sybil commented.

"Sybil's underbidding you," I remarked to Mrs. Robinson.

"This is some kind of a meeting place," Sybil continued her appraisal of the room, "many people come here . . . 1744 . . . and the name Ross. The whole house has an atmosphere which is not unpleasant, but rather *alive*."

Just as Mrs. Robinson had felt on first contact with the house, I thought. As for the meeting place, I later found out that the house was used as a Quaker meeting house in the 1740s and later, and even today the "Byberry Friends" meet down the road! John Worthington, the first owner of the house, was an overseer for the meeting house in 1752.

"There are many impressions here," Sybil explained as she psychometrized the room more closely, "many people meeting here, but this is superimposed on one dominant male person, this Ross."

After a moment of further walking about, she added, "The date 1774 seems to be very important."

She pointed at a "closet" to the right of the ancient fireplace, and explained that this personality seemed to be strongest there.

"It's a staircase," Mrs. Robinson volunteered, and opened the door of the "closet." Behind it a narrow, winding wooden staircase led to the upper floors.

I motioned to Sybil to sit down in a comfortable chair near the fireplace, and we grouped ourselves around her. We had perhaps thirty minutes left before we were to return to Philadelphia, but for the moment I did not worry about that. My main concern was the house: What would it tell us about its history? What tragedies took place here and what human emotions were spent in its old walls?

Soon we might know. Sybil was in deep trance within a matter of minutes.

"Ross," the voice speaking through Sybil said faintly now, "I'm Ross. John Ross. . . . Virtue in peace. . . ."

"Is this your house?"

"No."

"Then what are you doing here?"

"Praying. Hope for peace. Too much blood. People must pray for peace."

"Is there a war going on?"

"I say there's war . . . the enemies are gone. . . ."

"Are you a soldier?"

"Captain—John—Ross," the voice said, stressing each word as if it were painful to pronounce it.

"What regiment?" I shot back, knowing full well that regimental lists exist and can be checked out for names.

"Twenty-first."

The Colonial Soldier

"Cavalry or Infantry?"

"I—am—for—peace."

"But what branch of the Army were you in?"

"Twenty-first of Horse."

This is an old English expression for cavalry.

"Who is your superior officer?" I asked.

"Colonel Moss is bad . . . he must pray. . . ."

"Who commands?"

"Albright."

"Where did you serve?"

"Battle . . . here. . . ."

He claimed to be thirty-eight years old, having been born in 1726. This would make him thirty-eight in the year 1764. His place of birth was a little place named Verruck, in Holstein, and when he said this I detected a very faint trace of a foreign accent in the entranced voice of the medium.

"Are you German then?" I asked.

"German?" he asked, not comprehending.

"Are you American?"

"American—is good," he said, with appreciation in his voice. Evidently we had before us a mercenary of the British Army.

"Are you British?" I tried.

"Never!" he hissed back.

"Whom do you serve?"

"The thirteen . . . pray. . . ."

Was he referring to the thirteen colonies, the name by which the young republic was indeed known during the revolutionary war?

"This Albrecht. . . . What is his first name?"

"Dee-an-no . . . I don't like him. . . . Peace for this country!!! It was meant for peace."

I could not make out what he meant by Dee-an-no, or

what sounded like it. I then questioned the personality whether he was hurt.

"I wait for them to fetch me," he explained, haltingly, "sickness, make way for me!"

"Why are you in this house—what is there here?"

"Meeting place to pray."

"What religion are you?"

"Religion of peace and silence."

Suddenly, the medium broke into almost uncontrollable sighs and cries of pain. Tears flowed freely from Sybil's closed eyes. The memory of something dreadful must have returned to the communicator.

"I'm dying . . . hands hurt. . . . Where is my hand?"

You could almost see the severed hand, and the broken tone of voice realizing the loss made it the more immediate and dramatic.

"I—am—for peace. . . ."

"What sort of people come here?"

"Silent people. To meditate."

What better way to describe a Quaker meeting house?

"Don't stop praying," he beseeched us.

We promised to pray for him. But would he describe his activities in this house?

"Send for the Friend . . . dying."

He wanted spiritual guidance, now that he was at death's door. The term Friend is the official name for what we now call a Quaker.

Was there someone he wanted us to send for?

"William Proser . . . my brother . . . in England."

"Were you born in England?"

"No. William."

"He is your brother?"

"All—men—are—brothers."

194

The Colonial Soldier

He seemed to have trouble speaking. I started to explain what our mission was and that we wanted to help him find the elusive peace he so longed for.

"Name some of your fellow officers in the regiment," I then requested.

"Erich Gerhardt," the voice said. "Lieutenant Gerhardt."

"Was he in the cavalry? What regiment?"

"My—cavalry—Twenty-first—"

"What year did you serve together? What year are we in now?"

"Seventy-four."

"Where are you stationed?"

Sybil was completely immersed in the past now, with her face no longer hers; instead, we were watching a man in deep agony, struggling to speak again. Murray Burnett had his fingers at his lips, his eyes focused on the medium. It was clear he had never witnessed anything like it, and the extraordinary scene before him was bound to leave a deep and lasting impression, as indeed it did.

But the question went unanswered. Instead, Sybil was suddenly back again, or part of her, anyway. She seemed strangely distraught, however.

"Hands are asleep," she murmured, and I quickly placed her back into the hypnotic state so that the personality of Captain Ross might continue his testimony.

"Get me out, get me out," Sybil screamed now, "my hands . . . my hands are asleep. . . ."

I realized that the severed hand or hands of the Colonial soldier had left a strong imprint. Quickly I suggested that she go back into trance. I then recalled her to her own self, suggesting at the same time that no memory of the trance remain in her conscious mind.

Pearls of sweat stood on Sybil's forehead as she opened her

eyes. But she was in the clear. Nothing of the preceding hour had remained in her memory. After a moment of heavy silence, we rose. It was time to return to the city, but Murray did not care. He knew that his producer, Ted Reinhart, would stall for time by playing a tape, if need be. The Robinsons offered us a quick cup of coffee, which tasted even more delicious than it must have been, under the circumstances. Everybody was very tense and I thought how wise it had been of Mrs. Robinson to keep the children away from the séance.

Hurriedly, we picked up our gear and drove back to the station. It took us about one-fifth of the time it had taken us to come out. Murray Burnett showed his skill behind the wheel as he literally flew along the expressway. Traffic was light at this hour and we managed to get back just as the announcer said, "And now, ladies and gentlemen, Murray Burnett and his guests. . . ."

As if nothing had happened, we strode onto the platform and did a full hour of light banter. By the time we left Philadelphia to return to New York, though, Sybil was exhausted. When we staggered out of our coaches in New York, it was well past one in the morning. The silence of the night was a welcome relief from the turbulent atmosphere of the early evening.

The following day I started to research the material obtained in the Robinson homestead.

To begin with, the Robinsons were able to trace previous ownership back only to 1841, although the local historical society assured her that it was built in 1732. The early records are often sketchy or no longer in existence because so many wars—both of foreign origin and Indian—have been fought around the area, not counting fire and just plain carelessness.

The Robinsons were the ninth family to own the place since the Civil War period. Prior to that the only thing known for certain was that it was a Quaker meeting house, and this fit in with the references Sybil had made in trance.

The Colonial Soldier

But what about Ross?

The gentleman had claimed that he was Captain John Ross, and the year, at the beginning of our conversation, was 1764.

In W. C. Ford's *British Officers Serving in America 1754-1774*, I found, on page 88, that there was a certain Captain John Ross, commissioned November 8, 1764. This man of course was a Tory, that is, he would have fought on the side of the British. Now the Revolutionary War started only in April 1775, and the man had expressed a dislike for the British and admiration for the "thirteen," the American colonies. Had he somehow switched sides during the intervening years? If he was a German mercenary, this would not have been at all surprising. Many of these men, often brought here against their desire, either left the British armies or even switched sides. Later on he referred to the date 1774, and Sybil had said it was important. At that time the war was already brewing even though no overt acts had happened. But the atmosphere in this area was tense. It was the seat of the Continental Congress, and skirmishes between Tories and Revolutionaries were not uncommon, although they were on a small or even individual level. What traumatic experience had happened to Captain Ross at that time? Did he lose his hands then?

I needed additional proof for his identity, of course. The name John Ross is fairly common. A John Ross was Betsy Ross's husband. He was guarding munitions on the Philadelphia waterfront one night in 1776 when the munitions and Ross blew up. Another John Ross was a purchasing agent for the Continental Army, and he used much of his own money in the process. Although Robert Morris later tried to help him get his money back, he never really did, and only a year ago his descendants petitioned Congress for payment of this ancient debt of honor. Neither of these was our man, I felt, especially so as I recalled his German accent and the claim that he was born in a little place called Verruck in Holstein. That place name really had me stumped, but with the help of a librarian at the New York Public Library I got hold of some German source books. There is a tiny hamlet near Oldesloe, Holstein, called Viertbruch. An English-speaking person would pronounce this more like "Vertbrook." Although it is not on any ordinary map, it is listed in Mueller's *Grosses Deutsches Wortbuch*, published in Wuppertal in 1958, on page 1008.

Proser, his brother's name, is a German name. Why had he adopted an English name? Perhaps he had spent many years in England and felt it more expedient. He also mentioned belonging to the 21st Cavalry Regiment. The Captain John Ross I found in the records served in the 31st, not the 21st. On the other hand, there is, curiously enough, another Ross, first name David, listed for the 21st Regiment for the period in question, 1774.

I could not trace the superior named Albright or Albrecht, not knowing whether this was someone German or English. Since the first name given us by the communicator was unclear, I can't even be sure if the Philip Albright, a captain in the Pennsylvania Rifles 1776-1777, according to F. B. Heitman, *Historical Register of the Continental Army during the War of the Revolution*, is this man. This Philip Albright was a rebel, and if he was only a captain in 1776 he could not have been John Ross's commanding officer in 1774, unless he had changed sides, of course.

I was more successful with the fellow officer Lieutenant "Gerhardt," who also served in "his" 21st Regiment, Ross had claimed. Spellings of names at that period are pretty free, of course, and as I only heard the names without any indication as to proper spelling, we must make allowances for differences in the letters of these names. I did trace a Brevet Lieutenant Gerard (first name not given) of the Dragoons, a cavalry regiment, who served in the Pulaski Legion from September 3, 1778 to 1782.

The Colonial Soldier

Is this our man? Did he change sides after the Revolutionary War started in earnest? He could have been a regimental comrade of John Ross in 1774 and prior. The source for this man's data is F. B. Heitman's *Historical Register of the Continental Army*, Volume 1775-1783, page 189. The Pulaski Legion was not restricted to Polish volunteers who fought for the new republic, but it accepted voluntary help from any quarters, even former Britishers or mercenaries so long as they wanted to fight for a free America. Many Germans also served in that legion.

The Colonel Moss who was "bad" might have been Colonel Moses Allen, a Tory, who was from this area and who died February 8, 1779. He is listed in Saffell's *Records of the Revolutionary War*.

It was a confusing period in our history, and men changed their minds and sides as the need of the times demanded. Had the unfortunate soldier whom we had found trapped here in this erstwhile Quaker meeting house been one of those who wanted to get out from under, first to join what he considered "the good boys," and then, repelled by the continuing bloodshed, could he not even accept *their* war? Had he become religiously aware through his Quaker contacts and had he been made a pacifist by them? Very likely, if one is to judge the words of the colonial soldier from the year 1774 as an indication. His plea for peace sounds almost as if it could be spoken today.

Captain John Ross was not an important historical figure, nor was he embroiled in an event of great significance in the overall development of the United States of America. But this very anonymity made him a good subject for our psychometric experiment. Sybil Leek surely could not have known of Captain Ross, his comrades, and the Quaker connections of the old house on Byberry Road. It was her psychic sense that probed into the impressions left behind by history as it passed through and onward relentlessly, coating the house on Byberry Road with an indelible layer of human emotions and conflict.

I sincerely hope we managed to "decommission" Captain Ross in the process of our contact, to give him that much-desired "peace and silence" at last.

12

Charlottesville and the Revolution

When people think of the American Revolution, they think primarily of Boston and the Tea Party, Paul Revere and his ride, and Philadelphia and its Liberty Bell. Very few people realize that Charlottesville, Virginia, was the focal point of the emerging United States for a while—that it was at the little, conveniently situated town in northern Virginia that much of the early planning of the Revolution took place. That was so because some of the leaders of American independence, such as Thomas Jefferson and James Monroe, made their homes in and around Charlottesville. Foreign tourists who are eager to see Washington, D.C., and cannot get enough of its majestic government buildings should take an extra hour to fly down to Charlottesville to see where it all began.

I hadn't been to Charlottesville since 1964, when Horace Burr, professor of speech and director of drama at Madison College in Harrisonburg, Virginia, and Virginia Cloud, the noted librarian and historian, had invited me. At that time, however, my main interest was in ferreting out some of the local ghosts and discussing them in a book I was then writing. Professor Burr was instrumental in prearranging my visit in early February 1973, knowing what

201

I was hoping for, and clearing permission for me and a medium-istic friend to visit some private homes of the area. Virginia Cloud was on hand too, and it felt like old times revisited when my friend Ingrid Beckman and I emerged from the jet plane at the little Charlottesville airport. We were going to stay for two days, which had been tightly planned by Professor Burr and Miss Cloud. Even a television interview with a crew from nearby Richmond, Virginia, had been penciled into the schedule, and I gave it while standing on the historical staircase of the Burr house, Carrsgrove.

Immediately upon arriving, we checked in at the Monti-cello Hotel in downtown Charlottesville. In retrospect, it seems odd that such a patently third-rate provincial hotel should bear the illustrious name of Monticello. The rooms weren't at all what we had ordered, the service and food were below standard, and it occurred to me how Jefferson would have felt had he been forced to put up some of his friends at this hostelry. Fortunately, it didn't exist during Jefferson's lifetime.

It turned out that February 9 was also Professor Burr's birthday, and he had accepted an invitation for the evening from the president of the University. Nevertheless, he spent the afternoon with us. Promptly at two o'clock, he picked us up at the hotel and, together with Miss Cloud, who had arranged our visit, drove us to Foxhill Farm, now the home of Mrs. Isabelle Palmer, a prominent society leader in Charlottesville. The house is somewhat on the outskirts of the town itself, on a knoll set back from the street. Although of pre-Revolutionary origin, it has been nicely fixed up and contains the latest comforts. Its dozen or so rooms are distributed on two floors, with a large kitchen downstairs and an imposing dining room to the right of the entrance. Upstairs, there are mainly bedrooms. Behind the house is the loveliest of gardens, enclosed by a brick wall behind which extent the rolling hills of Virginia's horse country, as far as the eye can reach.

Mrs. Palmer received us with much cordiality, and, as she

had been briefed beforehand not to divulge anything about the house while Ingrid and I were inspecting it, only formalities and generalities were exchanged between us at first. As in my custom, I let my mediumistic associate go about the house as her intuition commanded her. Immediately on entering the large room to the right of the entrance, Ingrid stopped. She found herself now in the left-hand corner of what was obviously a dining room.

"What's the matter?" I asked, realizing that she was picking up some imprint from the past.

"I have a generally heavy feeling here. I can't describe it as yet, but the area is loaded with impressions," Ingrid replied, still trying to get her psychic bearings.

Ever since I had started to work with Ingrid, my own E.S.P. ability has also sharpened, and on occasion I was able to sense things along with her. Thus I heard myself say, "Walk around and see whether you feel anything. I get the feeling of a meeting of some importance having taken place here." I had no idea why I said it, but both Ingrid and I agreed that a meeting of some importance had taken place in that very room, that someone had been arguing and had gotten up to leave in order to warn someone about a matter of importance.

"I feel there is a series of meetings here, not just one," Ingrid added, and then we walked over to the kitchen area. Since Ingrid felt nothing particularly strong in that area, we proceeded upstairs.

As soon as Ingrid walked into the bedroom to the left of the stairs, she stopped. "Guests on government business stayed here," she said, touching the bed to receive stronger psychometric impressions. "I 'get' a woman here; she is the wife of someone who has gone away, and I think she is very anxious for him. I get the feeling that she is worried for the man to get through the lines, and she is sitting up in an all-night vigil."

While Ingrid was speaking, I received the impression of

the name Margaret, followed by the initial L. I have no idea why, but the imprint was quite strong.

"I have the feeling a lot of people went up and down the front stairway in the middle of the night," Ingrid said, "and that this is in a sense like a refuge."

I turned to Mrs. Palmer and Horace Burr, asking them to comment on the psychic impressions received by Ingrid and myself.

"Well," Professor Burr began, "this house, Foxhill Farm, stood halfway between Brown's Cove and the new village of Charlottesville at the time of the Revolutionary War. Our civilization came in through this part, through the valley, along the river. So this was actually a very important location; people who lived here were well-to-do, and it was a huge plantation. The owner was a certain John Rodes, and his son David was made sheriff of the county in 1775. During Colonial days, the post of sheriff was a very important government position, and Rodes had his own son filling that office.

"Since this house was a place halfway between the Revolutionary lines and the British, I felt it would be interesting to see what your psychic friend would get from the vibrations in the house," Burr added.

"What about the important meetings both Ingrid and I felt in the dining room downstairs?" I asked.

Professor Burr nodded emphatically. "Yes, if there were meetings they would undoubtedly have been held here."

At this point, Mrs. Palmer explained that the corner of the dining room where Ingrid had felt such strong vibrations had always puzzled her. It was on that spot that she had felt chills and had a sense of presence. Not being a medium, however, she could do very little with it. Nevertheless, she felt that whatever psychic activities might be present in her house would center around that corner of the dining room. I then questioned her about the room upstairs where Ingrid had had such a vivid impression. It turned out that the room was exactly above the library and not far from the area where the meetings had been held in the dining room. The house itself consisted originally of two separate houses that were joined together in the middle. The area where Ingrid had felt the strongest impressions had been built in 1765; the other, where she had felt nothing special, had been built in 1807.

I then directed a question to Burr. "Was there any particular meeting where people were sitting down at a long table, wearing a kind of severe dark brown coat, with lots of buttons running down the middle? Somebody at the end of the meeting would be getting up with a rather serious face, saying, 'I'll let him know,' and then take some papers and leave the assembly. This would have been very late at night or early in the morning, and someone would have to ride quite a distance to notify someone of a decision taken here for some area to join up with some other forces." As I finished speaking, I wondered where I had gotten all that information; it seemed to me that it was simply coming out of me, as if I had been *impressed* with it by some external source. I could tell by the look on Ingrid's face that she felt pretty much the same but that I had somehow expressed it first.

Burr thought this over for a moment. "It sounds very reasonable, since it was the time when they were recruiting and the sheriff would have had his hands in it, of course."

Again I followed a hunch. "Has anyone ever left here who was connected with this house and whose life was in jeopardy if he were caught?"

"Well, okay," Burr replied, "then let us go into the bloodstain on the floor, which you can see plainly even now." Sure enough, in the door jamb between the library and the next room there was a bloodstain deeply soaked into the wood.

Isabelle Palmer took up the explanation from this point on. "This has some connection with a Revolutionary person," she explained. "That is why when you mentioned refuge it hit home with me. Tradition has it that a wounded man came here during the Revolution and sought refuge. But we don't know who he was or whether he died here."

We walked back into the sumptuous library and sat down, surrounded by eighteenth-century oil paintings of great historical value. I asked about the men dressed in the reddish brown long coats which I had been impressed with a little while earlier. Could it have any meaning in terms of historical fact?

"Well," Burr replied, "that was the most typical homespun yarn that you could have in the 1770s in Piedmont, which is where we are. The material was produced on a loom and dyed with tobacco dyes, so the colors were dark brown."

Since the old pre-Revolutionary houses were once the centers of large plantations, they are not clustered in or around the town of Charlottesville but stand in lonely majesty in the countryside, even though much of the land has long since been sold off. Such was the case with Castalia, an imposing three-story manor house with red brick at the bottom, a veranda going around most of the house, and a portico dressing up the rest. The tall red brick chimneys, which supplied the fireplaces with outlets in the days before central heating, look like imposing flagpoles peering out into the Virginia hills. Castalia is surrounded by tall, old trees and is reached by a driveway from a dirt road which in turn branches off the main highway. Even in its reduced size, Castalia is the center of an estate which takes a full fifteen minutes to drive through.

As we were halfway between the town of Charlottesville and the estate, Virginia Cloud, who had been chatting incessantly, as is her custom, happened to say something about a ghost. Now, don't get me wrong. Virginia Cloud has a lot to say, and nothing she ever tells you is without interest. She probably knows more about motion pictures and stars than any living soul, and nearly everything there is to know about Charlottesville and the American Revolution.

"About that ghost," I said, and turned around. I was seated next to Horace Burr, and Ingrid and Virginia were in the rear seats.

"Well," Virginia said, "this very road we are riding on is the road where my friend Mrs. Emily Money Kelly had a remarkable experience with a ghost."

"Tell me more," I coaxed her, as if that were necessary.

"Emily lived nearby because her father was Colonel Money, an Englishman who worked for John Armstrong Chandler, a very famous gentleman of the area. One night Emily and her sister were on this long road which, as you know, connects Castle Hill with Castalia."

I knew that fact very well. In 1964 I had visited Castle Hill, where there is a haunted bedroom, allegedly visited at times by a lady ghost who appears only to people she doesn't like so she can tell them to leave "her" bedroom. At the time of my visit to Castle Hill, I had questioned the owner, Colonel Clark Lawrence, about any psychic occurrences. Politely, he informed me that he had none to report.

"Emily and her sister were turning into the driveway of their house, when they saw a rider very clearly—so clearly, in fact, that upon arriving at the door they asked one of their servants, 'Who was right in front of us when we came here?' The man seemed surprised. 'Why, Miss Emily, I've been out here all evening and I didn't see anybody.' Other people living in the area have also reported seeing a lonely rider ahead of them, heading up the road from Castle Hill to Castalia. Nobody knows who he is, or where he goes."

I thanked Virginia for her contribution to the local ghost lore, and just then the sleek blue car turned into the driveway leading up to Castalia. There we were welcomed by the owners, the Boocock family. We were exactly eighteen miles from Charlottesville and in the very heart of the Virginia horse country. The several ladies and gentlemen assembled to greet us in the large parlor downstairs were all members of the family, eager to contribute their experiences to the investigation. As I had requested that nothing be said about the house or the occurrences therein, only polite chitchat was exchanged at first. Ingrid took a look at the downstairs part of the house, and explained how pleasing it was to her artistic taste. But within a matter of minutes, she was on her way upstairs and I followed her, tape recorder and camera in hand. Behind me came Horace Burr and Virginia Cloud, followed at a respectful distance by the lady of the house.

The house was living proof that the Southern gentry still knows how to furnish homes. Elegantly decorated in the proper style, without so much as a single intrusion of modernism or so-called improvements, the interior of Castalia was a joy to the eye. Four-posters, heavy drapes, thick carpets, early nineteenth-century furniture, beautifully carved staircases and, above all, rooms upon rooms, space upon space, and all of it deep in the country, far away from pressures and the onrushing traffic.

As soon as we reached the second-floor landing, Ingrid made an immediate dash for a corner room, later identified as the chintz room. It had windows on both outside walls, giving a person an excellent view of the drive and thus of anyone coming up to the house. There was a period bed, or rather a double bed, in the center, and heavy drapes at the tall windows, reaching almost to the floor in the French manner. Opposite the bed stood a dresser with a large mirror. Horace and I kept back, close to the entrance door, while Ingrid walked slowly around the room.

"There is an impression here of an older woman; I get the feeling of an all-night vigil," she said finally. "I think she is worried about someone at a distance." I queried her about the person this woman worried over. "It is a man," Ingrid replied. "He's away on a war campaign. I think he is either a general or some other high-ranking officer; a leader and a patriot."

"Try to see what he looks like," I instructed her, "what his name is, what his connection is with this house, anything you can get on him."

Ingrid closed her eyes, breathed deeply for a moment, then reopened them again and said, "He is at a great distance right now, a hundred miles or more. She is worried that he may never return."

"Is he in any kind of action at the moment?"

"Yes. There is a decision, a turning point in the war, and she is worried that he may not come back from it. I get 1760 or '70. Her name is Margaret."

"What happened to this man? Does he come back?"

Ingrid's face took on a sad expression, almost as if she were feeling what "Margaret" must have felt at the time. "I don't think he comes back."

"What happens to her?"

"She stays here in great sadness."

"Is she still attached to this house, or do you merely feel her imprint?"

"Oh, I think she comes here. I think this is the room where she did most of her worrying. She comes back in the hopes that *he* will return."

"Did he die in battle?"

"Yes."

"How did she hear of it?"

"A carrier came with the news."

"How is it connected with this house?"

"He owned it; he was in the family."

"When the news came to her, was she in this room?"

"Yes, she was ill."

209

"As you speak, do you sense her close to you? Is she in some way telling you this? What was she dressed like?"

"I think she wore a nightgown," Ingrid replied, closing her eyes again to better describe what her psychic senses told her. "She wears perfume, her hair is pulled back, it is of dark brown color. She's a woman of perhaps forty-five. She likes to wear flowered clothes, gauzy material, and beads around her neck."

"What keeps her in this house?"

"He never returned and she is *still waiting.*"

"Is she aware of his death?"

"She's confused."

"Does she realize that her own death has occurred?"

"I don't think so."

Next, we entered the so-called lavender room, also on the second floor of the house. It was situated opposite the chintz room, on the right of the stairwell, but also facing toward the road so that one could observe it from the window. The lavender room was considerably smaller than the chintz room we had just left. I decided to leave Ingrid and Virginia alone in it for a few moments, to see whether they could gather up some impressions from the past. Meanwhile, I went outside to change film and tape.

When I returned, both ladies seemed agitated and said they had news for me. "I think a woman was brought in here. She was very ill and stayed here until her death," Ingrid said firmly. "I think it is the same woman I felt in the chintz room except that she actually stayed in this one. I think she received the shock when she was in the other room, and then her condition became hopeless and she was moved in here. I don't know whether it was because of drink, but she never recovered emotionally. She was in here for several years, and eventually she died here. In this room I feel only sadness and the long-drawn-out period of her suffering. I think she wants to tell her story, she is so lonely and sad."

I instructed Ingrid to try and contact the entity, in trance if possible. Obediently, Ingrid sat back in a deep, comfortable chair in the corner, closed her eyes and waited. Although full trance did not occur, she seemed very much under the influence of an outside entity. "David," Ingrid said, her voice barely audible. "David or Davis, she added, "I think that is the man. She is very confused and still waiting for him." I instructed Ingrid to inform the lady that the man had passed on and that she herself was no longer in the flesh. Did the spirit understand her condition? "She understands what I am saying," Ingrid replied, "but I don't think she pays attention."

I decided to follow a different route of questioning. "Ask her to reveal more about herself."

"I think she was a very delicate lady, with lots of perfumes and fineries and beads; she catered to herself. She was a socially prominent woman."

"Was there anything among her habits that was particularly outstanding, such as a hobby or interest of some sort?"

"I think she liked to read a lot. Poetry. Especially Emerson, I think. But she didn't do any more reading after her loss; she was too confused. She thinks she is still here. *She is afraid to leave.*"

As is my custom under such circumstances, I explained to the entity that she could join her loved one merely by calling out to him and displaying a sincere desire to join him. Did the spirit lady understand what I was saying to her? "She listens," Ingrid explained. "She is showing herself to me with a shawl now, a white shawl bordered with fringes. Maybe she does needlework. She is always watching out the windows. *But the news does not come. She grows old in this room.*"

"Does she understand why the man she is waiting for is not returning?"

"No. She is very stubborn."

But eventually, Ingrid and I persuaded her that there was no point in waiting any longer, and with our blessings we sent her away to the man who had also been waiting for her on *his* side of the road.

We continued our inspection of the large house, walking down half a flight of stairs and up another half on the other side of the house, which apparently had been built at a different time. The house presented a fascinating pattern of staircases and corridors, not laid out in a perfectly straight pattern but allowing for unexpected corners, turns, and hidden nooks. The master bedroom was located at the other end of the house, its windows looking down onto the land and toward the main road in the distance. It was a bright, large, and well-appointed room, beautifully decorated and well kept. Again, I let Ingrid step into it first by herself to pick up whatever she could in the way of psychic impressions.

"I don't feel anything here," Ingrid announced with a determined tone of voice. I had learned to respect her judgment, for whenever she felt nothing in the atmosphere of a room, there usually was nothing to be felt. On the other hand, whenever I had taken her to allegedly haunted rooms, she had picked up the scent without fail. I thanked her, and we descended to the ground floor, where the members of the family awaited us with great curiosity. Briefly, I filled them in on what Ingrid had discovered and in turn asked them to brief us on the house and make comments about Ingrid's discoveries.

Horace Burr was the first to speak. "The grandson of the famous Dr. Thomas Walker of Castle Hill, about whom you have written in *Ghosts I've Met*," he said, "had a grandson named Lewis. The house, as it stands now, was built around 1850, but there was an older house here before that time." Burr got up and showed me the dividing line where the old part ended and the newer portion began. About two-thirds of the living room was in the older section, while the frontal third actually occupied the newer part of the house. "So the first part, that is, the first room we were in, wasn't standing when the phenomena occurred," Burr explained. "Yet the apparition of a woman which has been observed by many of the people around here always occurred in the chintz room, the room where Ingrid correctly identified her. This was Mrs. Sally Lewis, the wife of Robert Lewis."

"Who saw her?" I asked.

"Mrs. Lila Boocock, the present Mrs. Boocock's sister-in-law. It happened prior to her marriage when she, her mother, and her intended were visiting here from New York. In the middle of the night she was awakened by a little woman with dark brown hair, pulled back, wearing a *shawl* and a striped taffeta dress. The woman was in her bedroom busying herself with a briefcase which Lila had brought with her and which contained some real estate papers. *The ghostly lady tried to go through it as if she were checking things out.* As Lila sat in bed, amazed at what she saw, she heard a sound reminding her of crisp onions being cut while the woman was going through her papers. Finally the woman walked straight over to the bed, with a faint smile on her face, and leaned over as if she wanted to say something. *The next moment she was gone.*"

Mrs. Lila Boocock lives in Florida now. The experience occurred in 1926.

I turned to my hostess, Mrs. Elizabeth Boocock. "Have you yourself had an experience along these lines?"

"Yes," she replied. "Before we actually lived here, we used to come down to visit, and we would take the bedroom in the left part. That was in 1929. One morning I woke up around five o'clock because I heard footsteps with a regular rhythm to them. It sounded like, one-two-three-stop. At first I thought that my husband was ill. He hadn't been very well and was in the bed next to me, so I turned on the lights. But he was sound asleep. After that, I heard the same footsteps again and again, always at five o'clock in the morning. Finally I asked my mother-in-law what it all meant, and she replied, 'Oh, that's Mrs. Lewis.' But I never heard it again after we moved into the house."

I turned to the attractive lady to her right, Gwendolyn Goss, Mrs. Boocock's daughter, asking for any first-hand experiences.

"When I was at school in 1943, I brought a roommate home for Thanksgiving weekend," she began. "My friend, Marie de France, and I stayed in the chintz room, and it was a very cold, windy night, so we had a fire going in the fireplace. We put our clothes over a chair near the fireplace and went to bed. Sometime after midnight I heard some noise, as if someone were moving around the room, and I assumed Marie had gotten up. At the same time, Marie thought I had gotten up, so we both got out of bed and turned on the lights. Imagine our surprise when we found all our clothes on the floor *and the chair turned toward the fireplace with an open book on it!* Neither of us had put the book there. All that time the wind was blowing hard and the room was icy cold."

"Someone must have sat in that chair, reading a favorite book by the fireplace," I interjected. Horace Burr gave me a significant look.

"When we first moved down here, we lived in this house for a while before we moved out to the cottage, which you can see out the window," Gwendolyn continued. "When mother mentioned again and again to me that she had heard footsteps of an unseen person overhead, I finally said, 'Why, that's ridiculous.' But one night I heard the footsteps myself and immediately went upstairs to look. They sounded like four very definite footsteps going in one direction, then turning around and coming back. Immediately I went upstairs to look above the room I was in, and there was nothing."

"What sort of footsteps were they?" I asked.

"It sounded almost as if someone were pacing up and down," Gwendolyn replied.

"But that wasn't all," she continued. "During the 1930s

214

my grandparents had gone to Europe for a while, and the house was locked up. Not only was it closed from the outside but each individual room in the house itself was also locked. When they sent word by cablegram that they were coming home and asked the maid and the farm manager to open the house for them, these people came in. When they got to the lavender room and unlocked the door, they found the bedspread off the bed and on the floor, the bureau scarf off it, and all the silver in a mess. It looked as if someone had gone through it in a fit of temper, yet there had been no one in the house. No one could have gotten in. A mouse couldn't have gotten in.

"On one occasion, Mrs. Boocock and her mother were sleeping in the room next to the chintz room, when she heard a crash in the middle of the night which sounded to her as if someone had jerked off the dresser scarf and everything had gone to the floor. When the two women checked, they found everything in order. This happened two or three times in a row, both in the chintz room and in the lavender room."

"It would seem that somebody was looking for something, wouldn't it?" I said. "But I wonder who the ghost was waiting for?" "I think I can answer that," Horace Burr said. "Mrs. Lewis's son had been hunting nearby when he shot himself accidentally, or so they say. That was in 1855. Naturally she was upset, pacing up and down, waiting for someone who never came. Ingrid mentioned someone who was part of the family, and she mentioned her reading Emerson. That would fit. George Lewis is buried here in the grounds."

A tall heavy-set man who had been listening to the conversations in patience and silence spoke up now. He turned out to be Gwendolyn's husband, Edward Goss. Since he was an expert in engineering matters, he wanted us to know that important structural changes had taken place in the house. Both the lavender room and the chintz room had been changed, in 1904 and then again in 1909. He understood that the late Mrs. Sally Lewis was "unhappy" about the changes in her house. He explained that during the Revolutionary period there was a double cabin about two minutes away from the main house, and that this cabin was built in 1747 by a man named Jack, not far from the Castalia spring, which had been named after the legendary spring on Mount Parnassus.

"About two years after Lila Boocock had seen the apparition of Mrs. Lewis in her bedroom," Goss said, "she happened to be introduced to a granddaughter of the late Mrs. Lewis. After describing the apparition in detail, she asked the granddaughter whether she recognized it. 'That is my grandmother,' the granddaughter said firmly. 'She was little and had straight, pulled-back hair. She wore a shawl and a striped taffeta dress.'"

"Did you yourself ever have an experience in the house?"

"Yes, I did. In 1947 the then owner of the house, Mrs. Marmie Boocock, was away in Florida, and the house was quite empty except for myself. One night I noticed a light shining from a distance, and when I went up to investigate, I realized the light was coming from the chintz room. Sure enough, the lights had been turned on in that room. Since I had been the only one in the house and hadn't turned them on, there was no natural explanation for it."

I suddenly recalled that Ingrid had "gotten" the name Margaret when we had first entered the chintz room. Certainly marmie and Margaret are close enough.

When we had first entered the house, I had asked Virginia Cloud to observe what she could, psychically speaking, and to make notes of her impressions. She too had a very strong impression in the chintz room of a woman named Louise, which of course, could have been Lewis. She "saw" her as a woman with white hair and blue eyes, wearing a kind of filmy nightgown, possibly with a cap on her head, and felt that she had lived quite a long time ago. Virginia senses that the woman had some anxiety about another person *whom she also felt present in the room.* The other person Virginia thought was a very vital individual, and she "got" the name Henry or Alexander. Local tradition has had it that a restless spirit from another century lived on in the patrician rooms of Castalia. Is it a Revolutionary wraith, or indeed Mrs. Lewis, waiting for her beloved son to return from the hunt?

As we were about to leave, I noticed a book on the table in the library downstairs. It was *A Pride of Lions,* by Lately Thomas. The book deals with the life of a local celebrity, John Armstrong Chandler. When Ingrid saw it, she let out a little cry. The book seemed to have been placed there, as if to greet her. You see, it was Ingrid who had designed the jacket for it.

The Farm is a most unlikely name for one of Charlottesville's oldest buildings. Actually, it is a handsome two-story brick house, with a prominent fireplace on one end. The downstairs is now divided into two rooms—a front room very much the way it was in colonial days, and a back room now used by the owner, the postmaster of Charlottesville, as a kind of storage room. Upstairs are two bedrooms. The house stands in a tree-studded lot right in the very center of Charlottesville. A little to the left of the house, the postmaster pointed out the spot where the old Kings Highway used to go through. It was here also that Ingrid felt the vibration of many men passing by.

On the outside of The Farm, a simple plaque reminds visitors that this is one of the most historical spots in the area. Carefully avoiding any opportunity for my mediumistic friend to see that plaque, Horace Burr, Virginia Cloud, Ingrid, and I arrived at The Farm at three o'clock in the afternoon and immediately proceeded to the main room downstairs, where Ingrid stood transfixed in front of the colonial fireplace. To her, the little house looked like any other pre-colonial stone building; there was nothing to indicate that it had been of any significance in the past. As Ingrid stared at the fireplace, another strange thing happened. Almost simultaneously and frequently complementing one another, she and I got impressions from the past, rapidly, as it were; we both said whatever came to our minds. "I'm getting something about sickness in this room," Ingrid said, while I heard myself say, "I get the feeling of people with long rifles, shooting from the upper story. They are wearing gray jackets and light-colored pants, and the rifles are very long. This is in the direction away from the fireplace." Both of us said that men were making plans in the house at one time, and that it had to do with the defense of the building.

"I have the feeling that wounded people are being brought in right down here," Ingrid said. "I get the name Langdon or Langley and the name Nat." She walked around the room and then returned to her position near the fireplace. "I think the people with the light-colored breeches and the brown waistcoats and the long rifles are watching the road nearby for someone to come up that road. This is like a block-house, and there is some great anxiety about someone on his way up here. This is a last-ditch defense; there are perhaps five or six men, and they are militia men. I get the feeling of them lying on their stomachs upstairs with those huge rifles pointing with their long barrels and bayonets on top of them. The bullets are homemade, and it is the middle of the night. And then I get the feeling of a skirmish."

"It is like a flank," I said, feeling my way through an indefinite something in the air. "Someone is coming from the *wrong direction* to defend it. They should be coming this way, but they're coming the other way. They are coming up rather than down, and this is a terrible catastrophe for the defenders. I think if they get through, then it is all over."

I asked Virginia Cloud whether she had felt anything in

the place. "I had a feeling of sickness here, as if it might be a hospital. I see Redcoats, Tories."

I turned to Horace Burr, asking him to comment on our
observations. He seemed plainly delighted. "Well, I thought the
most amazing thing that you said was this kind of replay of a group
of armed forces, a flank, because there was a very interesting little
maneuver that happened down the road, an attempt to cut off
the main body of the armed forces coming here. The attempt went
awry, though. The American troops were entrenched along the
road here, expecting the British to come *this* way. Unfortunately,
they came the *other* way, so the British did take Charlottesville
for one night. This is a very little known fact of history, and I'm
sure you wouldn't have been aware of it. What you said was so
interesting because it was one of those little events that are enor-
mously important but did not become generally known because
the stratagem didn't work."

"What about the defense outpost here and the men with
their rifles upstairs? Do they make any sense?"

"Yes, indeed. From upstairs you could see where this flank
should have been down the road, and so they probably were up
there looking out for the oncoming troops."

"What about their dress?"

"Of course, they were all colonial, not professional
soldiers."

"What about the name Nat?"

"This house was owned at the time by Nicholas
Merriweather Lewis. He was a colonel and George Washington's
aide. Nat was a colonial nickname for Nicholas."

"What about sick people in here?"

"This was an important center, and the owner's wife,
Mary Walker Lewis, was well known for her interest in the
public and public affairs. Her father owned Castle Hill. She
and her husband were first cousins, both descended from the

original Nicholas Merriweather, who had come here from Wales via Jamestown."

Why had Ingrid been so fascinated by the fireplace and the area immediately before it? Although she couldn't pinpoint it in so many words, she insisted that something terribly important had taken place in that very room. To be sure, no ghost had stayed behind in The Farm. But an indelible imprint of an important link with the past was indeed still alive in the atmosphere of the little house.

It was on June 14, 1781, that Colonel Banastre Tarleton, the British commander, had been seen by John Jouett, who then took his famous ride to warn Jefferson and the legislature of the approaching British. About that, anon. When Tarleton finally got to Charlottesville late the same day, proceeding along the old Kings Highway and destroying several wagonloads of Continental supplies on the way, he thwarted the carefully laid plans of the defenders of Charlottesville, two hundred men to whom the defense of the village had been entrusted. They had been planning an ambush in the gorge below Monticello. Captain John Marson, in command of the detachment, was disappointed, but there was nothing to be done. As Tarleton entered Charlottesville, he saw The Farm, with Mrs. Lewis standing at the door, far more curious than frightened. "I think maybe I'll stay here," Tarleton is quoted as saying, and decided to make The Farm his headquarters for the night. Mrs. Lewis had heard all sorts of stories about the handsome Tarleton. The Colonel was twenty-seven and very courteous. "Madam, you dwell in a little paradise," she quoted him in her diary.

Tarleton spent the night in front of the fireplace which had so attracted Ingrid, leaving the rest of the house to Mrs. Lewis, whose husband was away with the Continental Army. He spent the night wrapped in his greatcoat, in a chair which once stood in front of the fireplace but which was taken to Carrsgrove, the home of Horace Burr, several years ago.

It had been an unforgettable day, as Horace Burr put it, and the only night Tarleton spent in the area. Evidently the imprint of the expected but never realized ambush and the feelings of the men lying in wait for their feared foe had been left so strongly in the atmosphere of the house that Ingrid and, to some extent, I were able to tune in on it and reconstruct it.

What can one possibly say about Carrsgrove that the owners, Horace and Helen Burr, direct descendants of Aaron Burr, have not said at one time or another, either in person or in print? Carrsgrove is their home, and they live in it happily and with great style. But it is more than just a home; it is a landmark of great importance, meticulously maintained by Burr and gradually turned into a personal museum. Where else can you find a Gainsborough, a Hogarth portrait of the young King George III, and dozens upon dozens of fine paintings and art works of the seventeenth and eighteenth centuries? Where else can you find a complete blend of antiquities and today's way of life, a little garden with a terra cotta statuette, and, above all, so many important pieces of furniture directly associated with the American Revolution? Not only is Professor Burr the foremost art authority in Albemarle County, as the area is now called, but he can tell you within a fraction of a second who was married to whom two hundred years ago, who their children were, and who they married in turn; his genealogical knowledge is absolutely fascinating, if not frightening. However, all those whose births Horace Burr knows so intimately are the right kind of people, from the Virginia horse country's point of view—the old families. The Randolphs, the Carrs, the Merriweathers, the Lewises, and last but certainly not least, the Burrs.

When I visited the house for the first time in 1964, I was already overwhelmed by its historical atmosphere. People have lived continuously on the spot where Carrsgrove now stands, but the stone house was erected in 1748 by a certain David Reese. This was fourteen years before an Act of Assembly established the town to be called Charlottesville, in honor of Princess Charlotte of Mecklenburg-Strelitz, the wife of the new king, George III. From the Reese family the house passed into the Maury family.

A rising young lieutenant of only twenty years of age by the name of James Monroe, who had been with General Washington at Trenton, visited the house many times during the early years of the Revolutionary War. It was here on April 21, 1779, that the citizens of Albemarle County signed their own "Declaration of Independence." In 1787 the house passed into the hands of Mr. and Mrs. Hudson Martin, probably the first citizens of Charlottesville, except for Thomas Jefferson and the leaders of the Revolutionary War. Martin was George Washington's nephew and Mrs. Martin the daughter of colonel Nicholas Merriweather Lewis, owner of The Farm in town. Later the house attracted the attention of James Monroe's brother, Joseph Jones Monroe, who purchased it in 1797. Fortunately, James Dinsmore, the famous architect, was then at work at Monticello, the home of Thomas Jefferson, and he was persuaded to design the mantelpiece of the fireplace at Carrsgrove as well.

In 1799 James Monroe was elected governor of Virginia, and the following year he decided to buy Carrsgrove from his brother. For the next nine years Carrsgrove was the home of James Monroe, who was later to become President of the United States. His granite bust done from life now stands in the garden of Carrsgrove.

But Monroe was not the only great American who left his imprint in the atmosphere of Carrsgrove. In 1824, when Lafayette visited Charlottesville, a party was given in his honor at the house. During the War between the States, the infamous General George A. Custer made the house his headquarters, renaming it

Charlottsville and the Revolution

Piedmont, the name often given to that part of Virginia. Some alterations were made in 1896 by the then owner, Price Maury, who united the original stone house with two other buildings which were already standing in 1790. The Burrs acquired the house in 1955.

It had been decided to spend the late morning of our second day in Charlottesville at the Burr house, culminating in luncheon. Naturally, Ingrid knew nothing whatsoever about the house, and during the television interview I gave to the crew from Richmond I made sure that she did not have a chance to speak to anyone about it. Horace Burr thought we should try the library first, since the downstairs front portion of the house was in the oldest section. He was curious to see what Ingrid might discover in the beautifully appointed library, which would have done any English manor house proud.

It was quiet all around us when we entered the library. As I did so, I felt a strange chill traveling down my spine for which there seem to be no rational explanation. I had no foreknowledge of any ghostly manifestations in that part of the house, and to the best of my knowledge, the library was simply that. When I remarked upon it, Ingrid cut in to say that she too felt an unusual chill. "There is a lot of malice here, not toward anyone in this house, but there is a plan to *execute* someone."

I requested that she seat herself in a comfortable chair in the library and try for the semitrance state in which the deeper layers of consciousness might be contacted. After a few moments, Ingrid continued. "I think there are three men, and they are making plans to kill one person in an ambush. This has to do with politics, and we are somewhere in the 1730s or 1740s. *I can hear them talk around the fireplace..* The room is very tiny, not too much furniture in it. The floor is bare. I have a feeling they are killing this person unjustly."

I noticed how Horace Burr was hanging on every word

223

coming from her lips. "Why do they want to kill him?" I asked.

"He is a landowner. It has something to do with importing. They have a private grudge against him."

"Where is this ambush to take place?"

"About five or six miles from here. They're going to shoot him on his way home."

"Do they succeed?"

"Yes."

"Are they ever found out?"

"No." She added that the body was later discovered; it was not a presence she felt, but an imprint from the past.

"What was the explanation given for his death?"

"They said it was a robbery."

"Is there anything else you can find out about this man or the plot?"

"The man is a tradesman, but he is also interested in political office. Like a representative or a seat in the government."

"Can you catch his name?"

"He belongs to a prominent family. Something beginning with A."

Since Ingrid indicated that she could not get any more about the room, I turned to Horace Burr for verification of the material we had just heard.

"I know the family this concerns," he replied, "and since I have the invoice of what was in the house at that time, I know she is correct about the furniture."

"What about this ambush?"

"The builder of this house, David Reese, died only three years after he had moved in. It was a sudden and seemingly unexplained death. Just what happened to this man and why he died after such a short time, all these things make you kind of wonder."

"What about his running for the Assembly?"

Charlottsville and the Revolution

"Not to my knowledge. However, a somewhat later owner, Joseph Jones Monroe, did sit in the House of Burgesses."

We decided to go to the upper floor. Walking up the narrow staircase, Ingrid found her way directly to a small bedroom on the other side of the house. I had written about this room in 1965, but Ingrid had no idea where she was or what the room meant to anyone. In addition to a beautiful sixteenth-century bed, there was a hand-carved wooden chair in a prominent position—so prominent, in fact, that Ingrid could not help but sit down in it. I asked Ingrid to tell us about any impressions she might have about the room or the chair. Immediately she said, "I sense a tragedy here, and I think it involves a child."

"Oh, God," Burr exclaimed involuntarily. "Please go on."

"I think that someone may have sat in this chair and watched a child die or that something awful happened. I think it was a boy not older than seven. A disease that couldn't be treated. A lingering death. Something awful, like scarlet fever or cholera."

"What happened to the mother?"

"I sense that it is a woman's presence here trying to hold on to the life of a young child. She is alone somehow. The child is all she has. I think this was her home."

"Do you feel her presence here too?"

"Yes, but I sense the child very strongly. I think this was a child's room. The woman does everything she can with doctors, but nothing can be done. The child is delirious for a long time."

Since I knew from my own recollections of Carrsgrove and from the look Horace Burr gave me while Ingrid was speaking that she had accurately retold the story of the haunting in the room, I decided to test her in relation to the chair in which she was sitting. I pointed out a similar chair on the other side of the room. Evidently, they were a pair, both extremely well carved and at least two hundred or two hundred fifty years old. Ingrid insisted that her feelings concerned not an imprint from the past but an actual presence, something we usually call a ghost. As she was speaking, we all noticed a chandelier move considerably of its own volition. Later, after we had completed the session, we tried unsuccessfully to cause it to move by walking up and down the stairs, walking around the room itself, or doing whatever we could to create vibrations. The chandelier remained immobile.

But Ingrid could not get anything further about the chair. Somehow the overwhelming presence of the woman and the child canceled out any less potent impressions the chair might have carried. I turned to Horace Burr and asked him, as usual, for comments.

"Ingrid was very close to the tragedy which occurred here," he began. "The woman was sitting in this chair, and three feet from it is the spot where she killed herself. It was about her child, which she thought was hopelessly sick. As you know, Hans, we heard her sobbing voice many years after her death and thus discovered the tragedy which had occurred here many years before. But these could not be the chairs she sat in; they came later. The area, however, is correct. Incidentally, these are the oldest documented man-made things in America; they came over from Wales, first to Jamestown, and then to this area. These are the chairs that used to be in The Farm, and in one of them General Banastre Tarleton spent the night wrapped in his cloak in 1781. Incidentally, the unfortunate woman whose presence Ingrid felt here took poison because she felt the child would be deformed. Her dying gasps were heard at the other end of the hall, across the stairwell into the master bedroom, where her father was sleeping, and as he stepped out into the hall and heard her gasps, she died. The child however, grew up to be a perfectly normal and beautiful young woman."

Which proves that a powerful ghostly manifestation

from this century can very well overcome the rambling, though pungent, thoughts of an eighteenth-century British general, especially if he, as Tarleton did, enjoyed the hospitality of his Revolutionary "enemies" far more than was customary under the circumstances.

13

The Octagon Revisited

Back in 1965 I published a comprehensive account of the hauntings and strange goings-on at one of Washington's most famous houses. Frequently referred to as "the second White House" because it served in that capacity to President Madison during the War of 1812, the Octagon still stands as a superb monument to American architecture of the early nineteenth century. Most people hear more about the Pentagon than about the Octagon when referring to Washington these days, but the fact is that the Octagon, or eight-sided house, is still a major tourist attraction, although not for the same reasons that brought me there originally. As a matter of fact, The American Institute of Architects, who own the building, were and are quite reluctant to discuss their unseen tenants. It took a great deal of persuasion and persistence to get various officials to admit that there was something amiss in the old building.

After my first account appeared in *Ghosts I've Met*, which Bobbs-Merrill published in 1965, I received a number of calls from people in Washington who had also been to the Octagon and experienced anything ranging from chills to uncanny feelings. I also found that the executives of The American Institute of

Architects were no longer quite so unfriendly towards the idea of a parapsychologist investigating their famous old headquarters. They had read my account and found in it nothing but truthful statements relating to the history and psychic happenings in the house, and there really was nothing they could complain about. Thus, over the years I remained on good terms with the management of The American Institute of Architects. I had several occasions to test the relationship because once in a while there seemed to be a chance to make a documentary film in Washington, including, of course, the Octagon. It didn't come to pass because of the difficulties involved not with The American Institute of Architects but the more worldly difficulties of raising the needed capital for such a serious-minded film. It may yet come to pass.

Originally I became aware of the potential hauntings at the Octagon because of a *Life* magazine article in 1962. In a survey of allegedly haunted houses, *Life* claimed that some visitors to the Octagon had seen a shadow on the spot where a daughter of Colonel Tayloe, who had built the house, had fallen to her death. As far as I could ascertain at the time, there was a tradition in Washington that Colonel John Tayloe, who had been the original owner of the Octagon, had also been the grieving father of a daughter who had done the wrong thing marriage-wise. After she had run away from home, she had later returned with her new husband asking forgiveness from her stern father and getting short shrift. In desperation, so the tradition goes, she then flung herself from the third-floor landing of the winding staircase, landing on a spot near the base of the stairs. She died instantly. That spot, by the way, is one of those considered to be the most haunted parts of the Octagon.

A somewhat different version is given by Jacqueline Lawrence in a recent survey of Washington hauntings published by the Washington *Post* in October of 1969. According to Miss Law-

The Octagon Revisited

rence, Colonel Tayloe had more than one daughter. Another daughter, the eldest one, had fallen in love with a certain Englishman. After a quarrel with her father, who did not like the suitor, the girl raced up the stairs and when she reached the second landing, went over the bannister and fell two flights to her death. This, then, would have been not a suicide but an accident. As for the other daughter, the one who had brought home the wrong suitor according to tradition, Miss Lawrence reports that she did not marry the man after all. Her father thought of this young Washington attorney as a man merely after his daughter's money and refused to accept him. This was especially necessary as he himself had already chosen a wealthy suitor for his younger daughter. Again an argument ensued, during which he pushed the girl away from him. She fell over that same ill-fated bannister, breaking her neck in the fall. This also according to Miss Lawrence was an accident and not suicide or murder.

In addition to these two unfortunate girls, she also reports that a slave died on that same staircase. Pursued by a British naval officer, she threw herself off the landing rather than marry him. According to Miss Lawrence, the young man immediately leaped after her and joined her in death.

It is a moot question how easily anyone could fall over the bannister, and I doubt that anyone would like to try it as an experiment. But I wondered whether perhaps the story of the two girls had not in the course of time become confused into one tradition. All three deaths would have had to take place prior to 1814. In that year Washington was taken by the British, and after the burning of the White House President Madison and his family moved temporarily into the Octagon. They stayed there for one full year, during which the Octagon was indeed the official White House.

Only after President Madison and his family had left the Octagon did accounts of strange happenings there become known. People in Washington started to whisper that the house was haunted. Allegedly, bells could be heard when there was no one there to ring them. The shade of a girl in white had been observed slipping up the stairway. The usual screams and groans associated with phantoms were also reported by those in the know. According to Miss Lawrence, seven years after the Civil War five men decided to stay in the house after dark to prove to themselves that there was nothing to the stories about the haunting. They too were disturbed by footsteps, the sound of a sword rattling, and finally, human shrieks. Their names, unfortunately, are not recorded, but they did not stay the night.

After some correspondence with J. W. Rankin, Director of the Institute, my wife, Catherine, and I finally started out for Washington on May 17, 1963. The beautiful Georgian mansion greeted us almost as if it had expected us. At the time we did not come with a medium. This was our first visit and I wanted to gain first impressions and interview those who actually had come in contact with the uncanny, be it visual or auditory. First I asked Mr. Rankin to supply me with a brief but concise rundown on the history of the house itself. It is perhaps best to quote here my 1965 report in *Ghosts I've Met*.

Mr. Rankin received us with interest and showed us abound the house which was at that time fortunately empty of tourists and other visitors. It was he who supplied some of the background information on the Octagon, from which I quote:

The White House and the Octagon are relations, in a way. Both date from the beginning of government in the national capital; the White House was started first but the Octagon was first completed. Both have served as the official residence of the President.

It was early in 1797 that Colonel John Tayloe of Mount Airy, Virginia, felt the need for a town house. Mount Airy was

The Octagon Revisited

a magnificent plantation of some three thousand acres, on which the Colonel, among many activities, bred and raced horses, but the call of the city was beginning to be felt, even in that early day; Philadelphia was the Colonel's choice, but his friend General Washington painted a glowing picture of what the new national capital might become and persuaded him to build the Octagon in surroundings that were then far removed from urbanity.

Dr. William Thornton, winner of the competition for the Capitol, was Colonel Tayloe's natural selection of architect.

On April 19, 1797, Colonel Tayloe purchased for $1000 from Gustavus W. Scott—one of the original purchasers from the Government on November 21, 1796—Lot 8 in Square 170 in the new plot of Washington. Although, as the sketch of 1813 shows, the site was apparently out in a lonely countryside, the city streets had been definitely plotted, and the corner of New York Avenue and Eighteenth Street was then where it is today.

Obviously, from a glance at the plot plan, Colonel Tayloe's house derived its unique shape from the angle formed at the junction of these two streets. In spite of the name by which the mansion has always been known, Dr. Thornton could have had no intention of making the plan octagonal; the house planned itself from the street frontages.

Work on the building started in 1798 and progressed under the occasional inspection of General Washington, who did not live to see its completion in 1800. The mansion immediately took its place as a center of official and nonofficial social activities. Through its hospitable front door passed Madison, Jefferson, Monroe, Adams, Jackson, Decatur, Porter, Webster, Clay, Lafayette, Von Steuben, Calhoun, Randolph, Van Rensselaer, and their ladies.

Social activities were forgotten, however, when the War of 1812 threatened and finally engulfed the new nation's capital. On August 24, 1814, the British left the White House a fire-gutted ruin. Mrs. Tayloe's foresight in establishing the French

Minister—with his country's flag—as a house guest may have saved the Octagon from a like fate.

Colonel Tayloe is said to have dispatched a courier from Mount Airy, offering President Madison the use of the mansion, and the Madisons moved in on September 8, 1814.

For more than a year Dolly Madison reigned as hostess of the Octagon. In the tower room just over the entrance President Madison established his study, and here signed the Treaty of Ghent on February 17, 1815, establishing a peace with Great Britain which endures to this day.

After the death of Mrs. John Tayloe in 1855, the Octagon no longer served as the family's town house. That part of Washington lost for a time its residential character and the grand old mansion began to deteriorate.

In 1865 it was used as a school for girls. From 1866 to 1879 the Government rented it for the use of the Hydrographic Office. As an office and later as a studio dwelling, the Octagon served until about 1885, when it was entrusted by the Tayloe heirs to a caretaker.

Glenn Brown, a longtime secretary of The American Institute of Architects, suggested in 1889 that the house would make an appropriate headquarters for the Institute.

When the architects started to rehabilitate the building, it was occupied by ten Negro families. The fine old drawing room was found to be piled four feet deep with rubbish. The whole interior was covered with grime, the fireplaces closed up, windows broken, but the structure, built a century before, had been denied no effort or expense to make it worthy of the Tayloes, and it still stood staunch and sound against time and neglect.

Miraculously the slender balusters of the famous stairway continued to serve, undoubtedly helped by the fact that every fifth baluster is of iron, firmly jointed to the handrail and carriage. Even the Coade Stone mantels in drawing room and dining room, with their deeply undercut sculpture, show not a chip nor

The Octagon Revisited

scar. They had been brought from London in 1799 and bear that date with the maker's name.

On January 1, 1899, the Institute took formal possession of the rehabilitated mansion, its stable, smokehouse and garden.

So much for the house itself. I was given free rein to interview the staff, and proceeded to do so. Some of them are white, some black; all displayed a high degree of intelligence and dignity of the kind one often finds among the staff in old Southern mansions.

I carefully tabulated the testimony given me by the employees individually, and checked the records of each of them for reliability and possible dark spots. There were none.

In view of the fact that nobody was exactly eager to be put down as having heard or seen ghosts, far from seeking publicity or public attention, I can only regard these accounts as respectable experiences of well-balanced individuals.

The building itself was then in the care of Alric H. Clay. The museum part of the Octagon, as different from the large complex of offices of The American Institute of Architects, was under the supervision of Mrs. Belma May, assisted by a staff of porters and maids, since on occasion formal dinners or parties took place in the oldest part of the Octagon.

Mrs. May was not given to hallucinations or ghost stories, and in a matter-of-fact voice reported to me what she had experienced in the building. Most of her accounts were of very recent date.

Mrs. May saw the big chandelier swing of its own volition while all windows in the foyer were tightly shut; she mentioned the strange occurrence to a fellow worker. She also heard strange noises, not accounted for, and mostly on Saturdays. On one occasion, Mrs. May, accompanied by porters Allen and Bradley, found tracks of human feet in the otherwise undisturbed dust on the top floor, which had long been closed to the public. The tracks looked to her as "if someone were standing on toes, tiptoeing across the floor." It was from there that the daughter of Colonel Tayloe had jumped.

Mrs. May often smelled cooking in the building when there was no party. She also felt "chills" on the first-floor landing.

Caretaker Mathew reported that when he walks up the stairs, he often feels as if someone were walking behind him, especially on the second floor. This is still happening to him now.

Ethel Wilson, who helps with parties, reports "chills" in the cloakroom.

Porter Allen was setting up for a meeting on the ground floor in the spring of 1962 when he heard noises "like someone dragging heavy furniture across the floor upstairs." In March 1963 he and his colleague saw the steps "move as if someone was walking on them, but there was no one there." This happened at 9:30 A.M.

Porter Bradley has heard groaning, but the sound is hard to pin down as to direction. Several times he has also heard footsteps.

Alric H. Clay, in charge of buildings, was driving by with his wife and two children one evening in the spring of 1962, when he noticed that the lights in the building were on. Leaving his family in the car, he entered the closed building by the back door and found everything locked as it should be. However, in addition to the lights being on, he also noticed that the carpet edge was flipped up at the spot where the girl had fallen to her death in the 1800s.

Clay, not believing in ghosts, went upstairs; there was nobody around, so he turned the lights off, put the carpet back as it should be, and went downstairs into the basement where the light controls are.

At that moment, on the main floor above (which he had just left) he clearly heard someone walk from the drawing room to the door and back. Since he had just checked all doors and knew them to be bolted firmly, he was so upset he almost electrocuted himself at the switches. The steps were heavy and definitely those of a man.

In February of 1963 there was a late party in the building. After everybody had left, Clay went home secure in the knowledge that he alone possessed the key to the back door. The layout of the Octagon is such that nobody can hide from an inspection, so a guest playing a prank by staying on is out of the question.

At 3:00 A.M. the police called Clay to advise him that all lights at the Octagon were blazing and that the building was wide open. Mr. Woverton, the controller, checked and together with the police went through the building, turning off all lights once more. Everything was locked up again, in the presence of police officers.

At 7:00 A.M., however, they returned to the Octagon once more, only to find the door unlocked, the lights again burning. Yet, Clay was the only one with the key!

Only one prior account of any unusual goings-on at the Octagon had come to my attention before my visit in 1963. The July 1959 issue of The American Institute of Architects' Journal contains a brief account of the long service record of a certain employee named James Cypress. Although Mr. Cypress himself had never seen any ghosts, he did report that there was an unusual occurrence at one time when his wife was ill and in need of a doctor. The doctor had reported that he had seen a man dressed in the clothes of about 150 years ago coming down the spiral staircase. The doctor looked at the stranger somewhat puzzled. At that instant the apparition dissolved into thin air, leaving the medical man even more bewildered. A short time before publication of *Ghosts I've Met*, Joy Miller of the Associated Press wrote to me about the Octagon ghosts, adding a few more details to the story.

> *Legend has it that on certain days, particularly the anniversary of the tragic affair, no one may cross the hall at the foot of the stairway where the body landed without unconsciously going around an unseen object lying there.*

The story of the bells that ring without due cause also is embroidered in this account.

> *Once, so a story goes, a skeptic leaped up and caught hold of the wires as they started to ring. He was lifted off the floor but the ringing kept on. To keep superstitious servants, the house was entirely rewired, and this apparently did the trick.*

Of course, accounts of this kind are usually anonymous, as a parapsychologist I do not accept reports no matter how sincere or authentic they sound unless I can speak personally to the one to whom the event has occurred.

When I started to assemble material for this book, I wondered what had happened at the Octagon since 1963. From time to time I keep reading accounts of the hauntings that used to be, but nothing startling or particularly new had been added. It became clear to me that most of these newspaper articles were in fact based on earlier pieces and that the writers spent their time in the research libraries rather than in the Octagon. In April of 1969 I contacted The American Institute of Architects again, requesting permission to revisit the Octagon, quietly and discreetly but with a medium. The new executive director, William H. Scheick, replied courteously in the negative: "The Octagon is now undergoing a complete renovation and will be closed to visitors until this work is completed. We hope the Octagon will be ready for visitors in early 1970. I am sorry that you and your guest will not be able to see the building when you are in Washington."

But Mr. Scheick had not reckoned with the persistence and flexibility of an erstwhile ghost hunter. I telephoned him and after we had become somewhat better acquainted, he turned me over to a research staff member who requested that I let him remain anonymous. For the purpose of this account, then, I will refer to him simply as a research assistant. He was kind enough to accompany us on a tour of the Octagon, when we managed to come to Washington, despite the fact that the house was in repair or, rather, disrepair.

The date was May 6, 1969; the day was hot and humid, as so many days in May are in Washington. With me was my good friend Ethel Johnson Meyers, whom I had brought to Washington for the purpose of investigating several houses, and Mrs. Nicole Jackson, a friend who had kindly offered to drive us around. I can't swear that Mrs. Meyers had not read the account of my earlier investigation of the Octagon. We never discussed it particularly, and I doubt very much that she had any great interest in matters of this kind, since she lives in New York City and rarely goes to Washington. But the possibility exists that she had read the chapter, brief as it is, in my earlier book. As we will see in the following pages, it really didn't matter whether she had or had not. To her, primary impressions were always the thing, and I know of no instance where she referred back to anything she had done before or read before.

When we arrived at the Octagon, we first met with the research assistant. He received us courteously and first showed us the museum he had installed in the library. We then proceeded through the garden to the Octagon building itself, which is connected with the library building by a short path. Entering the building from the rear rather than the imposing front entrance as I had in 1963, we became immediately aware of the extensive work that was going on inside the old building. Needless to say, I regretted it, but I also realized the necessity of safeguarding the old structure. Hammering of undetermined origin and workmen scurrying back and forth were not particularly conducive to any psychic work, but we had no choice. From noon to one o'clock was the agreed-upon time for us, and I hoped that we could at least learn something during this brief period. I urged Ethel to find her own bearings the way she always does, and the three of us followed her, hoping to catch what might come from her lips clairvoyantly or perhaps even in trance.

Immediately inside the building, Ethel touched me, and I tried to edge closer to catch what came from her. She was quite herself and the impressions were nothing more than clairvoyant descriptions of what raced through her mind. We were standing in the room to the left of the staircase when I caught the name "Alice."

"What about Alice?" I asked. "Who is she?"

"I don't know. It just hit me."

"I won't tell you any more than that you should try to find your way around this general area we are in now, and upstairs as far as you feel like."

"Oh yes, my goodness, there's so many, they won't stay still long enough. There's one that has *quite a jaw*—I don't see the top of the face yet; just a *long jaw.*"

"Man or woman?"

"Man."

"Is this an imprint from the past or is this a *person?*"

"From the past."

"Go over to this bannister here, and touch the bannister and see whether this helps you establish contact."

"I see a *horse face.*"

"Is this part of his character or a physical impairment?"

"Physical impairment."

"What is his connection with this house?"

"I just see him here, as if he's going to walk out that door. Might have a high hat on, also. I keep hearing, 'Alice. Alice.' As if somebody's calling."

"Are there several layers in this house, then?"

"I would say there are several layers."

"Is there anything about this area we're standing in that is in any way interesting to you?" We were now in front of the fatal bannister.

"Well, this is much more vivid. This is fear."

She seemed visibly agitated now, gripping the bannister with both hands. Gently, I pried her loose and led her up a few steps, then down again, carefully watching her every move lest she join the hapless Tayloe girls. She stopped abruptly at the foot of the stairs and began to describe a man she sensed near the staircase—a phantom man, that is. Connected with this male ghost, however, was another person, Ethel indicated.

"Someone has been carried down these steps after an illness, and out of here. That's not the man, however. It seems to be a woman."

"What sort of illness?"

"I don't know. I just see the people carrying her down— like on a stretcher, a body, a sick person."

"Was this person alive at the time when she was carried down?"

"Alive, but very far gone."

"From where did she come?"

"I think from down here." Ethel pointed toward the spot beneath the bannister. "There is also a Will, but during this time I don't think Will is alive, when this happens. I also find the long-faced man walking around. *I can see through him.*"

"Is he connected with the person on the stretcher?"

241

"I would say so, because he follows it." Then she added, "Someone comes here who is still alive from *that*. Moved around."

"A presence, you mean?" She nodded. "This man with the horse face—what sort of clothes did he wear?"

"A formal suit with a long coat. turn of the century or the twenties?"

"The *nineteen*-twenties?"

"Somewhere in here, yes."

"And the person on the stretcher—do you see her?"

"No, she's covered up. It is the woman I still see in here."

"Why don't you go up those stairs, to about the first landing."

"I am afraid of that, *for some reason or other.*"

"Why do you suppose that is?"

"I don't like it."

"Did something happen in that area?"

"I don't know. I'm just getting a feeling as if I don't want to go. But I'll go *anyway.*"

"See whether you get any more impressions in doing that!"

"I'm getting a cerebral heaviness, in the back of the head."

"Was somebody hurt there?"

"I would say. Or—stricken."

"What is the connection? Take one or two steps only, and see whether you feel anything further in doing this. You're now walking up the stairs to the first landing."

"Oh, my head. Whew!"

"You feel—?"

"Numb."

"We're not going further than the first landing. If it is too difficult, don't do it."

"No. I'll take it for what it is." Suddenly, she turned. "Don't push me!"

"Somebody's trying to push you?"

"Yes."

I didn't feel like testing the matter. "All right, come back here. Let us stand back of the first landing."

"I get a George, too. And Wood, and something else. I'm holding onto my head, that hurts, very badly."

"Do you know who is this connected with, the injury to the head?"

"It sounds like Jacques."

"Is he connected with this house in any official capacity?"

"Well, this is a definite ghost. He's laughing at me. I don't like it!"

"Can you get any name for this person?"

"Again I get Jacques."

"Did anything tragic ever happen here?"

"I would say so. I get two individuals here—the long-faced man, and a shorter-faced man who is much younger."

"Are they of the same period?"

"No."

"Where does the woman on the stretcher fit in?"

"In between, or earlier."

"What is this tragic event? What happened here?"

"I can hardly get anything. It feels like my brains are gone."

"Where do you think it happened? In what part of the building?"

"Here, of course, *here*."

"Did somebody die here? Did somebody get hurt?"

"According to my head, I don't know how anybody got through this. It is like *blown off*. I can't feel it at all. I have to put my hand up to find it."

"Are the presences still here?"

Instead of replying, Ethel put up her hands, as if warding off an unseen attack. "Oh, no!"

243

"Why did you just move like this? Did you feel anyone present?"

"Yes—as if somebody was trying to get hold of me, and I don't want that. I don't know how long I can take the head business, right here . . ."

"All right, we'll go down. Tell them, whoever might be present, that if they have to say something, they should say it. Whatever information they have to pass on, we are willing to listen. Whatever problem they might have."

Ethel seemed to struggle again, as if she were being possessed.

"There's something foreign here, and I can't make out what is being said."

"A foreign language?"

"Yes."

"What language is it?"

"I'm not sure; it's hard to hear. It sounds more Latin than anything else."

"A Latin language? Is there anything about this house that makes it different from any other house?"

"There's a lot of foreign influence around it."

"Was it used in any way other than as a dwelling?"

"There were séances in this place."

"Who do you think held them?"

"Mary."

"Who is this Mary?"

"She parted her hair in the middle. Heavy girl. I've got to put my hand up, always to my head, *it hurts so.*"

"Do you get the names of the people involved in this horrible accident, or whatever it is that you describe, this painful thing?"

"That has to be Mary who's taken down the steps. I think it's this one."

"The tragedy you talk about, the pain . . ."

The Octagon Revisited

"It seems like it should be *here*, but it could have been somewhere else. I don't understand. There are two layers here."

"There may be many layers."

"There are so many people around here, it's so hard to keep them separate."

"Do you get the impression of people coming and going? Is there anything special about the house in any way?"

"I would say there is. *The highest people in the land have lived here.* I'm positively torn by the many things. Someone married here with the name of Alice. *That* has nothing to do with the head."

"Alice is another layer?"

"That's right."

"Mary has the injury to her head. Is the marriage of Alice later or earlier?"

"Much later." Then she added. "This house is terribly psychic, as it were—it is as if I have been able to find the easiest possible connections with a lot of people through what has been done here, psychically. There's a psychic circle around this place. From the past."

"Do you feel that these manifestations are still continuing?"

"I would say there are, yes. I don't know what all this rebuilding is doing to it, particularly when the painting starts. Has Lincoln had anything to do with this house? I feel that I see him here."

"What would be his connection with the house?"

"Nothing at all, but *he's been here.*"

"Why would he be her?"

"I see an imprint of him."

"As a visitor?"

"I would say, yes. Some other high people have been here, too."

"As high as he?"

"That's right."

"Before him or after him?"

"After."

"What about before? Has anybody been as high as he here?"

"I would say so." Ethel, somewhat sheepishly, continued. "The man with the long face, he looks like Wilson!"

At that I raised my eyebrows. The mention of President Lincoln, and now Wilson, was perhaps a little too much name-dropping. On the other hand, it immediately occurred to me that both of these dignitaries must have been present at the Octagon at one time or other in their careers. Even though the Octagon was not used as a second White House after the disastrous War of 1812, it had frequently been used as a major reception hall for official or semiofficial functions. We do not have any record as to President Lincoln's presence or, for that matter, Wilson's but it is highly likely that both of these men visited and spent time at the Octagon. If these occasions included some festivities, an emotional imprint might very well have remained behind in the atmosphere and Ethel would, of course, pick that up. Thus her mention of Lincoln and Wilson wasn't quite as outlandish as I had at first thought.

For several minutes now I had noticed a somewhat disdainful smile on the research assistant's face. I decided to discontinue questioning Ethel, especially as it was close to one o'clock now and I knew that the assistant wanted to go to lunch.

I wondered whether any of the foregoing material made any sense to him. Frankly, I didn't have much hope that it did, since he had been honest enough to communicate his lack of faith in the kind of work I was doing. But he had been kind enough to come along, so the very least I could do was use his services such as they might turn out to be.

The name Alice meant nothing to him, but then he was tuned in on the history of the Octagon rather than Washington history in general. Later, at the Wilson House I realized that Ethel was in some peculiar way catapulting her psychic readings. It appeared that Alice meant a good deal in the history of President Wilson.

What about Lincoln? The assistant shook his head.

"The family left the house about eighteen fifty-four, and I guess Lincoln was a Congressman then. He could have been here, but . . ."

"You're not sure?"

"I mean, he's not on the list that we have of people who have been here. I have no knowledge of it."

Colonel Tayloe died in 1854, and the house was owned by the family until after 1900 when the Institute bought it. But it was not occupied by the Tayloe family after the Colonel's death. I wondered why.

As to the names of the Tayloes' daughters, the research assistant wasn't very helpful either. He did have the names of some of the daughters, but he couldn't put his hands on them right now. He did not remember Mary. But, on reflection, there might have been.

I turned to Ethel. It was clear to me that the noise of the returning workmen, who had just finished their lunch hour, and the general tone of the conversation did not help to relax her. I thanked the assistant for his presence, and we left the building. But before we had walked more than a few steps, Ethel stopped suddenly and turned to me and said, "Somebody was murdered here, or badly wounded at least." She felt it was the woman on the stretcher. She was not completely sure that death had been due to murder, but it was certainly of a violent kind. I pointed at a portrait on the wall; the picture was that of Colonel Tayloe. Did Ethel recognize the man in the picture, I asked, without of course indicating who he was. Perhaps she knew anyway. She nodded immediately.

"That's the man. I saw him."

He was one of the men she had seen walking about with

a peculiar tall hat. She was quite sure. The face somehow had stuck in her mind. Ethel then pointed at another portrait. It was a photograph of Mrs. Wilson. She too had been at the Octagon. Ethel felt her presence.

"Would this be nineteen fifty-eight?" she asked somewhat unsure. The date seemed possible.

In evaluating Ethel's performance, I kept in mind that she had rarely if ever been wrong in pinpointing presences in haunted houses. Under the circumstances, of course, there was no possibility of Ethel going into full trance. Her contact with the entities was at the very best on the surface. Nevertheless, if three lady ghosts mentioned by Jacqueline Lawrence in her article had been present, then Ethel would surely have felt, seen, or otherwise indicated them. I am quite sure that Ethel never saw the article in the Washington *Post*. I am also equally sure that had she seen it, it would have made no difference to her, for she is a dedicated and honest medium. In the building itself she found her way to the psychic "hot spot" without my help, or in any way relying on my guidance. Had she been there before it would have made no difference, since the renovation had completely altered the impression and layout of the downstairs. I myself was hard put to find my way around, even though I had been to the Octagon on two previous occasions.

Thus, Ethel Johnson Meyers tended to confirm the original contention published by me in 1965. One girl ghost and one male ghost, daughter and father, would be the logical inhabitants of the Octagon at this time. Whether or not the entities themselves are aware of their plight is a moot question.

It appears to be equally difficult to ascertain the true nature of the girl's problem. Had she merely brought home a suitor whom her father did not like, or had she actually gotten married? Strange as it seems, the records are not clear in this case. What appears to be certain, at least to me, is her death by falling from

The Octagon Revisited

the upper story. Ethel Johnson Meyers would not have picked up the "passing condition" had she not genuinely felt it. Furthermore, these impressions were felt by the medium on the very spot where traditionally the girl landed. Thus, Ethel was able to confirm the continuous presence of an unfortunate young woman in what used to be her father's house. Since the two Presidents whom the medium felt in some way attached to the house are hardly of the ghostly kind, it remains for Colonel Tayloe himself to be the man whose footsteps have been identified by a number of witnesses.

The American Institute of Architects no longer considers the Octagon the kind of museum it was before the renovation. It prefers that it be known primarily as their headquarters. Also, it is doubtful that the frequent parties and social functions that used to take place inside its walls will be as frequent as in the past, if indeed the Institute will permit them altogether.

If you are a visitor to the nation's capital and are bent on unusual sights, by all means include the Octagon in your itinerary. Surely once the renovation is completed there can be no reason—I almost said no earthly reason—for a visitor to be denied the privilege of visiting the American Institute of Architects. And as you walk about the Octagon itself and look up at the staircase perhaps wondering whether you will be as fortunate, or unfortunate as the case may be, as to see one of the two phantoms, remember that they are only dimly aware of you if at all. You can't command a ghost to appear. If you manage to wangle an invitation to spend the night, perhaps something uncanny might happen—but then again, it might not. What you can be sure of, however, is that I haven't "deghosted" the Octagon by any means even though a medium, Ethel Johnson Meyers, was briefly almost on speaking terms with its two prominent ghosts.

It remains to be seen, or heard, whether further psychic phenomena take place at the Octagon in the future.

14

Assasination
of a President:
Lincoln, Booth,
and the Traitors Within

ive years after the assassination of President John F. Kennedy we are still not sure of his murderer or murderers, even though the deed was done in the cold glare of a public parade, under the watchful eyes of numerous police and security guards, not to mention admirers in the streets.

While we are still arguing the merits of various theories concerning President Kennedy's assassination, we sometimes forget that an earlier crime of a similar nature is equally unresolved. In fact, there are so many startling parallels between the two events that one cannot help but marvel.

One of the people who marveled at them in a particularly impressive way recently is a New York psychiatrist named Stanley Krippner, attached to Maimonides Medical Center, Brooklyn, who has set down his findings in the learned *Journal of Parapsychology.* Among the facts unearthed by Dr. Krippner is the remarkable "death circle" of presidential deaths: Harrison, elected in 1840, died in 1841; Lincoln, elected twenty years later, in 1860, died in 1865; Garfield, elected in 1880, was assassinated in 1881;

251

McKinley, elected in 1900, died by a murderer's hand in 1901; Harding, elected just twenty years after him, died in office in 1923; Roosevelt, re-elected in 1940, did likewise in 1945; and finally, Kennedy, elected to office in 1960, was murdered in 1963. Since 1840, every President voted into office in a year ending with a zero has died in office.

Dr. Krippner speculates that this cycle is so far out of the realm of coincidence that some other reason must be found. Applying the principle of sychronicity or meaningful coincidence established first by the late Professor Carl G. Jung, Dr. Krippner wonders if perhaps this principle might not hold an answer to these astounding facts. But the most obvious and simplest explanation of all should not be expected from a medical doctor: fate. Is there an overriding destiny at work that makes these tragedies occur at certain times, whether or not those involved in them try to avoid them? And if so, who directs this destiny—who, in short, is *in charge of the store?*

Dr. Krippner also calls attention to some amazing parallels between the two most noted deaths among U.S. Presidents, Kennedy's and Lincoln's. Both names have seven letters each, the wives of both lost a son while their husbands were in office, and both Presidents were shot in the head from behind on a Friday and in the presence of their wives. Moreover, Lincoln's killer was John Wilkes Booth, the letters of whose name, all told, add up to fifteen; Lee Harvey Oswald's name, likewise, had fifteen letters. Booth's birth year was 1829; Oswald's, 1939. Both murderers were shot down deliberately in full view of their captors, and both died two hours after being shot. Lincoln was elected to Congress in 1847 and Kennedy in 1947; Lincoln became President in 1860 and Kennedy in 1960. Both were involved in the question of civil rights for Negroes. Finally, Lincoln's secretary, named Kennedy, advised him not to go to the theater on the fateful day he was shot, and Kennedy's secretary, named Lincoln, urged him not to go to Dallas. Lincoln had a premonitory dream seeing himself killed and Kennedy's assassination was predicted by Jeane Dixon as early as 1952, by Al Morrison in 1957, and several other seers in 1957 and 1960, not to forget President Kennedy's own expressed feelings of imminent doom.

But far be it from me to suggest that the two Presidents might be personally linked, perhaps through reincarnation, if such could be proved. Their similar fates must be the result of a higher order of which we know as yet very little except that it exists and operates as clearly and deliberately as any other law of nature.

But there is ample reason to reject any notion of Lincoln's rebirth in another body, if anyone were to make such a claim. Mr. Lincoln's *ghost* has been observed in the White House by competent witnesses.

According to Arthur Krock of the New York *Times*, the earliest specter at the White House was not Lincoln but Dolley Madison. During President Wilson's administration, she appeared to a group of workers who were about to move her precious rose garden. Evidently they changed their minds about the removal, for the garden was not touched.

It is natural to assume that in so emotion-laden a building as the White House there might be remnants of people whose lives were very closely tied to the structure. I have defined ghosts as the surviving emotional memories of *people* who are not aware of the transition called death and continue to function in a thought world as they did at the time of their passing, or before it. In a way, then, they are psychotics unable or unwilling to accept the realities of the nonphysical world into which they properly belong, but which is denied them by their unnatural state of "hanging on" in the denser, physical world of flesh and blood. I am sure we don't know *all* the unhappy or disturbed individuals who are bound up with the White House, and some of them may not necessarily be from the distant past, either. But Abigail

Adams was seen and identified during the administration of President Taft. Her shade was seen to pass through the doors of the East Room, which was later to play a prominent role in the White House's most famous ghost story.

That Abraham Lincoln would have excellent cause to hang around his former center of activity, even though he died across town, is obvious: He had so much unfinished business of great importance.

Furthermore, Lincoln himself, during his lifetime, had on the record shown an unusual interest in the psychic. The Lincoln family later vehemently denied that séances took place in the White House during his administration. Robert Lincoln may have burned some important papers of his father's bearing on these sittings, along with those concerning the political plot to assassinate his father. According to the record, he most certainly destroyed many documents before being halted in this foolish enterprise by a Mr. Young. This happened shortly before Robert Lincoln's death and is attested to by Lincoln authority Emanuel Hertz in *The Hidden Lincoln*.

The spiritualists even go so far as to claim the President as one of their own. This may be extending the facts, but Abraham Lincoln was certainly psychic, and even during his term in the White House his interest in the occult was well known. The Cleveland *Plain Dealer*, about to write of Lincoln's interest in this subject, asked the President's permission to do so, or, if he preferred, that he deny the statements made in the article linking him to these activities. Far from denying it, Lincoln replied, "The only falsehood in the statement is that half of it has not been told. The article does not begin to tell the things I have witnessed."

The séances held in the White House may well have started when Lincoln's little boy Willie followed another son, Eddie, into premature death, and Mrs. Lincoln's mind gave way to a state of temporary insanity. Perhaps to soothe her feelings,

Assasination of a President

Lincoln decided to hold séances in the White House. It is not known whether the results were positive or not, but Willie's ghost has also been seen in the White House. During Grant's administration, according to Arthur Krock, a boy whom they recognized as the apparition of little Willie "materialized" before the eyes of some of his household.

The medium Lincoln most frequently used was one Nettie Colburn Maynard, and allegedly the spirit of Daniel Webster communicated with him through her. On that occasion, it is said, he was urged to proclaim the emancipation of the slaves. That proclamation, as everybody knows, became Lincoln's greatest political achievement. What is less known is the fact that it also laid the foundation for later dissension among his Cabinet members and that, as we shall see, it may indirectly have caused his premature death. Before going into this, however, let us make clear that on the whole Lincoln apparently did not need any mediums, for he himself had the gift of clairvoyance, and this talent stayed with him all his life. One of the more remarkable premonitory experiences is reported by Philip van Doren Stern in *The Man Who Killed Lincoln*, and also in most other sources dealing with Lincoln.

It happened in Springfield in 1860, just after Lincoln had been elected. As he was looking at himself in a mirror, he suddenly saw a double image of himself. One, real and lifelike, and an etheric double, pale and shadowy. He was convinced that it meant he would get through his first term safely, but would die before the end of the second. Today, psychic researchers would explain Lincoln's mirror experience in less fanciful terms. What the President saw was a brief "out-of-the-body experience," or astral projection, which is not an uncommon psychic experience. It merely means that the bonds between conscious mind and the unconscious are temporarily loosened and that the inner and the unconscious are temporarily loosened and that the inner or true self has quickly slipped out. Usually, these experiences take place in the dream state, but there are cases on record where the phenomenon occurs while awake.

The President's *interpretation* of the experience is of course another matter; here we have a second phenomenon come into play, that of divination; in his peculiar interpretation of his experience, he showed a degree of precognition, and future events, unfortunately, proved him to be correct.

This was not, by far, the only recorded dream experienced in Lincoln's life. He put serious stock in dreams and often liked to interpret them. William Herndon, Lincoln's onetime law partner and biographer, said to him that he always contended he was doomed to a sad fate, and quotes the President as saying many times, "I am sure I shall meet with some terrible end."

It is interesting to note also that Lincoln's fatalism made him often refer to Brutus and Caesar, explaining the events of Caesar's assassination as caused by laws over which neither had any control; years later, Lincoln's murderer, John Wilkes Booth, also thought of himself as the new Brutus slaying the American Caesar because destiny had singled him out for the deed!

Certainly the most widely quoted psychic experience of Abraham Lincoln was a strange dream he had a few days before his death. When his strangely thoughtful mien gave Mrs. Lincoln cause to worry, he finally admitted that he had been disturbed by an unusually detailed dream. Urged, over dinner, to confide his dream, he did so in the presence of Ward Hill Lamon, close friend and social secretary as well as a kind of bodyguard. Lamon wrote it down immediately afterward, and it is contained in his biography of Lincoln: "About ten days ago," the President began, "I retired very late. I had been up waiting for important dispatches from the front. I could not have been long in bed when I fell into a slumber, for I was weary. I soon began to dream. There seemed to be a death-like stillness about me. Then I heard subdued sobs, as if a number of people were weeping. I thought I left my bed and wandered downstairs. There the silence was broken by the same pitiful sobbing, but the mourners were invisible. I went from room to room; no living person was in sight, but the same mournful sounds of distress met me as I passed along. It was light in all the rooms; every object was familiar to me; but where were all the people who were grieving as if their hearts would break? I was puzzled and alarmed. What could be the meaning of all this? Determined to find the cause of a state of things so mysterious and so shocking, I kept on until I arrived at the East Room, which I entered.

"There I met with a sickening surprise. Before me was a catafalque, on which rested a corpse wrapped in funeral vestments. Around it were stationed soldiers who were acting as guards; and there was a throng of people, some gazing mournfully upon the corpse, whose face was covered, others weeping pitifully.

"'Who is dead in the White House?' I demanded of one of the soldiers. 'The President,' was his answer; 'he was killed by an assassin!' Then there came a loud burst of grief from the crowd, which awoke me from my dream. I slept no more that night. . . ."

Lincoln always knew he was a marked man, not only because of his own psychic hunches, but objectively, for he kept a sizable envelope in his desk containing all the threatening letters he had received. That envelope was simply marked "Assassination," and the matter did not frighten him. A man in his position is always in danger, he would argue, although the Civil War and the larger question of what to do with the South after victory had split the country into two factions, making the President's position even more vulnerable. Lincoln therefore did not take his elaborate dream warning seriously, or at any rate, he pretended not to. When his friends remonstrated with him, asking him to take extra precautions, he shrugged off their warnings with the lighthearted remark, "Why, it wasn't me on that catafalque. It was some other fellow!"

257

But the face of the corpse had been covered in his dream and he really was whistling in the dark.

Had fate wanted to prevent the tragedy and give him warning to avoid it?

Had an even higher order of things decided that he was to ignore that warning?

Lincoln had often had a certain recurrent dream in which he saw himself on a strange ship, moving with great speed toward an indefinite shore. The dream had always preceded some unusual event. In effect, he had dreamed it precisely in the same way preceding the events at Fort Sumter, the Battles of Bull Run, Antietam, Gettysburg, Stone River, Vicksburg, and Wilmington. Now he had just dreamed it again on the eve of his death. This was the thirteenth of April, 1865, and Lincoln spoke of his recurrent dream in unusually optimistic tones. To him it was an indication of impending good news. That news, he felt, would be word from General Sherman that hostilities had ceased. There was a Cabinet meeting scheduled for April 14 and Lincoln hoped the news would come in time for it. It never occurred to him that the important news hinted at by this dream was his own demise that very evening, and that the strange vessel carrying him to a distant shore was Charon's boat ferrying him across the Styx into the non-physical world.

But had he really crossed over?

Rumors of a ghostly President in the White House kept circulating. They were promptly denied by the government, as would be expected. President Theodore Roosevelt, according to Bess Furman in *White House Profile*, often fancied that he felt Lincoln's spirit, and during the administration of Franklin D. Roosevelt, in the 1930s, a girl secretary saw the figure of Abraham Lincoln in his onetime bedroom. The ghost was seated on the bed, pulling on his boots, as if he were in a hurry to go somewhere. This happened in mid-afternoon.

Assasination of a President

Eleanor Roosevelt had often felt Lincoln's presence and freely admitted it.

Now it had been the habit of the administration to put important visitors into what was formerly Lincoln's bedroom. This was not done out of mischief, but merely because the Lincoln room was among the most impressive rooms the White House contained. We have no record of all those who slept there and had eerie experiences, for people, especially politically highly placed people, don't talk about such things as ghosts.

Yet, the late Queen Wilhelmina did mention the constant knockings at her door followed by footsteps—only to find the corridor outside deserted. And Margaret Truman, who also slept in that area of the White House, often heard knocking at her bedroom door at 3 A.M.. Whenever she checked, there was nobody there. Her father, President Truman, a skeptic, decided that the noises had to be due to "natural" causes, such as the dangerous settling of the floors. He ordered the White House completely rebuilt, and perhaps this was a good thing: It would surely have collapsed soon after, according to the architect, General Edgerton. Thus, if nothing else, the ghostly knockings had led to a survey of the structure and subsequent rebuilding. Or was that the reason for the knocks? Had Lincoln tried to warn the later occupants that the house was about to fall down around their ears?

Not only Lincoln's bedroom, but other old areas of the White House are evidently haunted. There is, first of all, the famous East Room, where the lying in state took place. By a strange quirk of fate, President Kennedy also was placed there after his assassination. Lynda Bird Johnson's room happened to be the room in which Willie Lincoln died, and later on, Truman's mother. It was also the room used by the doctors to perform the autopsy on Abraham Lincoln. It is therefore not too surprising that President Johnson's daughter did not sleep too well in the room. She heard footsteps at night, and the phone would ring and no one would be on the other end. An exasperated White House telephone operator would come on again and again, explaining she did not ring her!

But if Abraham Lincoln's ghost roams the White House because of unfinished business, it is apparently a ghost free to do other things as well, something the average specter can't do, since it is tied only to the place of its untimely demise.

Mrs. Lincoln lived on for many more years, but ultimately turned senile and died not in her right mind at the home of her sister. *Long before* she became unbalanced, however, she journeyed to Boston in a continuing search for some proof of her late husband's survival of bodily death. This was in the 1880s, and word had reached her that a certain photographer named William Mumler had been able to obtain the likenesses of dead people on his photographic plates under strict test conditions. She decided to try this man, fully aware that fraud might be attempted if she were recognized. Heavily veiled in mourning clothes, she sat down along with other visitors in Mumler's experimental study. She gave the name of Mrs. Tyndall; all Mumler could see was a widow in heavy veils. Mumler then proceeded to take pictures of all those present in the room. When they were developed, there was one of "Mrs. Tyndall." In back of her appears a semi-solid figure of Abraham Lincoln, with his hands resting upon the shoulders of his widow, and an expression of great compassion on his face. Next to Lincoln was the figure of their son Willie, who had died so young in the White House. Mumler showed his prints to the assembled group, and before Mrs. Lincoln could claim her print, another woman in the group exclaimed, "Why, that looks like President Lincoln!" Then Mrs. Lincoln identified herself for the first time.

There is, by the way, no photograph in existence showing Lincoln with his son in the manner in which they appeared on the psychic photograph.

Assasination of a President

Another photographic likeness of Lincoln was obtained in 1937 in an experiment commemorating the President's one-hundredth birthday. This took place at Cassadaga, Florida, with Horace Hambling as the psychic intermediary, whose mere *presence* would make such a phenomenon possible.

Ralph Pressing, editor of the *Psychic Observer*, was to supply and guard the roll of film to be used, and the exposures were made in dim light inside a séance room. The roll film was then handed to a local photographer for developing, without telling him anything. Imagine the man's surprise when he found a clearly defined portrait of Abraham Lincoln, along with four other, smaller faces, superimposed on the otherwise black negative.

I myself was present at an experiment in San Francisco, when a reputable physician by the name of Andrew von Salza demonstrated his amazing gift of psychic photography, using a Polaroid camera. This was in the fall of 1966, and several other people witnessed the proceedings, which I have reported in my book *Psychic Photography—Threshold of a New Science?*

After I had examined the camera, lens, film, and premises carefully, Dr. von Salza took a number of pictures with the Polaroid camera. On many of them there appeared various "extras," or faces of people superimposed in a manner excluding fraud or double exposure completely. The most interesting of these psychic impressions was a picture showing the face of President Lincoln, with President Kennedy next to him!

Had the two men, who had suffered in so many similar ways, found a bond between them in the nonphysical world? The amazing picture followed one on which President Kennedy's face appeared alone, accompanied by the word "War" written in white ectoplasm. Was this their way to warn us to "mend our ways"?

Whatever the meaning, I am sure of one thing: The phenomenon itself, the experiment, was genuine and in no way the result of deceit, accident, self-delusion, or hallucination. I have published both pictures for all to see.

There are dozens of good books dealing with the tragedy of Abraham Lincoln's reign and untimely death. And yet I had always felt that the story had not been told fully. This conviction was not only due to the reported appearances of Lincoln's ghost, indicating restlessness and unfinished business, but also to my objective historical training that somehow led me to reject the solutions given of the plot in very much the same way many serious people today refuse to accept the findings of the Warren Commission as final in the case of President Kennedy's death. But where to begin?

Surely, if Lincoln had been seen at the White House in recent years, that would be the place to start. True, he was shot at Ford's Theatre and actually died in the Parker House across the street. But the White House was his home. Ghosts often occur where the "emotional center" of the person was, while in the body, even though actual death might have occurred elsewhere. A case in point is Alexander Hamilton, whose shade has been observed in what was once his personal physician's house; it was there that he spent his final day on earth, and his unsuccessful struggle to cling to life made it his "emotional center" rather than the spot in New Jersey where he received the fatal wound.

Nell Gwyn's spirit, as we shall see in a later chapter, appeared in the romantic apartment of her younger years rather than in the staid home where she actually died.

Even though there might be imprints of the great tragedy at both Ford's Theatre and the Parker House, Lincoln himself would not, in my estimation, "hang around" there!

My request for a quiet investigation in the White House went back to 1963 when Pierre Salinger was still in charge and John F. Kennedy was President. I never got an answer, and in March 1965 I tried again. This time, Bess Abell, social secretary to Mrs. Johnson, turned me down "for security reasons." Patiently, I wrote back explaining I merely wanted to spend a half hour or so with a psychic, probably Mrs. Leek, in two rarely used areas: Lincoln's bedroom and the East Room. Bess Abell had referred to White House policy of not allowing visitors to the President's "private living quarters." I pointed out that the President, to my knowledge, did not spend his nights in Lincoln's bedroom, nor was the East Room anything but part of the ceremonial or official government rooms and hardly "private living quarters," especially as tourists are taken through it every hour or so. As for security, why, I would gladly submit anything I wrote about my studies for their approval.

Back came another pensive missive from Bess Abell. The President and Mrs. Johnson's "restrictive schedules" would not permit my visit.

I offered, in return, to come at any time, day or night, when the Johnsons were out of town.

The answer was still no, and I began to wonder if it was merely a question of not wanting anything to do with ESP?

But a good researcher never gives up hope. I subsequently asked Senator Jacob Javits to help me get into the White House, but even he couldn't get me in. Through a local friend I met James Ketchum, the curator of the State rooms. Would he give me a privately conducted tour exactly like the regular tourist tour, except minus tourists to distract us?

The answer remained negative.

On March 6, 1967, Bess Abell again informed me that the only individuals eligible for admission to the two rooms I wanted to see were people invited for State visits and close personal friends. On either count, that left us out.

I asked Elizabeth Carpenter, whom I knew to be favorably inclined toward ESP, to intervene. As press secretary to Mrs. Johnson, I thought she might be able to give me a less contrived excuse, at the very least. "An impossible precedent," she explained, if I were to be allowed in. I refused to take the tourist tour, of course, as it would be a waste of my time, and dropped the matter for the time being.

But I never lost interest in the case. To me, finding the missing link between what is officially known about Lincoln's murderer and the true extent of the plot was an important contribution to American history.

The events themselves immediately preceding and following that dark day in American history are known to most readers, but there are, perhaps, some details which only the specialist would be familiar with and which will be found to have significance later in my investigation. I think it therefore useful to mention these events here, although they were not known to me at the time I undertook my psychic investigation. I try to keep my unconscious mind free of all knowledge so that no one may accuse my psychics of "reading my mind," or suggest similar explanations for what transpires. Only at the end of this amazing case did I go through the contemporary record of the assassination.

The War between the States had been going on for four years, and the South was finally losing. This was obvious even to diehard Confederates, and everybody wanted only one thing: to get it over with as quickly as possible and resume a normal life once again.

While the South was, by and large, displaying apathy, there were still some fanatics who thought they could change the course of events by some miracle. In the North, it was a question of freeing the slaves and restoring the Union. In the South, it was not only a question of maintaining the economic system they had come to consider the only feasible one, but also one of maintaining the feudal, largely rural system their ancestors had known in Europe and which was being endangered by the industrialized

Assasination of a President

North with its intellectuals, labor forces, and new values. To save the South from such a fate seemed a noble cause to a handful of fanatics, among them also John Wilkes Booth, the man who was to play so fateful a role. Ironically, he was not even a true Southerner, but a man born on the fringe of the South, in Maryland, and his family, without exception, considered itself to be of the North.

John Wilkes Booth was, of course, the lesser known of the Booth brothers and scions of a family celebrated in the theater of their age, and when Edwin Booth, "the Prince of Players," learned of the terrible crime his younger brother had committed, he was genuinely shocked, and immediately made clear his position as a longtime supporter of Abraham Lincoln.

But John Wilkes Booth did not care whether his people were with him or not. Still in his early twenties, he was not only politically immature but also romantically inspired. He could not understand the economic changes that were sure to take place and which no bullet could stop.

And so, while the War between the States was drawing to a close, Booth decided to become the savior of his adopted Dixie, and surrounded himself with a small and motley band of helpers who had their secret meetings at Mrs. Mary Surratt's boarding house in Washington.

At first, they were discussing a plot to abduct President Lincoln and to deliver him to his foes at the Confederate capitol in Richmond, but the plot never came into being. Richmond fell to the Yankees, and time ran out for the cause of the Confederacy. As the days crept by and Booth's fervor to "do something drastic" for his cause increased, the young actor started thinking in terms of killing the man whom he blamed for his country's defeat. To Booth, Lincoln was the center of all he hated, and he believed that once the man was removed all would be well.

Such reasoning, of course, is the reasoning of a demented

mind. Had Booth really been an astute politician, he would have realized that Lincoln was a moderate compared to some members of his Cabinet, that the President was indeed, as some Southern leaders put it when news of the murder reached them, "the best friend the South had ever had."

Had he appraised the situation in Washington correctly, he would have realized that any man taking the place of Abraham Lincoln was bound to be far worse for Southern aspirations than Lincoln, who had deeply regretted the war and its hardships and who was eager to receive the seceded states back into the Union fold with as little punishment as possible.

Not so the war party, principally Stanton, the Secretary of War, and Seward, the Secretary of State. Theirs was a harsher outlook, and history later proved them to be the winners—but also the cause for long years of continuing conflict between North and South, conflict and resentment that could have been avoided had Lincoln's conciliatory policies been allowed to prevail.

The principal fellow conspirators against Lincoln were an ex-Confederate soldier named Lewis Paine; David Herold, a druggist's clerk who could not hold a job; George Atzerodt, a German-born carriagemaker; Samuel Arnold, a clerk; Michael O'Laughlin, another clerk; Mrs. Mary Surratt, the Washington boarding house keeper at whose house they met; and finally, and importantly, John Harrison Surratt, her son, by profession a Confederate spy and courier. At the time of the final conspiracy Booth was only twenty-six, Surratt twenty-one, and Herold twenty-three, which perhaps accounts for the utter folly of their actions.

The only one, besides Booth, who had any qualities of leadership was young Surratt. His main job at the time was traveling between Washington and Montreal as a secret courier for the Washington agents of the Confederacy and the Montreal, Canada headquarters of the rebels. Originally a clerk with the Adams Express Company, young Surratt had excellent connec-

Assasination of a President

tions in communications and was well known in Washington government circles, although his undercover activities were not.

When Booth had convinced Surratt that the only way to help the Confederacy was to murder the President, they joined forces. Surratt had reservations about this course, and Mrs. Surratt certainly wanted no part of violence or murder. But they were both swept up in the course of events that followed.

Unfortunately, they had not paid enough attention to the presence in the Surratt boarding house on H Street of a young War Department clerk named Louis Weichmann. Originally intending to become a priest, young Weichmann was a witness to much of the coming and going of the conspirators, and despite his friendship for John Surratt, which had originally brought him to the Surratt boarding house, he eventually turned against the Surratts. It was his testimony at Mrs. Surratt's trial that ultimately led to her hanging.

Originally, Mrs. Surratt had owned a tavern in a small town thirteen miles south of Washington then called Surrattsville and later, for obvious reasons, renamed Clinton, Maryland. When business at the tavern fell off, she leased it to an innkeeper named John Lloyd, and moved to Washington, where she opened a boarding house on H Street, between Sixth and Seventh Streets, which house still stands.

Certainly she was present when the plans for Lincoln's abduction were made, but she never was part of the conspiracy to kill him. That was chiefly Booth's brain child, and all of his confederates were reluctant, in varying degrees, to go along with him; nevertheless, such was his ability to impress men that they ultimately gave in to his urgings. Then, too, they had already gotten into this conspiracy so deeply that if one were caught they'd all hang. So it seemed just as well that they did it together and increased their chances of getting away alive.

Booth himself was to shoot the President. And when he

discovered that the Lincolns would be in the State box at Ford's Theatre, Washington, on the evening of April 14, 1865, it was decided to do it there. Surratt was to try to "fix the wires" so that the telegraph would not work during the time following the assassination. He had the right connections, and he knew he could do it. In addition, he was to follow General Grant on a train that was to take the general and his wife to New Jersey. Lewis Paine was to kill Secretary Seward at the same time.

Booth had carefully surveyed the theater beforehand, making excellent use of the fact that as an actor he was known and respected there. This also made it quite easy to get inside the strategic moment. The play on stage was "Our American Cousin" starring Laura Keene. Booth's plans were furthermore helped by a stroke of luck—or fate, if you prefer, namely, one of the men who was supposed to guard the President's box was momentarily absent from his post.

The hour was shortly after 10 P.M. when Booth quickly entered the box, killed Lincoln with a small Derringer pistol, struggled with a second guard and then, according to plan, jumped over the box rail onto the stage below.

Lincoln lived through the night but never regained consciousness. He expired in the Parker House across the street, where he had been brought. Booth caught his heel on an American flag that adorned the stage box, and fell, breaking his leg in the process. Despite intense pain, he managed to escape in the confusion and jump on the horse he had prepared outside.

When he got to the Navy Yard bridge crossing the Anacostia River, the sentry on this road leading to the South stopped him. What was he doing out on the road that late? In wartime Washington, all important exits from the city were controlled. But Booth merely told the man his name and that he lived in Charles County. He was let through, despite the fact that a nine o'clock curfew was being rigidly enforced at that moment.

Assasination of a President

Many later historians have found this incident odd, and have darkly pointed to a conspiracy: It may well be that Surratt did arrange for the easy passage, as they had all along planned to use the road over the Anacostia River bridge to make good their escape.

A little later, Booth was joined on the road by David Herold. Together they rode out to the Surratt tavern, where they arrived around midnight. The purpose of their visit there at that moment became clear to me only much later. The tavern had of course been a meeting place for Booth and Surratt and the others before Mrs. Surratt moved her establishment to Washington. Shortly after, the two men rode onward and entered the last leg of their journey. After a harrowing escape interrupted by temporary stays at Dr. Mudd's office at Bryantown—where Booth had his leg looked after—and various attempts to cross the Potomac, the two men holed up at Garrett's farm near Port Royal, Virginia. It was there that they were hunted down like mad dogs by the Federal forces. Twelve days after Lincoln's murder, on April 26, 1865, Booth was shot down. Even that latter fact is not certain: Had he committed suicide when he saw no way out of Garrett's burning barn, with soldiers all around it? Or had the avenger's bullet of Sergeant Boston Corbett found its mark, as the soldier had claimed?

It is not my intent here to go into the details of the flight and capture, as these events are amply told elsewhere. The mystery is not so much Booth's crime and punishment, about which there is no doubt, but the question of who *really* plotted Lincoln's death. The State funeral was hardly over when all sorts of rumors and legends concerning the plot started to spring up.

Mrs. Surratt was arrested immediately, and she, along with Paine, Atzerodt, and Herold were hanged after a trial marked by prejudice and the withholding of vital information, such as Booth's own diary, which the Secretary of War had ordered confiscated and which was never entered as an exhibit at the trial. This, along with the fact that Stanton was at odds politically with Lincoln, gave rise to various speculations concerning Stanton's involvement in the plot. Then, too, there was the question of the role John Surratt had played, so much of it covered by secrecy, like an iceburg with only a small portion showing above the surface!

After he had escaped from the United States and gone to Europe and then to Egypt, he was ultimately captured and extradited to stand trial in 1867. But a jury of four Northerners and eight Southerners allowed him to go free, when they could not agree on a verdict of guilty. Surratt moved to Baltimore, where he went into business and died in 1916. Very little is known of his activities beyond these bare facts. The lesser conspirators, those who merely helped the murderer escape, were convicted to heavy prison terms.

There was some to-do about Booth's body also. After it had been identified by a number of people who knew him in life, it was buried under the stone floor of the Arsenal Prison in Washington, the same prison where the four other conspirators had been executed. But in 1867, the prison was torn down and the five bodies exhumed. One of them, presumed to be Booth's, was interred in the family plot in Greenmount Cemetery, Baltimore. Yet a rumor arose, and never ceased, that actually someone else lay in Booth's grave and, though most historians refuse to take this seriously, according to Philip Van Doren Stern, "the question of whether or not the man who died at Garrett's Farm was John Wilkes Booth is one that doubtless will never be settled."

No accounts of any psychic nature concerning Booth have been reported to date, and Booth's ghost does not walk the corridors of Ford's Theatre the way Lincoln's does in the White House. The spot where Garrett's farm used to stand is no longer as it was, and a new building has long replaced the old barn.

Assasination of a President

If I were to shed new light or uncover fresh evidence concerning the plot to kill Lincoln, I would have to go to a place having emotional ties to the event itself. But the constant refusal of the White House to permit me a short visit made it impossible for me to do so properly.

The questions that, to me, seem in need of clarification concerned, first of all, the strange role John H. Surratt had played in the plot; secondly, was Booth really the one who initiated the murder, and was he really the leader of the plot? One notices the close parallel between this case and the assassination of President Kennedy.

As I began this investigation, my own feelings were that an involvement of War Secretary Stanton could be shown and that there probably was a northern plot to kill Lincoln as well as a southern desire to get rid of him. But that was pure speculation on my part, and I had as yet nothing to back up my contention. Then fate played a letter into my hands, out of left field, so to speak, that gave me new hope for a solution to this exciting case.

A young girl by the name of Phyllis Amos, of Washington, Pennsylvania, had seen me on a television show in the fall of 1967. She contacted me by letter, and as a consequence I organized an expedition to the Surratt tavern, the same tavern that had served as home to Mrs. Mary Surratt and as a focal point of the Lincoln conspiracy prior to the move to H Street in Washington.

Phyllis's connection with the old tavern goes back to 1955. It was then occupied by a Mrs. Ella Curtain and by Phyllis's family, who shared the house with this elderly lady. Mrs. Curtain's brother, B. K. Miler, a prosperous supermarket owner nearby, was the actual owner of the house, but he let his sister live there. Since it was a large house, they subleased to the Amos family, which then consisted of Mr. and Mrs. Amos and their two girls, about two years apart in age.

Phyllis, who is now in her twenties, occupied a room on the upper floor; across the narrow hall from her room was Ella Curtain's room—once the room where John Wilkes Booth had hidden his guns. To the right of Phyllis's bedroom and a few steps down was a large room where the conspirators met regularly. It was shielded from the curious by a small anteroom through which one would have to go to reach the meeting room. Downstairs were the parents' room and a large reception room. The house stood almost directly on the road, surrounded by dark green trees. A forlorn metal sign farther back was the sole indication that this was considered a historical landmark: If you didn't know the sign was there, you wouldn't find it unless you were driving by at very slow speed.

Mrs. Amos never felt comfortable in the house from the moment they moved in, and after eight months of occupancy the Amos family left. But during those eight months they experienced some pretty strange things. One day she was alone in the house when it suddenly struck her that someone was watching her intently. Terrified, she ran to her bedroom and locked the door, not coming out until her husband returned. The smaller of the two girls kept asking her mother who the strange men were she saw sitting on the back stairs. She would hear them talk in whispers up there.

The other occupant of the house, Mrs. Curtain, was certainly not a steadying influence on them. On one occasion she saw the figure of a woman "float" down the front steps. That woman, she felt sure, was Mary Surratt. The house had of course been Mary Surratt's true home, her only safe harbor. The one she later owned in Washington was merely a temporary and unsafe abode. Mightn't she have been drawn back here after her unjust execution to seek justice, or at the very least be among surroundings she was familiar with?

The floating woman returned several times more, and ultimately young Phyllis was to have an experience herself. It was in April of 1955 and she was in bed in her room, wide awake. Her bed stood parallel to the room where the conspirators used to meet, separated from it only by a thin wall, so that she might have heard them talk had she been present at the time. Suddenly, she received several blows on the side of her face. They were so heavy that they brought tears to her eyes. Were the ghosts of the conspirators trying to discourage her from eavesdropping on their plans?

Both Phyllis and her mother have had ESP experiences all their lives, ranging from premonitions to true dreams and other forms of precognition.

I decided to contact the present owner and ask for permission to visit with a good medium. Thomas Miller, whose parents had owned the Surratt tavern and who now managed it prior to having it restored, at great cost, to the condition it was in a hundred years ago, readily assented. So it was that on a very chilly day in November of 1967, Sybil Leek and I flew down to Washington for a look at the ghosts around John Wilkes Booth: If I couldn't interview the victim, Lincoln, perhaps I could have a go at the murderer?

A friend, Countess Gertrude d'Amecourt, volunteered to drive us to Clinton. The directions the Millers had given us were not too clear, so it took us twice as long as it should have to get there. I think we must have taken the wrong turn off the highway at least six times and in the end got to know them all well, but got no nearer to Clinton. Finally we were stopped by a little old Negro woman who wanted to hitch a ride with us. Since she was going in the same direction, we let her come with us, and thanks to her we eventually found Miller's supermarket, about two hours later than planned. But ghosts are not in a hurry, even though Gertrude had to get back to her real estate office, and within minutes we set out on foot to the old Surratt tavern, located only a few blocks from the supermarket. Phyllis Amos had come down from Pennsylvania to join us, and as the wind blew harder and harder and our teeth began to chatter louder and louder in the unseasonable chill of the late afternoon, we pushed open the dusty, padlocked door of the tavern, and our adventure into the past began.

Before I had a chance to ask Sybil Leek to wait until I could put my tape recording equipment into operating condition, she had dashed past us and was up the stairs as if she knew where she was headed. She didn't, of course, for she had no idea why she had been brought here or indeed where she was. All of us—the Millers, Phyllis, Gertrude d'Amecourt, and myself—ran up the stairs after Sybil. We found her staring at the floor in what used to be the John Wilkes Booth bedroom. Staring at the hole in the floor where the guns had been hidden, she mumbled something about things being hidden there . . . not budging from the spot. Thomas Miller, who had maintained a smug, skeptical attitude about the whole investigation until now, shook his head and mumbled, "But how would she know?"

It was getting pretty dark now and there was no electric light in the house. The smells were pretty horrible, too, as the house had been empty for years, with neighborhood hoodlums and drunks using it for "parties" or to sleep off drunken sprees. There is always a broken back window in those old houses, and they manage to get in.

We were surrounding Sybil now and shivering in unison. "This place is different from the rest of the house," Sybil explained, "cold, dismal atmosphere . . . this is where something happened."

"What sort of thing do you think happened here?"

"A chase."

How right she was! The two hunted men were indeed on a chase from Washington, trying to escape to the South. But again, Sybil would not know this consciously.

"This is where someone was a fugitive," she continued now, "for several days, but he left this house and went to the woodland."

Booth hiding out in the woods for several days after passing the tavern!

"Who is this man?" I asked, for I was not at all sure who she was referring to. There were several men connected with "the chase," and for all we knew, it could have been a total stranger somehow tied up with the tavern. Lots of dramatic happenings attach themselves to old taverns, which were far cries from Hilton hotels. People got killed or waylaid in those days, and taverns, on the whole, had sordid reputations. The *good* people stayed at each other's homes when traveling.

"Foreign . . . can't get the name . . . hiding for several days here . . . then there is . . . a brother . . . it is very confusing."

The foreigner might well have been Atzerodt, who was indeed hiding at the tavern at various times. And the brother?

"A man died suddenly, violently," Sybil took up the impressions she seemed to be getting now with more depth. We were still standing around in the upstairs room, near the window, with the gaping hole in the floor.

"How did he die?" I inquired.

"Trapped in the woods . . . hiding from soldiers, I think."

That would only fit Booth. He was trapped in the woods and killed by soldiers.

"Why?"

"They were chasing him . . . he killed someone."

"Who did he kill?"

"I don't know . . . birthday . . . ran away to hide . . .

275

I see a paper . . . invitation . . . there is another place we have to go to, a big place . . . a big building with a gallery . . ."

Was she perhaps describing Ford's Theatre now?

"Whose place is it?" I asked.

Sybil was falling more and more under the spell of the place, and her consciousness bordered now on the trance state.

"No one's place . . . to see people . . . I'm confused . . . lot of people go there . . . watching . . . a gathering . . . with music . . . I'm not going there!!"

"Who is there?" I interjected. She must be referring to the theater, all right. Evidently what Sybil was getting here was the entire story, but jumbled as psychic impressions often are, they do not obey the ordinary laws of time and space.

"My brother and I," she said now. I had gently led her toward another corner of the large room where a small chair stood, in the hope of having her sit in it. But she was already too deeply entranced to do it, so I let her lean toward the chair, keeping careful watch so she would not topple over.

"My brother is mad . . ." she said now, and her voice was no longer the same, but had taken on a harder, metallic sound. I later wondered about this remark: Was this Edwin Booth, talking about his renegade brother John who was indeed considered mad by many of his contemporaries? Edwin Booth frequently appeared at Ford's Theatre, and so did John Wilkes Booth.

"Why is he mad?" I said. I decided to continue the questioning as if I were agreeing with all she—or he—was saying, in order to elicit more information.

"Madman in the family . . ." Sybil said now, "killed—a—friend. . . ."

"Whom did he kill?"

276

"No names . . . he was mad. . . ."

"Would I know the person he killed?"

"Everybody—knows. . . ."

"What is your brother's name?"

"John."

"What is *your* name?"

"Rory."

At first it occurred to me this might be the name of a character Edwin Booth had played on the stage and he was hiding behind it, if indeed it *was* Edwin Booth who was giving Sybil this information. But I have not found such a character in the biographies of Edwin Booth. I decided to press further by reiterating my original question.

"Whom did John kill?"

An impatient, almost impertinent voice replied, "I won't tell you. You can read!"

"What are you doing in this house?"

"Helping John . . . escape. . . ."

"Are you alone?"

"No . . . Trevor. . . ."

"How many of you are there here?"

"Four."

"Who are the others?"

"Traitors. . . ."

"But what are their names?"

"Trevor . . . Michael . . . John. . . ."

These names caused me some concern afterward: I could identify Michael readily enough as Michael O'Laughlin, school chum of Booth, who worked as a livery stable worker in Baltimore before he joined forces with his friend. Michael O'Laughlin was one of the conspirators, who was eventually sentenced to life imprisonment. But on Stanton's orders he and the other three "lesser" conspirators were sent to the Dry Tortugas, America's own version of Devil's Island, off Florida, and it was there that Michael O'Laughlin died of yellow fever in 1868.

John? Since the communicator had referred to his brother's name as John, I could only surmise this to mean John Wilkes Booth. But Trevor I could not identify. The only conspirator whose middle name we did not know was Samuel Arnold, also an ex-classmate of Booth. Was Trevor perhaps the familiar name by which the conspirators referred to this Maryland farmhand and Confederate deserter?

I pressed the point further with Sybil.

"Who is in the house?"

"Go away. . . ."

I explained my mission: To help them all find peace of mind, freedom, deliverance.

"I'm going to the city. . . ." the communicator said.

"Which city?"

"The big city."

"Why?"

"To stop him . . . he's mad . . . take him away . . . to the country to rest . . . help him . . . give him rest. . . ."

"Has he done anything wrong?"

"He . . . he's my brother!"

"Did he kill anyone?"

"Killed that man. . . . "

"Why did he kill him?"

Shouting at me, the entranced medium said, "He was unjust!"

"Toward whom?"

"He was unjust toward the Irish people."

Strange words, I thought. Only Michael O'Laughlin could be considered a "professional" Irishman among the conspirators, and one could scarcely accuse Lincoln of having mistreated the Irish.

"What did he do?" I demanded to know.

"He did nothing. . . ."

"Why did he kill him then?"

"He was mad."

"Do you approve of it?"

"Yes!! He did not like him because he was unjust . . . the law was wrong . . . his laws were wrong . . . free people . . . he was confused. . . ."

Now if this were indeed Edwin Booth's spirit talking, he would most certainly not have approved of the murder. The resentment for the sake of the Irish minority could only have come from Michael O'Laughlin. But the entity kept referring to his brother, and only Edwin Booth had a brother named John, connected with this house and story! The trance session grew more and more confusing.

"Who else was in this?" I started again. Perhaps we could get more information on the people *behind* the plot. After all, we already knew the actual murderer and his accomplices.

"Trevor . . . four. . . ."

"Did you get an order from someone to do this?"

There was a long pause as the fully entranced psychic kept swaying a little, with eyes closed, in front of the rickety old chair.

I explained again why I had come, but it did not help. "I don't believe you," the entity said in great agitation, "Traitors. . . ."

"You've long been forgiven," I said, "but you must speak freely about it now. What happened to the man he killed?"

"My brother—became—famous. . . ."

This was followed by bitter laughter.

"What sort of work did your brother do?"

"Writing . . . acting. . . ."

"Where did he act?"

"Go away . . . don't search for me. . . ."

"I want to help you."

"Traitor . . . shot like a dog . . . the madman. . . ."

Sybil's face trembled now as tears streamed freely from her eyes. Evidently she was reliving the final moments of Booth's agony. I tried to calm the communicator.

"Go away . . ." the answer came, "go away!"

But I continued the questioning. Did anyone put him up to the deed?

"He was mad," the entity explained, a little calmer now.

"But who is guilty?"

"The Army."

"Who in the Army?"

"He was wild . . . met people . . . they said they were Army people . . . Major General . . . Gee . . . I ought to go now!!"

Several things struck me when I went over this conversation afterward. To begin with, the communicator felt he had said too much as soon as he had mentioned the person of Major General Gee, or G., and wanted to leave. Why? Was this something he should have kept secret?

Major General G.? Could this refer to Grant? Up to March 1864 Grant was indeed a major general; after that time Lincoln raised him to the rank of lieutenant general. The thought seemed monstrous on the face of it, that Grant could in any way be involved with a plot against Lincoln. Politically, this seemed unlikely, because both Grant and Lincoln favored the moderate treatment of the conquered South as against the radicals, who demanded stern measures. Stanton was a leading radical, and if anyone he would have had a reason to plot against Lincoln. And yet, by all appearances, he served him loyally and well. But Grant had political aspirations of a personal nature, and he succeeded Lincoln after Johnson's unhappy administration.

I decided to pursue my line of questioning further to see where it might lead.

I asked Sybil's controlling entity to repeat the name of this Army general. Faintly but clear enough it came from her entranced lips:

"Gee . . . G-E-E . . . Major General Robert Gee."

Then it wasn't Grant, I thought. But who in blazes was it? If there existed such a person I could find a record, but what if it was merely a cover name?"

"Did you see this man yourself?"

"No."

"Then did your brother tell you about him?"

"Yes."

"Where did they meet?"

Hesitatingly, the reply came.

"In the city. This city. In a club. . . ."

I decided to change my approach.

"What year is this?" I shot at him.

"Forty-nine."

"What does forty-nine mean to you?"

"Forty-nine means something important. . . ."

"How old are you now?"

"Thirty-four."

He then claimed to have been born in Lowell, Virginia, and I found myself as puzzled as ever: It did not fit Edwin, who was born in 1833 on the Booth homestead at Belair, Maryland. Confusion over confusion!

"Did anyone else but the four of you come here?" I finally asked.

"Yes . . . Major . . . Robert Gee. . . ."

"What did he want?"

"Bribery."

"What did he pay?"

"I don't know."

"Did he give him any money?"

"Yes."

"What was he supposed to do?"

"Cause a disturbance. In the gallery. Then plans would be put into operation. To hold up the law."

"Did your brother do what he was supposed to do?"

"He was mad . . . he killed him."

"Then who was guilty?"

"Gee. . . ."

"Who sent Gee? For whom did he speak?"

We were getting close to the heart of the matter and the others were grouping themselves closely around us, the better to hear. It was quite dark outside and the chill of the November afternoon crept into our bones with the result that we started to tremble with the wet cold. But nobody moved or showed impatience. American history was being relived, and what did a little chill matter in comparison?

"He surveyed . . ."

"Who worked with him?"

"The government."

"Who specifically?"

"I don't know."

It did not sound convincing. Was he still holding out on us?

"Were there others involved? Other men? Other women?"

A derisive laughter broke the stillness. "Jealous . . . jealousy . . . his wife. . . ."

"Whose wife?"

"The one who was killed . . . shot."

* * *

Assasination of a President

That I found rather interesting, for it is a historical fact that Mrs. Lincoln was extremely jealous and, according to Carl Sandburg, perhaps the most famous Lincoln biographer, never permitted her husband to see a woman alone—for any reason whatever. The Lincolns had frequent spats for that reason, and jealousy was a key characteristic of the President's wife.

"Why are we in this room?" I demanded.

"Waiting for . . . what am I waiting for?" the communicator said, in a voice filled with despair.

"I'd like to know that myself," I nodded. "Is there anything of interest for you here?"

"Yes . . . I have to stay here until John comes back. Where's John?"

"And what will you do when he comes back?"

"Take him to Lowell . . . my home. . . ."

"Whom do you live with there?"

"Julia . . . my girl . . . take him to rest there."

"Where is John now?"

"In the woods . . . hiding."

"Is anyone with him?"

"Two . . . they should be back soon."

Again the entity demanded to know why I was asking all those questions and again I reassured him that I was a friend. But I'd have to know everything in order to help him. Who then was this Major General Gee?

"Wants control," the voice said, "I don't understand the Army . . . politics . . . he's altering the government. . . ."

"Altering the government?" I repeated, "On whose side is he?"

"Insurgent side."

"Is he in the U. S. Government?"

"My brother knows them . . . they hate the government."

"But who are they? What are their names?"

"They had numbers. Forty-nine. It means the area. The area they look after."

"Is anyone in the government involved with these insurgents?"

"John knows . . . John's dead . . . knew too much . . . the names . . . he wasn't all . . . he's mad!"

"Who killed him?"

"Soldier."

"Why did he kill him?" I was now referring to John Wilkes Booth and the killing of the presidential assassin by Sergeant Boston Corbett, allegedly because "God told him to," as the record states.

"Hunted him."

"But who gave the order to kill him?"

"The government."

"You say, he knew too much. What *did* he know?"

"I don't know the names, I know only I wait for John. John knows the names. He was clever."

"Was anyone in this government involved?"

"Traitors . . . in the *head of the Army*. . . . Sher . . . must not tell you, John said not to speak. . . ."

"You must speak!" I commanded, almost shouting.

"Sherman . . . Colonel . . . he knows Sherman. . . . John says to say nothing. . . ."

"Does Sherman know about it?"

"I don't know. . . . I am not telling you any more . . ." he said, trembling again with tears, "Everybody asks questions . . . You are not helping me."

"I will try to help you if you don't hold back," I promised. "Who paid your brother?"

"Nothing . . . promised to escape . . . look after him . . . promised a ticket. . . ."

"How often did your brother see this officer?"

"Not too often. Here. John told me . . . some things. John said not to talk. He is not always mad."

"Who is the woman with him?" I tried, to see if it would trick him into talking about others.

"She's a friend," the communicator said without hesitation.

"What is her name?"

"Harriet."

"Where does she live?"

"In the city."

"How does he know her?"

"He went to play there . . . he liked her. . . ."

Evidently this was some minor figure of no importance to the plot. I changed directions again. "You are free to leave here now. John wants you to go," I said, slowly. After all, I could not let this poor soul, whoever he was, hang on here for all eternity!

"Where are we?" he asked, sounding as confused as ever.

"A house. . . ."

"My house? . . . No, Melville's house. . . ."

"Who is Melville?"

"Friend of Gee. Told me to come here, wait for John."

"You are free to go, free!" I intoned.

"Free?" he said slowly, "Free country?"

"A hundred years have gone by. Do you understand me?"

"No."

The voice became weaker as if the entity were drifting away. Gradually Sybil's body seemed to collapse and I was ready to catch her, should she fall. But in time she "came back" to herself. Awakening, as if she had slept a long time, she looked around herself, as completely confused as the entity had been. She remembered absolutely nothing of the conversation between the ghost and myself.

For a moment none of us said anything. The silence was finally broken by Thomas Miller, who seemed visibly impressed with the entire investigation. He knew very well that the hole in the floor was a matter *he* was apt to point out to visitors in the house, and that no visitors had come here in a long time, as the house had been in disrepair for several years. How could this strange woman with the English accent whom he had never met before in his life, or for that matter, how could I, a man he only knew by correspondence, know about it? And how could she head straight for the spot in the semi-darkness of an unlit house? That was the wedge that opened the door to his acceptance of what he had witnessed just now.

"It's cold," Sybil murmured, and wrapped herself deeper into her black shawl. But she has always been a good sport, and did not complain. Patiently, she waited further instructions from me. I decided it was time to introduce everybody formally now, as I had of course not done so on arrival in order to avoid Sybil's picking up any information or clues.

Phyllis Amos then showed us the spot where she had been hit by unseen hands, and pointed out the area where her younger sister Lynn, seven at the time and now nineteen, had heard the voices of a group of men whom she had also seen huddled together on the back stairs.

"I too thought I heard voices here," Phyllis Amos commented. "It sounded like the din of several voices but I couldn't make it out clearly."

I turned to Thomas Miller, who was bending down now toward the hole in the floor.

"This is where John Wilkes Booth hid his guns," he said, anticlimactically. "The innkeeper, Lloyd, also gave him some brandy, and then he rode on to where Dr. Mudd had his house, in Bryantown."

Assasination of a President

"You heard the conversation that came through my psychic friend, Mr. Miller, I said. "Do you care to comment on some of the names? For instance, did John Wilkes Booth have a brother along those lines?"

"My father bought this property from John Wilkes' brother," Miller said, "the brother who went to live in Baltimore after John Wilkes was killed; later he went to England."

That, of course, would be Edwin Booth, the "Prince of Players," who followed his sister Asia's advice to try his luck in the English theater.

I found this rather interesting. So Surratt's tavern had once belonged to Edwin Booth—finger of fate!

Mr. Miller pointed out something else of interest to me. While I had been changing tapes, during the interrogation of the communicator speaking through Sybil, I had missed a sentence or two. My question had been about the ones behind the killing.

"S-T-..." the communicator had whispered. Did it mean Stanton?

"John Wilkes Booth was very familiar with this place, of course," Miller said in his Maryland drawl. "This is where the conspirators used to meet many times. Mary Surratt ran this place as a tavern. Nothing has changed in this house since then."

From Thomas Miller I also learned that plans were afoot to restore the house at considerable cost, and to make it into a museum.

We thanked our host and piled into the car. Suddenly I remembered that I had forgotten my briefcase inside the house, so I raced back and recovered it. The house was now even colder and emptier, and I wondered if I might hear anything unusual—

but I didn't. Rather than hang around any longer, I joined the others in the car and we drove back to Washington.

I asked Countess d'Amecourt to stop once more at a house I felt might have some relationship with the case. Sybil, of course, had no idea why we got out to look at an old house on H Street. It is now a Chinese restaurant and offers no visible clues to its past.

"I feel military uniforms, blue colors here," Sybil said as we all shuddered in the cold wind outside. The house was locked and looked empty. My request to visit it had never been answered.

"What period?"

"Perhaps a hundred years . . . nothing very strong here . . . the initial S . . . a man . . . rather confusing . . . a meeting place more than a residence . . . not too respectable . . . meeting house for soldiers . . . Army. . . ."

"Is there a link between this house and where we went earlier this afternoon?"

"The Army is the link somehow. . . ."

After I had thanked the Countess d'Amecourt for her help, Sybil and I flew back to New York.

For days afterward I pondered the questions arising from this expedition. Was the "S" linking the house on H Street—which was Mary Surratt's Washington boarding house—the same man as the "S-T- . . ." Sybil had whispered to me at Mary Surratt's former country house? Were both initials referring to Secretary Stanton and were the rumors true after all?

The facts of history, in this respect, are significant. Lincoln's second term was actively opposed by the forces of the radical Republicans. They thought Lincoln too soft on the rebels and feared that he would make an easy peace with the Confederacy. They were quite right in this assumption, of course, and all through Lincoln's second term of office, his intent was clear. That is why, in murdering Abraham Lincoln, Booth actually did the South a great disservice.

In the spring of 1864, when the South seemed to be on its last legs, the situation in Washington also came to a point where decisions would have to be made soon. The "hawks," to use a contemporary term, could count on the services of Stanton, the War Secretary, and of Seward, Secretary of State, plus many lesser officials and officers, of course. The "doves" were those in actual command, however—Lincoln himself, Grant, and Vice President Johnson, a Southerner himself. Logically, the time of crisis would be at hand the moment Grant had won victory in his command and Sherman, the other great commander, on his end of the front. By a strange set of circumstances, the assassination took place precisely at that moment: Both Grant and Sherman had eminently succeeded and peace was at hand.

Whenever Booth's motive in killing Lincoln has been described by biographers, a point is made that it was both Booth's madness and his attempt to avenge the South that caused him to commit the crime. Quite so, but the assassination made a lot more sense in terms of a *northern* plot by conveniently removing the chief advocate of a soft peace treaty just at the right moment!

This was not a trifling matter. Lincoln had proposed to go beyond freeing the slaves: to franchise the more intelligent ones among them to vote. But he had never envisioned general and immediate equality of newly freed blacks and their former masters. To the radicals, however, this was an absolute must as was the total takeover of southern assets. While Lincoln was only too ready to accept any southern state back into the Union fold that was willing to take the oath of loyalty, the radicals would hear of no such thing. They foresaw a long period of military government and rigid punishment for the secessionist states.

Lincoln often expressed the hope that Jefferson Davis and his chief aides might just leave the country to save him the embarrassment of having to try them. Stanton and his group, on the other hand, were pining for blood, and it was on Stanton's direct orders that the southern conspirators who killed Lincoln were shown no mercy; it was Stanton who refused to give in to popular sentiment against the hanging of a woman and who insisted that Mrs. Surratt share the fate of the other principal conspirators.

Stanton's stance at Lincoln's death—his remark that "now he belongs to the ages" and his vigorous pursuit of the murderers in no way mitigates against a possible secret involvement in a plot to kill the President. According to Stefan Lorant, he once referred to his commander-in-chief Lincoln as "the original gorilla." He frequently refused to carry out Lincoln's orders when he thought them "too soft." On April 11, three days prior to the assassination, Lincoln had incurred not only Stanton's anger but that of the entire Cabinet by arranging to allow the rebel Virginia legislature to function as a state government. "Stanton and the others were in a fury," Carl Sandburg reports, and the uproar was so loud Lincoln did not go through with his intent. But it shows the deep cleavage that existed between the liberal President and his radical government on the very eve of his last day!

Then, too, there was the trial held in a hurry and under circumstances no modern lawyer would call proper or even constitutional. Evidence was presented in part, important documents—such as Booth's own diary—were arbitrarily suppressed and kept out of the trial by order of Secretary Stanton, who also had impounded Booth's personal belongings and any and all documents seized at the Surratt house on H Street, giving defense attorneys for the accused, especially Mrs. Mary Surratt, not the slightest opportunity to build a reasonable defense for their clients.

Assasination of a President

That was as it should be, from Stanton's point of view: fanning the popular hatred by letting the conspirators appear in as unfavorable a light as possible, a quick conviction and execution of the judgment, so that no sympathy could rise among the public for the accused. There was considerable opposition to the hanging of Mrs. Surratt, and committees demanding her pardon were indeed formed. But by the time these committees were able to function properly, the lady was dead, convicted on purely circumstantial evidence: Her house had been the meeting place for the conspirators, but it was never proven that she was part of the conspiracy. In fact, she disapproved of the murder plot, according to the condemned, but the government would not accept this view. Her own son John H. Surratt, sitting the trial out in Canada, never lifted a hand to save his mother—perhaps he thought Stanton would not dare execute her.

Setting aside for the moment the identity of the spirit communicator at the Surratt tavern, I examined certain aspects of this new material: Certainly Sherman himself could not have been part of an anti-Lincoln plot, for he was a "dove," strictly a Lincoln man. But a member of his staff—perhaps the mysterious colonel—might well have been involved. Sybil's communicator had stated that Booth knew all about those Army officers who were either using him or were in league with him, making, in fact, the assassination a dual plot of southern avengers and northern hawks. If Booth knew these names, he might have put the information into his personal diary. This diary was written during his flight, while he was hiding from his pursuers in the wooded swamplands of Maryland and Virginia.

At the conspiracy trial, the diary was not even mentioned, but at the subsequent trial of John H. Surratt, two years later, it did come to light. That is, Lafayette Baker, head of the Secret Service at the time of the murder, mentioned its existence, and it was promptly impounded for the trial. But when it was produced as evidence in court, only two pages were left in it—the rest had been torn out by an unknown hand! Eighteen pages were missing. The diary had been in Stanton's possession from the moment of its seizure until now, and it was highly unlikely that Booth himself had so mutilated his own diary the moment he had finished writing it! To the contrary, the diary was his attempt to justify himself before his contemporaries, and before history. The onus of guilt here falls heavily upon Secretary Stanton again.

It is significant that whoever mutilated the diary had somehow spared an entry dated April 21, 1865:

"Tonight I will once more try the river, with the intention to cross; though I have a greater desire and almost a mind to return to Washington, and in a measure clear my name, which I feel I can do.'

Philip Van Doren Stern, author of *The Man Who Killed Lincoln*, quite rightfully asks, how could a self-confessed murderer clear his name unless he knew something that would involve other people than himself and his associates? Stern also refers to David Herold's confession in which the young man quotes Booth as telling him that there was a group of *thirty-five men in Washington* involved in the plot.

Sybil's confused communicator kept saying certain numbers, "forty-nine" and "thirty-four." Could this be the code for Stanton and a committee of thirty-four men?

Whoever they were, not one of the northern conspirators ever confessed their part in the crime, so great was the popular indignation at the deed.

John H. Surratt, after going free as a consequence of the inability of his trial jury to agree on a verdict, tried his hand at lecturing on the subject of the assassination. He only gave a single lecture, which turned out a total failure. Nobody was interested.

But a statement Surratt made at that lecture fortunately has come down to us. He admitted that another group of conspirators had been working independently and simultaneously to strike a blow at Lincoln.

That Surratt would make such a statement fits right in with the facts. He was a courier and undercover man for the Confederacy, with excellent contacts in Washington. It was he who managed to have the telegraph go out of order during the murder and to allow Booth to pass the sentry at the Navy Yard bridge without difficulty. But was the communicator speaking through Mrs. Leek not holding back information at first, only to admit finally that John Wilkes *knew* the names of those others, after all?

This differs from Philip Van Doren Stern's account, in which Booth was puzzled about the identities of his "unknown" allies. But then, Stern didn't hold a trance session at the Surratt tavern, either. Until our visit in November of 1967, the question seemed up in the air.

Surratt had assured Booth that "his sources" would make sure that they all got away safely. In other words, Booth and his associates were doing the dirty work for the brain trust in Washington, with John Surratt serving both sides and in a way linking them together in an identical purpose—though for totally opposite reasons.

Interestingly enough, the entranced Sybil spoke of a colonel who knew Sherman, and who would look after him . . . he would supply a ticket . . . ! That ticket might have been a steamer ticket for some foreign ship going from Mexico to Europe, where Booth could be safe. But who was the mysterious Major General Gee? Since Booth's group was planning to kill Grant as well, would he be likely to be involved in the plot on the northern end?

Lincoln had asked Grant and Mrs. Grant to join him at Ford's Theatre the fateful evening; Grant had declined, explaining that he wished to join his family in New Jersey instead. Perhaps that was a natural enough excuse to turn down the President's invitation, but one might also construe it differently: Did he *know* about the plot and did he not wish to see his President shot?

Booth's choice of the man to do away with Grant had fallen on John Surratt, as soon as he learned of the change in plans. Surratt was to get on the train that took Grant to New Jersey. But Grant was not attacked; there is no evidence whatever that Surratt ever took the train, and he himself said he didn't. Surratt, then, the go-between of the two groups of conspirators, could easily have warned Grant himself: The Booth group wanted to kill Lincoln *and* his chief aides, to make the North powerless; but the northern conspirators would have only wanted to have Lincoln removed and certainly none of their own men. Even though Grant was likely to carry out the President's "soft" peace plans, while Lincoln was his commander-in-chief, he was a soldier accustomed to taking orders and would carry out with equal loyalty the hard-line policies of Lincoln's successor! Everything here points to Surratt as having been, in effect, a double agent.

But was the idea of an involvement of General Grant really so incredible?

Wilson Sullivan, author of a critical review of a recently published volume of *The Papers of Andrew Johnson*, has this to say of Grant, according to the *Saturday Review of Literature*, March 16, 1968:

"Despite General Grant's professed acceptance of Lincoln's policy of reconciliation with the Southern whites, President Grant strongly supported and implemented the notorious Ku Klux Act in 1871."

This was a law practically disenfranchising Southerners and placing them directly under federal courts rather than local and state authorities.

It was Grant who executed the repressive policies of the radical Republican Congress and who reverted to the hard-line policies of the Stanton clique after he took political office, undo-ing completely whatever lenient measures President Johnson had instituted following the assassination of his predecessor.

But even before Grant became President, he was the man in power. Since the end of the Civil War, civil administrations had governed the conquered South. In March 1867, these were replaced by military governments in five military districts. The commanders of these districts were directly responsible to General Grant and disregarded any orders from President Johnson. Civil rights and state laws were broadly ignored. The reasons for this perversion of Lincoln's policies were not only vengeance on the Confederacy, but political considerations as well: By delaying the voting rights of Southerners, a Republican Congress could keep itself in office that much longer. Wilson Sullivan feels that this attitude was largely responsible for the emergence of the Ku Klux Klan and other racist organizations in the South.

Had Lincoln lived out his term, he would no doubt have implemented a policy of rapid reconciliation, the South would have regained its political privileges quickly, and the radical Republican party might have lost the next election.

That party was led by Secretary Stanton and General Grant!

What a convenient thing it was to have a southern con-spiracy at the proper time! All one had to do is get aboard and ride the conspiracy to the successful culmination—then blame it all on the South, thereby doing a double job, heaping more guilt upon the defeated Confederacy and ridding the country of the *one* man who could forestall the continuance in power of the Stanton-Grant group!

That Stanton might have been the real leader in the northern plot is not at all unlikely. The man was given to rebellion when the situation demanded it. President Andrew Johnson had tried to continue the Lincoln line in the face of a hostile Congress and even a Cabinet dominated by radicals. In early 1868, Johnson tried to oust Secretary Stanton from his Cabinet because he realized that Stanton was betraying his policies. But Stanton defied his chief and barricaded himself in the War Department. This intolerable situation led to Johnson's impeachment proceedings, which failed by a single vote.

There was one more tragic figure connected with the events that seemed to hold unresolved mysteries: Mrs. Mary Surratt, widow of a Confederate spy and mother of another. On April 14, 1865, she invited her son's friend, and one of her boarders, Louis Weichman, to accompany her on an errand to her old country home, now a tavern, at Surrattsville. Weichmann gladly obliged Mrs. Surratt and went down to hire a buggy. At the tavern, Mrs. Surratt got out carrying a package which she described to Weichmann as belonging to Booth. This package she handed to tavernkeeper John Lloyd inside the house to safekeep for Booth. It contained the guns the fugitives took with them later, after the assassination had taken place.

Weichmann's testimony of this errand, and his description of the meetings at the H Street house, were largely responsible for Mrs. Surratt's execution, even though it was never shown that she had anything to do with the murder plot itself. Weichmann's testimony haunted him all his life, for Mrs. Surratt's "ghost," as Lloyd Lewis puts it in *Myths After Lincoln*, "got up and walked" in 1868 when her "avengers" made political capital of her execution, charging Andrew Johnson with having railroaded her to death.

Mrs. Surratt's arrest at 11:15 P.M., April 17, 1865, came as a surprise to her despite the misgivings she had long harbored about her son's involvement with Booth and the other plotters. Lewis Paine's untimely arrival at the house after it had already been raided also helped seal her fate. At the trial that followed, none of the accused was ever allowed to speak, and their judges were doing everything in their power to link the conspiracy with the Confederate government, even to the extent of producing false witnesses, who later recanted their testimonies.

If anyone among the condemned had the makings of a ghost, it was Mary Surratt.

Soon after her execution and burial, reports of her haunting the house on H Street started. The four bodies of the executed had been placed inside the prison walls and the families were denied the right to bury them.

When Annie Surratt could not obtain her mother's body, she sold the lodging house and moved away from the home that had seen so much tragedy. The first buyer of the house had little luck with it, however. Six weeks later he sold it again, even though he had bought it very cheaply. Other tenants came and went quickly, and according to the Boston *Post*, which chronicled the fate of the house, it was because they saw the ghost of Mrs. Surratt clad in her execution robe walking the corridors of her home! That was back in the 1860s and 1870s. Had Mary Surratt found peace since then? Her body now lies buried underneath a simple gravestone at Mount Olivet Cemetery.

The house at 604 H Street, N.W. still stands. In the early 1900s, a Washington lady dined at the house. During dinner, she noticed the figure of a young girl appear and walk up the stairs. She recognized the distraught girl as the spirit of Annie Surratt, reports John McKelway recently in the Washington *Star*. The Chinese establishment now occupying the house does not mind the ghosts, either mother or daughter. And Ford Theatre has just been restored as a legitimate theatre, to break the ancient jinx. Whether the President of the United States will attend any performances is not known at this time.

Both Stern and Emanuel Hertz quote an incident in the life of Robert Lincoln, whom a Mr. Young discovered destroying many of his father's private papers. When he remonstrated with Lincoln, the son replied that "the papers he was destroying contained the documentary evidence of the treason of a member of Lincoln's Cabinet, and he thought it best for all that such evidence be destroyed."

Mr. Young enlisted the help of Nicholas Murray Butler, later head of Columbia University, New York, to stop Robert Lincoln from continuing this destruction. The remainder of the papers were then deposited in the Library of Congress, but we don't know how many documents Robert Lincoln had already destroyed when he was halted.

There remains only the curious question as to the identity of our communicator at the Surratt tavern in November 1967.

"Shot down like a dog," the voice had complained through the psychic.

"Hunted like a dog," Booth himself wrote in his diary. Why would Edwin Booth, who had done everything in his power to publicly repudiate his brother's deed, and who claimed that he had little direct contact with John Wilkes in the years before the assassination—why would he want to own this house that was so closely connected with the tragedy and John Wilkes Booth? Who would think that the "Prince of Players," who certainly had no record of any involvement in the plot to kill Lincoln, should be drawn back by feelings of guilt to the house so intimately connected with his brother John Wilkes?

But he did own it, and sell it to B. K. Miller, Thomas Miller's father!

I couldn't find any Lowell, Virginia on my maps, but there is a Laurel, Maryland not far from Surrattsville, or today's Clinton.

Much of the dialogue fits Edwin Booth, owner of the house. Some of it doesn't, and some of it might be deliberate coverup.

Assasination of a President

Mark you, this is not a "ghost" in the usual sense, for nobody reported Edwin Booth appearing to them at this house. Mrs. Surratt might have done so, both here and at her town house, but the principal character in this fascinating story has evidently lacked the inner torment that is the basis for ghostly manifestations beyond time and space. Quite so, for to John Wilkes Booth the deed was the work of a national hero, not to be ashamed of at all. If anything, the ungrateful Confederacy owed him a debt of thanks.

No, I decided, John Wilkes Booth would not make a convincing ghost. But Edwin? Was there more to his relationship with John Wilkes than the current published record shows? "Ah, there's the rub . . ." the Prince of Players would say in one of his greatest roles.

Then, too, there is the peculiar mystery of John Surratt's position. He had broken with John Wilkes Booth weeks before the murder, he categorically stated at his trial in 1867. Yes, he had been part of the earlier plot to abduct Lincoln, but murder, no. That was not his game.

It was my contention, therefore, that John Surratt's role as a dual agent seemed highly likely from the evidence available to me, both through objective research and psychic contacts. We may never find the mysterious colonel on Sherman's staff, nor be able to identify with *certainty* Major General "Gee." But War Secretary Stanton's role looms ominously and in sinister fashion behind the generally accepted story of the plot.

If Edwin Booth came through Sybil Leek to tell us what he knew of his brother's involvement in Lincoln's death, perhaps he did so because John Wilkes never got around to clear his name himself. Stanton may have seen to that, and the disappearing diary and unseeming haste of the trial all fall into their proper places.

It is now over a hundred years after the event. Will we have to wait that long before we know the complete truth about another President's murder?

15

The Case
of the Lost Head

One of the most famous ghosts of the South is railroad conductor Joe Baldwin. The story of Joe and his lantern was known to me, of course, and a few years ago *Life* magazine even dignified it with a photograph of the railroad track near Wilmington, North Carolina, very atmospherically adorned by a greenish lantern, presumably swinging in ghostly hands.

Then one fine day in early 1964, the legend became reality when a letter arrived from Bill Mitcham, Executive Secretary of the South Eastern North Carolina Beach Association, a public-relations office set up by the leading resort hotels in the area centering around Wilmington. Mr. Mitcham proposed that I have a look at the ghost of Joe Baldwin, and try to explain once and for all—scientifically—what the famous "Maco Light" was or is.

In addition, Mr. Mitcham arranged for a lecture on the subject to be held at the end of my investigation and sponsored jointly by the Beach Association and Wilmington College. He promised to roll out the red carpet for Catherine and me, and roll it out he did.

Seldom in the history of ghost hunting has a parapsychologist been received so royally and so fully covered by press, tele-

301

vision and radio, and if the ghost of Joe Baldwin is basking in the reflected glory of all this attention directed towards his personal Ghost Hunter, he is most welcome to it.

If it were not for Joe Baldwin, the bend in the railroad track which is known as Maco Station (a few miles outside of Wilmington) would be a most unattractive and ordinary trestle. By the time I had investigated it and left, in May of 1964, the spot had almost risen to the prominence of a national shrine and sight-seeing groups arrived at all times, especially at night, to look for Joe Baldwin's ghostly light.

Bill Mitcham had seen to it that the world knew about Joe Baldwin's headless ghost and Hans Holzer seeking same, and not less than seventy-eight separate news stories of one kind or another appeared in print during the week we spent in Wilmington.

Before I even started to make plans for the Wilmington expedition, I received a friendly letter from a local student of psychic phenomena, William Edward Cox, Jr., and a manuscript entitled "The Maco Ghost Light." Mr. Cox had spent considerable time observing the strange light, and I quote:

> A favorite "ghost story" in the vicinity of Wilmington, N.C., is that of "Joe Baldwin's Ghost Light," which is alleged to appear at night near Maco, N.C., 12 miles west of Wilmington on the Atlantic Coast Line Railroad.
>
> On June 30–July 1, 1949, this writer spent considerable time investigating the phenomenon. The purpose was to make an accurate check on the behavior of the light under test conditions, with a view toward ascertaining its exact nature.
>
> This light has been observed since shortly after the legend of the Joe Baldwin ghost light "was born in 1867." It is officially reported in a pamphlet entitled "The Story of the Coast Line, 1830–1948." In its general description it resembles a 25-watt electric light slowly moving along the tracks toward the observer, whose best point of observation is on the track itself

The Case of the Lost Head

at the point where the tracks, double at that point, are crossed by a branch of a connecting roadway between U.S. Highway 74–76 and U.S. Highway 19.

The popular explanation is that Conductor Baldwin, decapitated in an accident, is taking the nocturnal walks in search of his head. . . .

After testing the various "natural" theories put forward for the origin of the nocturnal light, Mr. Cox admits:

Although the general consensus of opinion is that the lights stem from some relatively rare cause, such as the paranormal, *"ignis fatuus,"* etc., the opinions of residents of the Maco vicinity were found by this observer to be more divided. The proprietor of the Mobilgas Service Station was noncommittal, and a local customer said he had "never seen the light." A farmer in the area was quite certain that it is caused by automobile headlights, but would not express an opinion upon such lights as were customarily seen there before the advent of the automobile.

The proprietress of the Willet Service Station, Mrs. C.L. Benton, was firmly convinced that it was of "supernatural origin," and that the peculiar visibility of automobile headlights to observers at Maco must be more or less a subsequent coincidence.

She said that her father "often saw it as he loaded the wood burners near there over 60 years ago."

The basic question of the origin and nature of the "Maco Light," or the original light, remains incompletely answered. The findings here reported, due as they are to entirely normal causes, cannot accurately be construed as disproving the existence of a light of paranormal origin at any time in the distant past (or, for that matter, at the present time).

The unquestionable singularity of the phenomenon's being in a locale where it is so easily possible for automobiles to produce an identical phenomenon seems but to relegate it to the enigmatic "realm of forgotten mysteries."

So much for Mr. Cox's painstaking experiment conducted at the site in 1949.

The coming of the Ghost Hunter (and Mrs. Ghost Hunter) was amply heralded in the newspapers of the area. Typical of the veritable avalanche of features was the story in *The Charlotte Observer*:

Can Spook Hunter De-Ghost Old Joe?

The South Eastern N.C. Beach Association invited a leading parapsychologist Saturday to study the ghost of Old Joe Baldwin.

Bill Mitcham, executive director of the association, said he has arranged for Hans Holzer of New York to either prove or disprove the ghostly tales relating to Old Joe.

Holzer will begin his study May 1.

Tales of Joe Baldwin flagging down trains with false signals, waving his lantern on dark summer nights have been repeated since his death in 1867.

Baldwin, a conductor on the Wilmington, Manchester and Augusta Railroad, was riding the rear coach of a train the night of his death. The coach became uncoupled and Baldwin seized a lantern in an effort to signal a passenger train following.

But the engineer failed to see the signal. In the resulting crash, Baldwin was decapitated.

A witness to the wreck later recalled that the signal lantern was flung some distance from the tracks, but that it burned brightly thereafter for some time.

Soon after the accident, there were reports of a mysterious light along the railroad tracks at Maco Station in Brunswick County.

304

The Case of the Lost Head

> Two lanterns, one green and one red, have been used by trainmen at Maco Station so that engineers would not be confused or deceived by Joe Baldwin's light.

Most helpful in a more serious vein was the Women's Editor of the *Wilmington Star-News*, Theresa Thomas, who has for years taken an interest in the psychic and probably is somewhat sensitive herself. On April 8, 1964, she asked her readers:

Have You Ever Seen the Maco Light?

> Have you ever seen Old Joe Baldwin? Or his light, that is? As far as we know, nobody has actually seen Joe himself.
> But if you have seen his lantern swinging along the railroad track at Maco, you can be of great help to Hans Holzer, Ghost Hunter, who will be in Wilmington April 29th.
> Either write out your experience and send it to us, or call and tell us about it.

Then the feminine point of view crashed the scientific barrier a little as Miss Thomas added:

> His [Mr. Holzer's] wife is just as fascinating as he. She is a painter and great-great-great-granddaughter of Catherine The Great of Russia. Mrs. Holzer was born Countess Catherine Buxhoeveden in a haunted castle in Meran, the Tyrol, in the Italian Alps. And she paints—haven't you guessed?—haunted houses.

My visit was still three weeks away, but the wheels of publicity where already spinning fast and furiously in Wilmington.

Theresa Thomas' appeal for actual witnesses to the ghostly phenomena brought immediate results. For the first time people of standing took the matter seriously, and those who had seen the light, opened up. Miss Thomas did not disguise her enthusiasm. On April 12, she wrote:

It seems a great many people have seen Old Joe Baldwin's light at Maco and most of them are willing—even eager—to talk about it.

Among the first to call was Mrs. Larry Moore, 211 Orange Street, who said she had seen the light three or four times at different seasons of the year.

The first time it was a cloudy, misty winter night and again in summer, misty again. Her description of the light was "like bluish yellow flame." She and her companions walked down the track and the light came closer as they approached the trestle. When they reached the center of the trestle with the light apparently about 10 feet away, it disappeared.

Mrs. Thelma Daughtry, 6 Shearwater Drive, Wrightsville Beach, says she saw it on a misty spring night. It was about 7 or 8 o'clock in the evening and the reddish light appeared to swing along at about knee height.

Mrs. Margaret Jackson, of 172 Colonial Circle, a native of Vienna, Austria, saw it about seven years ago on a hazy night. She was with several other people and they all saw the light, a "glary shine" steady and far away but always the same distance ahead of them.

Dixie Rambeau, 220 Pfeiffer Avenue, saw it about 1 A.M. Friday morning. She says it was "real dark" and the light appeared as a red pinpoint at a distance up the track, as it neared it became yellowish white, then closer still it was a mixed red and white.

She recalls that she and her companions watched it come closer to the left side of the track and that as it came close the reflection on the rail almost reached them. At about 10 feet away it reversed its process and as they walked toward it, it disappeared. Once it appeared to cross over. They watched it five or six times, she said.

The Case of the Lost Head

Mrs. Marvin Clark, 406 Grace Street, a practical nurse, states that she and her husband saw the light 15 years ago. It was about midnight on a cloudy, rainy night. They were standing in the middle of the track and "it looked like a light on a train coming at full speed."

Mrs. Clark described the light as "the color of a train light."

"We picked up our little girl and ran. All of us have always seen reflections of automobiles but beyond a doubt it was the Maco Light."

Mrs. Lase V. Dail of Carolina Beach also has a story to tell. It seems she and her husband came home late one night from Fayetteville.

She writes: "As we left the cut off and headed into 74–76 highway, I shall never forget the experience we had . . ." She goes on, "All at once a bright light came down the road toward us, first I figured it was a car. But decided if so it had only one light. On it came steadily toward us.

"Then I figured it was a train, yet I heard nothing, and as suddenly as it appeared it vanished. I can say it was quite a weird feeling. I have often thought of it. I have heard many versions, but never one like this."

Three days later, Miss Thomas devoted still another full column to people who had witnessed the ghost light.

Mrs. Marjorie H. Rizer of Sneads Ferry writes: "I have seen the light three times. The last and most significant time was about a year and a half ago. My husband, three young sons and a corpsman from the United States Naval Hospital at Camp Lejeune were with me and we saw the same thing. It was about 10:30 P.M. and we were returning from a ball game. We decided to go to Maco since we were so near and the young man with us didn't believe there was anything to our story.

"The sky was cloudy and a light mist was falling. We

307

parked the car beside the track and sure enough, there was the light down the track. I stayed in the car with my sons, and my husband and the corpsman walked down the track toward the light.

"The light would alternately dim and then become very bright. The two men walked perhaps a quarter of a mile down the track before they returned. They said the light stayed ahead of them, but my sons and I saw the light between them and us.

"It looked as if the light would come almost to where we were parked and then it would wobble off down the track and disappear. In a moment it would reappear and do the same time after time.

"When we had been there for about an hour and started to leave, a train approached going toward Wilmington. The light was a short distance away from us. As the train passed the light, it rose and hovered over the train. We could clearly see the top of the train as the light became very bright.

"It stayed over the train until it had passed then disappeared back down near the track and finally it looked as if someone had thrown it off into the woods.

"As we pulled away from the track the light came back on the track and weaved backward and forward down the track as it had been doing."

And still the letters poured in. On April 22, after half a column devoted to my imminent arrival in the area, Miss Thomas printed a letter from a young man who had taken some interesting pictures·

He is J. Everett Huggins, home address 412 Market Street, Wilmington. The letter is addressed to Bill Mitcham and reads in part: "I read with interest the articles on your 'ghost survey,' especially since I saw the Maco light less than two weeks ago and was actually able to catch Old Joe on film.

"On the nights of April 1 and 2 a schoolmate of mine

The Case of the Lost Head

and I went to Maco Station in the hopes of seeing the light. We saw nothing on Friday, April 1, but we had more success on Saturday, when it was a little darker. Around 10:30 we saw a yellow light about 100 yards down the track from us (this distance is only a guess). It seemed to be about 10 feet above the tracks and looked as if it were moving slowly toward us for a while, then it went back and died out.

"The light appeared maybe three times in succession for periods up to what I would estimate to be about thirty seconds.

"I attempted to take two time exposures with my camera. Unfortunately I did not have a tripod, and so I had to hold the camera in my hands, which made clear results impossible. The pictures are not spectacular—just a small spot on each of the color transparencies—but they are pictures. If you are interested I will have some copies made.

"My friends had kidded me about the light, so I noted some details to try to end their skepticism. The headlights of cars traveling west on Highway 74 could be seen in the distance, and no doubt many who think they see Old Joe only see these lights. Old Joe could be distinguished in several ways, however. First, the light had a yellower tone than did the auto headlights.

"Secondly, unlike the headlights which grow brighter and brighter and then suddenly disappear, the Maco light would gradually grow brighter and then gradually fade out. Thirdly, the Maco light produced a reflection on the rails that was not characteristic of the headlights.

"More interesting was the fact that the reflection on the rails was seen only on a relatively short stretch of track. By observing the reflection, we could tell that the light moved backward and forward on the rails. It always remained directly above the tracks.

"I had seen the light once before, in 1956. It was on a cold winter night, and the light was brighter."

As the day of our arrival grew nearer, the tempo of the press became more hectic. On April 26, Arnold Kirk wrote in the *Wilmington Star-News:*

> This tiny Brunswick County village, nestled in a small clearing a few miles west of Wilmington off U.S. Highway 74, is rapidly gaining acclaim as the "Ghost Capital" of North Carolina.
>
> Its few dozen inhabitants, mostly farmers of moderate means, have suddenly found their once-peaceful nights disturbed by scores of vehicles sparring for vantage points from which to view the famous "Maco Light."
>
> While the legend of the light and old Joe Baldwin, the "ghost" of Maco, has long been known, its popularity has become intense only in recent months.
>
> Elaborate plans have already been made to welcome Holzer to the Port City. The mayors of all the towns in New Hanover and Brunswick counties, in addition to county commissioners from both counties, have agreed to be at the New Hanover County Airport Wednesday at 7:43 P.M. when the "ghost hunter's" plane arrives.
>
> *Lanterns at Airport*—Also on hand to greet the noted parapsychologist will be 1,000 high-school students, carrying, appropriately enough, lighted lanterns! The lanterns were purchased by the city years ago to offer warmth to trees and plants during blustery winter months.
>
> Adding to the fanfare of the event will be the first public offering of "The Ballad of Old Joe Baldwin," written by the senior English class of New Hanover High School.

The reception was a bash that would have made Old Joe Baldwin feel honored. A little later, we tried to sneak out to Maco and have a first glance at the haunted spot. The results were disappointing.

It was not so much that the ghost did not show, but what

The Case of the Lost Head

did show up was most disturbing. *The Wilmington Star* summed it up like this:

An unwilling Old Joe Baldwin exercised his ghostly pre-rogative Wednesday night by refusing to perform before what may have been his largest audience.

Huddled in small clusters along the railroad tracks near the center of this tiny Brunswick County village, an estimated 250 persons stared into the gloomy darkness in hopes of catching a glimpse of the famous "Maco Light."

But the light would not offer the slightest flicker.

Holzer's announced visit to the scene of Baldwin's ghastly demise gave no comfort to the few dozen residents of Maco. By 10 o'clock, dozens of cars lined both sides of the narrow Maco road and scores of thrill-seeking teenagers had spilled onto the railroad track.

If Joe Baldwin had decided to make an appearance, his performance no doubt would have been engulfed in the dozens of flashlights and battery-powered lanterns searching through the darkness for at least a mile down the track.

Several times, the flashlights and lanterns were mistaken for the "Maco Light," giving hope that the mysterious glow would soon appear.

A large portion of the track was illuminated by the headlights of a jeep and small foreign car scurrying back and forth along both sides of the track. A young girl created an anxious moment when she mistook a firefly as the "Maco Light" and released a penetrating scream that sliced through the pitch-darkness.

Holzer's visit to Maco on Wednesday night was mostly for the benefit of photographers and reporters who met the noted parapsychologist at the New Hanover County airport earlier that night.

His second visit to the crossing will be kept a closely guarded secret in hopes the "ghost hunter" will be able to conduct his investigation of the light without being interrupted by pranksters and playful teenagers.

Soon I realized that it would be impossible for us to go out to the tracks alone. Crowds followed us around and crowds were ever present at the spot, giving rise to a suspicion in my mind that these people were not in a working mood while we were visiting their area. Evidently we were the most exciting thing that had happened to them for some time.

Finally, the day of a scheduled press conference arrived, and at ten o'clock in the morning, before a battery of kleig lights and microphones set up at the magnificent new Blockade Runner Hotel on the beach, I started to talk in person to those who had come to tell me about their encounters with Joe Baldwin's ghost.

In addition to those who had written to Miss Thomas and reaffirmed their original stories, others came forward who had not done so previously. There was William McGirt, an insurance executive, who called the light "buoyant," flicking itself on and off, as it were, and fully reflected on the iron rails. But you cannot see it looking east, he told me, only when you look towards Maco Station.

Margaret Bremer added to her previously told story by saying the light looked to her "like a kerosene lantern swaying back and forth."

Her husband, Mr. Bremer, had not planned on saying anything, but I coaxed him. He admitted finally that twelve years ago, when his car was standing straddled across the track, he saw a light coming towards him. It flickered like a lamp and when it came closer, it flared up. As an afterthought, he added, "Something strange—suddenly there seemed to be a rush of air, as if a train were coming from Wilmington."

"Was there?" I inquired cautiously.

The Case of the Lost Head

"No, of course not. We wouldn't have had the car across the track if a train were expected."

Mrs. Laura Collins stepped forward and told me of the time she was at the trestle with a boy who did not believe in ghosts, not even Joe Baldwin's. When the light appeared, he sneered at it and tried to explain it as a reflection. Six feet away from the boy, the light suddenly disappeared and reappeared in back of him—as if to show him up! Mrs. Collins, along with others, observed that misty weather made the light appear clearer.

Next in the parade of witnesses came Mrs. Elizabeth Finch of Wilmington, who had offered her original testimony only the day before.

"It appeared to me many times," she said of the light, "looked like a lantern to me. Two years ago, we were parked across the tracks in our car—we were watching for a train of course, too—when I saw two dazzling lights from both sides. It was a winter evening, but I suddenly felt very hot. There was a red streak in front of the car, and then I saw what was a dim outline of a man walking with a lantern and swinging it. Mind you, it was a bare outline," Mrs. Finch added in emphasis, "and it did have a head . . . just kept going, then suddenly he disappeared inside the tracks."

"Did you ever have psychic experiences before, Mrs. Finch?" I wanted to know.

"Yes, when we lived in a house in Mansonborough, I used to hear noises, steps, even voices out of nowhere—later, I was told it was haunted."

I thanked Mrs. Finch, wondering if the local legend had impressed her unconscious to the point where she did see what everyone had said was there—or whether she really saw the outline of a man.

I really have no reason to doubt her story. She struck me as a calm, intelligent person who would not easily make up a story just to be sensational. No, I decided, Mrs. Finch might very well have been one of the very few who saw more than just the light.

"I tell you why it can't be anything ordinary," Mr. Trussle, my next informant, said. "Seven years ago, when I saw the light on a damp night about a mile away from where I was standing, I noticed its very rapid approach. It disappeared fast, went back and forth as if to attract attention to something. It was three foot above the track, about the height of where a man's arm might be.

"At first, it seemed yellowish white; when I came closer, it looked kind of pinkish. Now an ordinary car headlight wouldn't go back and forth like that, would it?"

I agreed it was most unlikely for an automobile headlight to behave in such an unusual manner.

Mrs. Miriam Moore saw it three times, always on misty, humid nights. "I had a funny ringing in my ears when I reached the spot," she said. She was sure what she saw was a lamp swinging in a slow motion. Suddenly, she broke into a cold sweat for no reason at all. I established that she was a psychic person, and had on occasion foretold the death of several members of her family.

E. S. Skipper is a dapper little man in the golden years of life, but peppery and very much alert. He used to be a freight shipper on the Atlantic Coast Line and grew up with the Maco Light the way Niagara kids grow up with the sight of the Falls.

"I've seen it hundreds of times," he volunteered. "I've seen it flag trains down—it moved just like a railroad lantern would. On one occasion I took my shot gun and walked towards it. As I got nearer, the light became so bright I could hardly look. Suddenly, it disappeared into the old Catholic cemetery on the right side of the tracks."

"Cemetery?" I asked, for I had not heard of a cemetery in this area.

Mr. Skipper was quite certain that there was one. I promised to look into this immediately. "Since you came so close to the light, Mr. Skipper," I said, "perhaps you can tell me what it looked like close up."

"Oh, I got even closer than that—back in 1929, I remember it well. It was two o'clock in the morning. I got to within six foot from it."

"What did you see?"

"I saw a flame. I mean, in the middle of the light, there was unmistakably, a flame burning."

"Like a lantern?"

"Like a lantern."

I thanked Mr. Skipper and was ready to turn to my last witness, none other than Editor Thomas herself, when Mrs. E.R. Rich, who had already given her account in the newspaper, asked for another minute, which I gladly gave her.

"Ten years ago," Mrs. Rich said, "we were at the track one evening. My son Robert was in the car with me, and my older son went down the track to watch for the light. Suddenly not one but two lights appeared at the car. They were round and seemed to radiate, and sparkle—for a moment, they hung around, then one left, the other stayed. My feet went ice cold at this moment and I felt very strange."

"Miss Thomas," I said, "will you add your own experiences to this plethora of information?"

"Gladly," the Women's Editor of the *Star-News* replied. "There were three of us, all newspaper women, who decided a few weeks ago to go down to the trestle and not see anything."

"I beg your pardon?"

"We'd made up our minds not to be influenced by all the publicity Joe Baldwin's ghost was getting."

"What happened?"

"When we got to the track, dogs were baying as if disturbed by something in the atmosphere. We parked on the dirt road that runs parallel to the track, and waited. After a while, the light appeared. It had a yellow glow. Then, suddenly, there were two lights, one larger than the other, swaying in the night sky.

"The lights turned reddish after a while. There was no correlation with car lights at all. I thought at first it was a train bearing down on us, that's how big the lights appeared. Just as suddenly the lights disappeared. One light described an arc to the left of the track, landing in the grass."

"Just as those old tales say Joe's lantern did, eh?"

"It seems so, although it is hard to believe."

"What else did you notice?"

"I had a feeling that I was not alone."

And there you have it. Mass hysteria? Self-hypnosis? Suggestion? Could all these people make up similar stories?

Although the Maco Light is unique in its specific aspects, there are other lights that have been observed at spots where tragedies have occurred. There are reports of apparitions in Colorado taking the form of concentrated energy, or light globes. I don't doubt that the human personality is a form of energy that cannot be destroyed, only transmuted. The man who heard the sound of a train, the psychic chill several people experienced, the flame within the light, the two lights clearly distinguished by the newspaper women—possibly Joe's lantern and the headlight of the onrushing train—all these add up to a case.

That evening, at Bogden Hall, before an audience of some five hundred people of all ages, I stated my conviction that the track at Maco Station was, indeed, haunted. I explained that the shock of sudden death might have caused Joe Baldwin's etheric self to become glued to the spot of the tragedy, re-enacting the final moments over and over again.

I don't think we are dealing here with an "etheric impression" registered on the atmosphere and not possessing a life of its own. The phantom reacts differently with various people and seems to me a true ghost, capable of attempting communication with the living, but not fully aware of his own status or of the futility of his efforts.

I was, and am, convinced of the veracity of the phenomenon and, by comparing it to other "weaving lights" in other areas, can only conclude that the basic folklore is on the right track, except that Joe isn't likely to be looking for his head—he is rather trying to keep an imaginary train from running into his uncoupled car, which of course exists now only in his thought world.

And until someone tells Joe all's well on the line now, he will continue to wave his light. I tried to say the right words for such occasions, but I was somewhat hampered by the fact that I did not have Mrs. Ethel Meyers, my favorite medium, with me; then, too, the Wilmington people did not like the idea of having their town ghost go to his reward and leave the trestle just another second rate railroad track.

The folks living alongside it, though, wouldn't have minded one bit. They can do without Joe Baldwin and his somewhat motley admirers.

Suddenly the thought struck me that we had no proof that a Joe Baldwin had ever really existed in this area. The next morning I went to the Wilmington Public Library and started to dig into the files and historical sources dealing with the area a hundred years ago. Bill Mitcham and I started to read all the newspapers from 1866 onwards, but after a while we gave up. Instead, I had a hunch which, eventually, paid off. If Joe Baldwin was physically fit to work on the railroad in so hazardous a job as that of a train man, he must have been well enough to be in the Armed Forces at one time or another.

I started to search the Regimental Records from 1867 on backwards. Finally I found in volume V, page 602, of a work called *North Carolina Regiments*, published in 1901, the following entry:

> "Joseph Baldwin, Company F, 26th N.C.T., badly wounded in the thigh. Battle of Gettysburg. July 1, 1863."

It was the only Joseph Baldwin listed in the area, or, for that matter, the state.

I also inquired about the old Catholic cemetery. It was, indeed, near the railroad track, but had been out of use for many years. Only oldsters still remembered its existence. Baldwin may have been Catholic, as are many residents in the area. Time did not permit me to look among the dilapidated tombstones for a grave bearing the name of Joe Baldwin.

But it would be interesting to find it and see if *all* of Joe Baldwin lies buried in sacred ground!

16

The Gray Man of Pawley's Island

One of the best known ghosts of South Carolina's low country is the so-called Gray Man of Pawley's Island. A number of local people claim they have seen him gazing seaward from the dunes, especially when a hurricane is about to break. He is supposed to warn of impending disaster. Who the Gray Man of Pawley's Island is is open to question. According to A *Perceptive Survey of South Carolina Ghosts* by Worth Gatewood, published in 1962, he may be the original Percival Pawley who so loved his island that he felt impelled to watch over it even after he passed on. But Mr. Gatewood gives more credence to a beautiful and romantic account of the origin of the specter. According to this story a young man who was to be married to a local belle left for New York to attend to some business but on his way back was shipwrecked and lost at sea. After a year's time the young woman married his best friend and settled down on Pawley's Island with her new husband. Years later the original young man returned, again shipwrecked and rescued by one of his former fiancée's servants.

When he realized that his love had married in the meantime, he drowned himself at the nearby shore. All this happened, if we believe it happened, a long time ago, because the Gray Man has been seen ever since 1822, or perhaps even earlier than that. A Mrs. Eileen Weaver, according to Mr. Gatewood's account, saw the specter on her veranda and it was indeed a dim outline of a man in gray. There had been unexplained footsteps on her veranda and doors opening and closing by themselves, untouched by human hands.

A businessman by the name of William Collins who did not believe in ghosts, not even in South Carolina ghosts, found himself on the lookout to check on the rising surf on the morning of famed Hurricane Hazel. As he was walking down the dunes he noticed the figure of a man standing on the beach looking seaward. Collins challenged him, thinking that perhaps he was a neighbor who had come out to check on the rising tide, but the stranger paid no attention. Busy with his task, Collins forgot about this and by the time he looked up the stranger had gone. According to the weather forecast, however, the hurricane had shifted directions and was not likely to hit the area, so Collins and his family went to bed that night, sure that the worst was over. At five o'clock in the morning he was aroused from bed by heavy pounding on his door. Opening it, he could feel the house shake from the wind rising to tremendous force. On his veranda stood a stranger wearing a gray fishing cap and a common work shirt and pants, all of it in gray. He told Collins to get off the beach since the storm was coming in. Collins thanked him and ran upstairs to wake his family. After the excitement of the storm had passed Collins wondered about the man who had warned him to get off the island. Intelligently he investigated the matter, only to find that no one had seen the man, nor had any of his neighbors had a guest fitting his description. The state highway patrolman on duty also had not seen anyone come or go, and there is only one access road, the causeway over the marshes.

The Gray Man of Pawley's Island

* * *

Mrs. G. lives in the state of Kansas. She is a respectable real estate operator who has been in business for many years. She and her husband share a lovely, upper-middle class home in one of the finer residential areas.

The occult was the furthest thing from her mind when someone laughingly suggested they try their hands at a ouija board rather than continue playing bridge as was their custom on slow afternoons. As so many others, Mrs. G. not for a moment took the ouija board seriously nor did she think that anything could come of it she couldn't handle. To her surprise there was an immediate response. The indicator moved under her hands, and this surprised Mrs. G. very much since she knew very well that she was not doing the moving.

Before long the disconnected letters made sense and spelled out words. Imagine her surprise and subsequent horror when Mrs. G. discovered that she was receiving a message from a man she had once known and who was now dead! Her former suitor had dropped dead of a heart attack some years before, but they had been estranged ever since she had refused his offer of marriage. Mrs. G. was quite happy in her present marriage and had given William, the man she once knew well, no further thought for years. All of a sudden there he was communicating with her through a piece of wood. At first she tried to laugh off the whole thing and explained the resurgence of her old suitor by some trick of the memory. Perhaps she had liked him better than she was consciously aware of and in some unknown fashion his name surfaced again while she was playing with this board. But the discarnate personality showed that it was indeed he, the man she had known some years before, who was sending her those messages, moving her hands against her wishes over the board. Before long she was made to write down his messages with a pencil. They were clear and concise. William wanted to make up for lost time. He didn't care that he had been dead and gone for several years. He had never stopped loving her, had hated her husband for marrying her, and was now quite prepared to take his rightful place with her, the way he saw it.

Mrs. G. protested, taking the entity seriously now, but the more she protested, the stronger he became. He was no longer satisfied to send her messages through the ouija board or automatic writing. A few days later she felt him in her bed. There was no mistaking it: William, in some unspeakably horrible way, was making love to her. She could sense the outlines of his body, even though she could not see it. There was definite weight and pressure against her body, as he lay upon her.

She cried out in horror and begged him to go away. She took her refuge in replying that hell would await William if he did not cease and desist, but it was of no avail. Eventually she found her way to me and a session with hypnosis. I reasoned with William. I asked him to leave the body of the unwilling Mrs. G. but this didn't do any good either. Shortly after her return to Kansas, the phenomena recommenced.

Almost every psychiatrist would say that since this case involved a woman in the change of life, such a phenomena could not be caused by possessing entities but by some form of sexually connected hysteria. It is always possible that cases of this kind are indeed due to internal biological changes in a woman's body and personality. But from the practical point of view, it is of little difference whether the possessing entity is an outsider or a split-off, alienated part of the individual's own personality. In either case, possession exists and must be dealt with.

In the case of Mrs. G., much depended upon her own attitude. I became convinced that the possessing entity was not entirely unwelcome. The evil fascination of this dead man, who had been her suitor and whom she had rejected, somehow had triggered within her a sense of reverse frustration which allowed her to reject his physical advances from the beyond while at the same time wallowing in the very evil force they represented.

I advised Mrs. G. to leave ouija boards and other occult gadgets alone in the future and to find emotional outlets in other quarters. Presumably, she had done so, or perhaps she has come to terms with William. At any rate, I have heard nothing further from her.

There are many cases where the possessor could not be part of the person's own personality. The evil one possessing the flesh-and-blood person can be identified as a real person who once lived, but of whom the victim knows nothing or had no connection with. I do not think it likely that a rational, well-adjusted individual could invent a relationship with a person who once lived but is now dead, and of whom the victim has no knowledge beforehand. If anything, an individual might invent a nonexistent personality and mask it as a possessor. But when we have proof that the personality existed as a human being, we must look to true possession as the only answer.

David G. is a prominent broadcaster and writer in a major city. His career had been going well for years, but lately there had been difficulties with management, and in the end he had resigned his position. For several months prior to the events I'm about to describe, Mr. G. had been in a highly nervous condition, depressed, and generally not quite himself.

He and his wife and children lived in a modernized townhouse in the heart of the city. They had spent considerable time and effort to create from an ordinary brownstone house a jewel of a modern residence three stories high, filled with fine furniture and the technical apparatus Mr. G. required for his broadcasting activities. It was a happy house, as houses went. They had been in it for some time without noticing anything unusual.

323

Then they noticed that the atmosphere seemed strangely charged. Little things began to bother them. Doors would not stay shut. Footsteps would reverberate when no one was walking. The G.'s had no interest or belief in the supernatural, but one day Mr. G. himself saw a hairbrush fly of its own volition off its shelf in the bathroom and hit the wall so hard that the brush broke in two.

He had built himself a tool shop down in the cellar. Tools would disappear from one corner and reappear in another spot where they did not belong. As he turned around in puzzlement, he found the tool gone from its incorrect location, only to see it back where it should have been in the first place, a moment later. It was as if someone were trying to play games with him. At night, lights would turn themselves on. In several instances the G.'s saw the switch being turned by unseen fingers. The footsteps indicated some sort of presence in the house.

At first they thought it was a young person, but they couldn't be sure. Mr. G. hastily consulted books on parapsychology and realized that the presence of his son Michael, age thirteen, might furnish the energies in some as yet little understood way. This knowledge calmed him considerably, since there was now a seemingly natural explanation for the phenomena. He, of course, did not tell Michael anything about this. A few days later, towards four o'clock in the morning, Mr. G. could not sleep so he decided to do some work in his tool shop downstairs. As he approached the shop, unseen hands flung the door open for him. In the subsequent weeks this happened at least twenty times. On one occasion a taxi driver who had come to fetch him for an early-morning broadcast also witnessed the amazing performance.

Mr. G. had bought the house in 1958 from a local man initialed L. But L. only owned the house for a few short years. The man who would know more about it than anyone else was the late Dr. D., who was born in it and had lived there for fifty years. The house itself was considerably older, though no one knew exactly when it had been built. Since G. had remodeled it completely, using only the original walls, it would be hard to determine its age merely from appearances. As the phenomena continued to plague the G.'s, Mr. G. thought several times of consulting someone like myself to get rid of the problem but his busy career and other problems did not allow him to follow through. Then one fine day the need to do something about the phenomena was graphically brought into focus again. One afternoon in 1961, Mr. G.'s wife was found dead. The verdict was suicide, but Mr. G. could never accept this as final. There had been no quarrel, no disagreements whatever, and no unhappiness between them. Why would Mrs. G. have wanted to take her own life? The horrible tragedy made Mr. G.'s own condition even worse than it had been due to professional reverses of the past months.

For a few weeks the house fell strangely silent; then the phenomena began again, more urgently, more sinister than ever before. Mr. G. however was in no mood to cope with them now. His own nervous condition was such that he felt himself at the breaking point. It was precisely at this moment that he called me to help him. I took Ethel Johnson Meyers with me and in June of 1962, we visited Mr. G. in his townhouse. After she had looked the place over for a few minutes, Mrs. Meyers confirmed that there was "a presence" in the house. She had no idea where she was or who her famous host was. In trance, her own personality was replaced by someone filled with hatred, complaining bitterly that he had been deceived by his friends and by his wife. His best friend had taken his money and his wife, Helen. His name was Henry, he had been in Wall Street and he had been sold short. "I am Titus Andronicus, Titus the Fool," he said with a fine sense of satire, referring to Shakespeare's unfortunate hero. Somehow, in the strange way in which these things seem to work in the world beyond, the confused entity staying on in what was once his house mistook Mr. G.'s wife for the unfaithful wife who had left him with his best friend. In a moment of hatred he had caused her death.

The emotional impact of all this seemed almost too much for the medium. Shortly after, she broke from her trance and had to be calmed down for several minutes. As soon as she was fully herself again, she looked around the room as if she were only now conscious of her surroundings, and remarked—"Somebody fell to death here of a broken neck." Nobody said a word. Mr. G. was visibly upset by all this, but he thanked us for having come to make things a little easier for him. Twice more I returned to Mr. G.'s house with Mrs. Meyers. On those occasions the earlier material was confirmed and broadened but nothing essentially new was found. What was different, however, was the very personal contact Mrs. Meyers was able to make for Mr. G. with his late wife in the house she had loved so much.

Immediately after the first séance I went to work trying to research the house. I could only go back to 1879 for the house itself, but the building lot had been in use continuously since 1760, according to the records in the Hall of Records, Conveyances and Deeds. I then discovered that there had been a protracted will fight between the heirs of one particular owner, and that for years two branches of the family, the Joneses and the Masons, had been pitted one against the other. Bitterness had marked this period during which petition after petition was filed with the supreme court. Finally, the court handed down a partition rule in July, 1855. The man who received the lot on which Mr. G.'s house stood *had the first name of Henry.*

Several months passed, and the house seemed quieter. Then I received another call from Mr. G. Even though the entity had had a chance to express himself and was aware of having taken the wrong life, apparently he was not fully satisfied. What did Henry want of him now? Mr. G. wondered. I realized that the continued presence of young people in the house and of the highly nervous Mr. G. himself might be supplying the energies on which the disturbed mind of the discarnate Henry M. feasted. Under the circumstances I advised Mr. G. to sell the house as soon as he could. This was done, and Mr. G. moved to another neighborhood. He has had no problems, either personal or professional, ever since.

17

The House
on Plant Avenue

Plant Avenue is a charming suburban boulevard running through one of the better sectors of Webster Groves, Missouri, in itself a better-than-average small town, near St. Louis. Plant Avenue is not known for anything in particular except perhaps that it does have some plants, mainly very old trees that give it a coolness other streets lack, even in the heat of summer when this part of the country can be mighty unpleasant.

Webster Groves wasn't much of a landmark either until *Life* magazine published an article on its high school activities, and then it had a short-lived flurry of excitement as the "typical" American upper-middle-class town with all its vices and virtues. But now the town has settled back to being just one of many such towns and the people along Plant Avenue sigh with relief that the notoriety has ebbed. They are not the kind that enjoy being in the headlines and the less one pays attention to them, the happier they are.

In the three hundred block of Plant Avenue there are mainly large bungalow type houses standing in wide plots and surrounded by shrubbery and trees. One of these houses is a two-story wood and brick structure of uncertain style, but definitely distinguished looking in its own peculiar way. The roof suggests old English influences and the wide windows downstairs are perhaps southern, but the overall impression is that of a home built by an individualist who wanted it his way and only his way. It does not look like any other house on the block, yet fits in perfectly and harmoniously. The house is somewhat set back and there is a garden around it, giving it privacy. From the street one walks up a front law, then up a few stairs and into the house. The downstairs contains a large living room, a day room and a kitchen with a rear exit directly into the garden. From the living room, there is a winding staircase to the upper floor where the bedrooms are located.

The house was built in the final years of the last century by a man of strange character. The neighborhood knew little enough about this Mr. Gehm. His business was the circus and he seems to have dealt with various circus performers and represented them in some way. He was not a good mixer and kept mainly to himself and ultimately died in the house he had built for himself.

This much was known around the neighborhood, but to tell the truth, people don't much care what you do so long as you don't bother them, and the real estate agent who took on the house after Mr. Gehm passed away was more concerned with its wiring and condition than Mr. Gehm's unusual occupation. As the house had a certain nobility about it, perhaps due to the German background of its builder, it seemed a good bet for resale and so it turned out to be.

In 1956 the house passed into the hands of Mr. and Mrs. S. L. Furry, who had been married twenty years at the time, and had two young daughters, now long married also.

Mrs. Furry's ancestry was mainly English and she worked for the Washington University Medical school in St. Louis, having been a major in psychology in college.

Thus she found herself more than shaken when she dis-

The House on Plane Avenue

covered some peculiarities about the house they had moved into—
such as being awakened, night after night at precisely two A.M.
with a feeling of having been shaken awake. On one occasion,
she clearly heard a heavy hammer hit the headboard of her bed,
turned on the lights only to discover everything intact where she
was sure she would find splinters and a heavy indentation. Soon
this was amplified by the sound of something beating against the
windows at night. "It sounds just like a heavy bird," Mrs. Furry
thought, and shuddered. There was nothing visible that could
have caused the sounds.

One morning she discovered one of the heavy wall
sconces, downstairs, on the floor. Yet it had been securely fastened
to the wall the night before. On examination she discovered no
logical reason for how the piece could have fallen.

By now she realized that the footsteps she kept hearing
weren't simply caused by overwrought nerves due to fatigue or simply
her imagination. The footsteps went up and down the stairs, day and
night, as if someone were scurrying about looking for something and
not finding it. They always ended on the upstairs landing.

At first, she did not wish to discuss these matters with her
husband because she knew him to be a practical man who would
simply not believe her. And a woman is always vulnerable when
it comes to reporting the psychic. But eventually he noticed her
concern and the problem was brought out into the open. He readily remarked he had heard nothing to disturb his sleep and advised
his wife to forget it.

But shortly after, he sheepishly admitted at the breakfast
table that he, too, had heard some odd noises. "Of course, there
must be a logical explanation," he added quickly. "It is very likely
only the contraction and expansion of the old house. Lots of old
houses do that." He seemed satisfied with this explanation, but
Mrs. Furry was not. She still heard those scurrying footfalls and
they did not sound to her like a house contracting.

Eventually, Mr. Furry did not insist on his explanation, but had no better one to offer and decided to shrug the whole thing off. One night he was awakened in the bedroom adjoining his wife's boudoir because of something *strange*: he then noticed a filmy, white shape go *through the door* into the hall and proceed into their little girl's room. He jumped out of bed and looked into the room, but could see nothing. "Must have been the reflection of car lights from the street," he concluded. But it never happened again, and cars kept passing the house at all hours.

The years went on and the Furry's got somewhat used to their strange house. They had put so much money and work into it, not to say love, that they were reluctant to let a ghost dislodge them. But they did become alarmed when their three-year-old child kept asking at breakfast, "Who is the lady dressed in black who comes into my room at night?" As no lady in black had been to the house at any time, this of course upset the parents.

"What lady?" Mrs. Furry demanded to know.

"The lady," the three-year-old insisted. "She's got a little boy by the hand."

Some time later, the child complained about the lady in black again. "she spanks me with a broom, but it doesn't hurt," she said. Mrs. Furry did not know what to do. Clearly there was something in the house the real estate people had failed to tell her about. After nine years, they found a better house—one more suitable to their needs—and moved. Again, the house on Plant Avenue was for sale. It wasn't long until a new tenant for the handsome house appeared.

In the middle of November 1965, the Walshes rented the house and moved in with two of their three children, ten-year-old Wendy and twenty-year-old Sandy. They had of course not been told anything about the experiences of the previous owners and they found the house pleasant and quiet, at least at first.

The House on Plane Avenue

A short time after moving in, Mrs. Walsh was preparing dinner in the kitchen. She was alone except for her dog. The time was six-thirty. Suddenly, she noticed the dog cringe with abject fear. This puzzled her and she wondered what the cause was. Looking up, she noticed a white cloud, roughly the shape and height of a human being, float in through the open door leading into the living room. The whole thing only lasted a moment but she had never seen anything like it.

"A ghost!" she thought immediately, for that was exactly what it looked like. Clare Walsh is not a simple-minded believer in the supernatural. She has a master's degree in biochemistry and did research professionally for five years. But what she saw was, indeed a ghost! She wasn't frightened. In fact, she felt rather good, for her sneaking suspicions had been confirmed. On the day she first set foot into the house, when they had not yet taken it, she had had a deep feeling that there was a presence there. She dismissed it as being a romantic notion at the time, but evidently her intuition had been correct. With a sigh Mrs. Walsh accepted her psychic talents. This wasn't the first time that they had shown themselves.

At the time her husband's ship was torpedoed, she dreamed the whole incident in detail. When she was a child, her aunt died, and she saw her aunt's apparition before anyone in the family knew she had passed on. Since then she had developed a good deal of telepathy, especially with her daughters.

She dismissed the apparition she had seen in the kitchen, especially since nothing similar followed. But the nights seemed strangely active. At night, the house came to life. Noises of human activity seemed to fill the halls and rooms and in the darkness Mrs. Wash felt unseen presences roaming about her house at will. It wasn't a pleasant feeling but she decided to brave it out and wait for some kind of opening wedge, whereby she could find out more about the background of her house. In February of 1966, her neighbors next door invited them to dinner.

Over dinner, the question of the house came up and casually Mrs. Walsh was asked how quiet the house was. With that, she confessed her concern and reported what she had seen and heard. The neighbors—a couple named Kurus—nodded to each other with silent understanding.

"There seems to be a pattern to these noises," Mrs. Walsh said, "it's always at 4 A.M. and upstairs."

The Kurus had almost bought the house themselves but were dissuaded from it by the experiences of another neighbor who lived across the street. The man had been a frequent houseguest at the house and while there, had encountered ghostly phenomena sufficient to convince him that the house was indeed haunted. The Kurus then bought the house next door instead. When Mrs. Walsh obtained the name of the man across the street, she called him and asked what he knew about their house.

"The original owner has hidden some valuables in a number of places, niches, all over the house." the gentleman explained, "and now he's looking for his treasures."

One of those secret hiding places apparently was the fireplace downstairs. Upon putting down the receiver, Mrs. Walsh started to examine the fireplace. There was a strange hollow sound in one spot, but unless she took tools to pry it open, there was no way of telling what, if anything, was hidden there.

The vague promise of hidden treasure was not sufficient to outweigh the pride of ownership in a handsome fireplace, so she did not proceed to cut open the fireplace, but instead went to bed.

About midnight she was awakened by a peculiar, musty odor in the room. She got up and walked about the room, but the musty odor lingered on. It reminded her of the smell of death.

The next morning she told her husband about it.

"Ridiculous," he laughed, but the following morning the same odor invaded his bedroom and he, too, smelled it. Since Mr. Walsh works for a large chemical concern odors are his business, in a manner of speaking. But he could not classify the peculiar odor he was confronted with in his own house.

After that, not much happened beyond the 4 A.M. noises that kept recurring with punctuality—almost of Germanic character.

But Mrs. Walsh noticed that the door to the attic was always open. The stairs leading up to the attic from the second story have a stair whose tread lifts. Underneath the stairs she discovered a hollow space! So the tales of hidden treasure might have some basis of fact after all, she mused. The secret space was once completely closed, but the catch had long disappeared.

On one occasion, when Mr. Walsh was down with the flu, he used an adjoining bedroom. While Mrs. Walsh was resting she heard the attic door open and close again four times, and thought it was her husband going to the bath room. But he had only been up once that night. The other three times, it was another person, one they could not see.

As time went on, Mrs. Walsh kept notes of all occurrences, more as a sport than from fear. Both she and her husband, and soon the children, kept hearing the footsteps going up to the attic, pausing at the now empty hiding place. Each following morning the attic door, securely closed the night before, was found wide open. It got to be such a routine they stopped looking for *real* people as the possible culprits. They knew by now they wouldn't find anyone.

One morning she went up to the attic and closed the door again, then continued with her breakfast work in the kitchen. Suddenly she had the strange urge to return to the attic once more. Almost as if led by a force outside of herself, she dropped the bread knife and went up the stairs. The door was open again, and she stepped through it into a small room they had never used for anything but storage. It was chock-full of furniture, all of it securely fastened and closed.

To her amazement, when she entered the little room, things were in disorder. The heavy chest of drawers at one side had a drawer opened wide. She stepped up to it and saw it was filled with blueprints. She picked one of them up, again as if led by someone, and at the bottom of the blueprint saw the name "Henry Gehm."

She had been looking in the attic for a supposedly hidden doorway and had never been able to locate it. Was it after all just gossip and was there no hidden door?

At this moment, she had held the blueprints of the house in her hands, she received the distinct impression she should look in a certain spot in the attic. As she did, she noticed that the furniture against that wall had recently been moved. No one of flesh and blood had been up there for years, of course, and this discovery did not contribute to her sense of comfort. But as she looked closer she saw there was now a door where before a large piece of furniture had blocked the view!

Who had moved the furniture?

She felt a chill run down her back as she stood there. It wasn't the only time she had felt cold. Many times a cold blast of air, seemingly out of nowhere, had enveloped her in the bedroom or in the kitchen. As she thought of it now, she wondered why she had not investigated the source of that air but taken it for granted. Perhaps she did not want to know the results.

The events in the attic occurred on March 1, 1966. The following day, she was awakened quite early by incessant footsteps in the hallway. Someone was walking up and down, someone she could not see.

She got up. At that moment, she was distinctly impressed with the *command* to take out an old music box that had belonged to her mother. The box had not played for years and was in fact out of order. She opened the box and it started to play. It has remained in working order ever since. Who had fixed it and was this a reward for having looked at the blueprints for "someone"?

On March 5, she was roused from deep sleep once more at the "witching hour" of 4 A.M., but the house was quiet, strangely so, and she wondered why she had been awakened. But she decided to have a look downstairs. In the dining room, the breakfront which she had left closed the night before, stood wide open. The teaspoons in one of the drawers had been rearranged by unseen hands! A plant had a shoot broken off and the twig lay on the table nearby. Since the dog had not been in the room, there was no one who could have done this.

The next day, her sleep was interrupted again at 4 o'clock. This time the drawer containing her underclothes was all shaken up. Suddenly it dawned on her that her ten-year-old daughter might have spoken the truth when she reported "someone" in her mother's bedroom opening and closing the dresser when Mrs. Walsh knew for sure she had not been in the room.

She realized now what it was. The bedroom she occupied had been Henry Gehm's room. If he had hidden anything in it, he might be mistaking her dresser for his own furniture and still keep looking.

On March 8 Mrs. Walsh was in the basement, and her ten-year-old girl, Wendy, was in the garden playing. The house was quite empty.

Suddenly, she heard the sound of a child running at a mad pace through the dining room and kitchen. It must be Sandy, she thought, and called out to her. She received no reply. She went upstairs to investigate and found the house empty and quiet. Yet the footsteps had been those of a child, not the same footfalls she had so often heard on the stairs and in the attic. So there were two of them now, she thought, with a shudder.

It was then also that she recalled the baby hair she had found under the couch shortly after they had first moved in. At the time she had dismissed it as unimportant, even though no one with *blond* hair lived in the house. The hair was very fine, clearly blond and seemed like the hair of a very young child.

"Like angel's hair," she thought and wondered.

Five days later all but Mr. Walsh were out of the house, in church. He was still in bed, but after the family had left for church he came downstairs, and fixed himself breakfast in the kitchen. At that moment, he thought he heard Wendy running upstairs.

He assumed the child was not well and had been left behind, after all. Worried, he went upstairs to see what was the matter. No child. He shook his head and returned to his breakfast, less sure that the house didn't have "something strange" in it.

Upon the return of the others, they discussed it and came to the conclusion that the house was haunted by at least two, possibly three, people. It was a large enough house, but to share one's home with people one could not see was not the most practical way to live.

A few days later Mrs. Walsh was again in the basement, doing the laundry. A sweater hanging from the rafters on the opposite side of the basement suddenly jumped down from the rafters, hanger and all, and landed in front of her. The windows were firmly closed and there was no breeze. What amazed Mrs. Walsh even more was the way the sweater came down. Not straight as if pulled by gravity, but in an ark, as if held by unseen hands.

"Mrs. Gehm," she heard herself exclaiming. "What did you do that for?"

There she was talking to a ghost.

What is your first name, anyway? she heard herself think.

Instantly, a counterthought flashed into her mind. My name is Mary.

On March 16, she woke again early in the morning with the sure sensation of not being alone. Although she could not see anyone, she knew there was someone upstairs again. However she decided to stay in bed this time. First thing in the morning, as soon as it was *light*, she ventured up the stairs to the attic. In the little room the furniture had been completely reshuffled! She then recalled having heard a dull thud during the night.

A trunk had been moved to the center of the room and opened; a doll house had been placed from one shelf to a much lower shelf, and a tool box she had never seen before had suddenly appeared in the room. There were fresh markings in the old dust of the room. They looked like a child's scrawl. . . .

Mrs. Walsh looked at the scrawl. It looked as if someone had made a crude attempt to write a name in the dust. She tried to decipher it, but could not. The next day she returned to the room. No one had been there. The children were by now much too scared to go up there.

The scribbled signature was still there, and not far from it, someone had made a handprint in the dust. *A small child's hand!*

As Mrs. Walsh stared at the print of the child's hand, it came back to her how she had the month before heard a child's voice crying somewhere in the house. None of her children had been the cause of the crying, she knew, and yet the crying persisted. Then on another occasion, a humming sound such as children like to make, had come to her attention, but she could determine no visible source for it.

Two days later, still bewildered by all this, she found herself again alone in the house. It was afternoon, and she clearly heard the muffled sound of several voices talking. She ran up the stairs to the attic—for it seemed to her that most of the phenomena originated here—and sure enough the door to the attic, which she had shut earlier, was wide open again.

Early the next morning Mrs. Walsh heard someone calling a child up in the attic. Who was up there? Not any of the Walshes, she made sure. Slowly it dawned upon her that a family from the past was evidently unaware of the passage of time and that the house was no longer theirs. But how to tell them?

A busy family it was, too. At 5 A.M. one morning a type-writer was being worked. The only typewriter in the house stood in Wendy's room. Had she used it? She hadn't, but that morning she found her typewriter *had* been used by someone. The cover had been put back differently from the way she always did it. A doll she had left next to the machine the night before, was now on top of it.

That night, while the family was having dinner in the kitchen, the lights in the living were turned on by unseen forces. Pieces of brightly wrapped candy disappeared from a tray and were never seen again.

The dog, too, began to change under the relentless turn of events. She would refuse to sleep in the basement or go near certain spots where most of the psychic phenomena had occurred. The seven-year-old dog, once the very model of a quiet suburban canine, soon turned into a neurotic, fear-ridden shadow of her former self.

It got to be a little too much for the Walshes.

The treasure Mr. Gehm was hunting had no doubt long ago been found and taken away by some earlier tenant or stranger. As for the house itself, the ghosts could have it, if they wanted it that much. The Walshes decided to build a new home of their own, from scratch. No more old homes for them. That way, they would not inherit the ghosts of previous owners.

They notified the owner of their intent to move and as soon as the new home was ready, they moved out.

Even on the last day, the sounds of footsteps scurrying up the stairs could be heard.

Plant Avenue gossips can add another chapter to the lore of the Gehm house, but the sad little girl up in the attic won't have any playmates now. Even if they couldn't see her, the children knew she was *there*.

And that's all a ghost can hope for, really.

340

18

The Whaley House
Ghosts

I first heard about the ghosts at San Diego's Whaley House through an article in *Cosmic Star*, Merle Gould's psychic newspaper, back in 1963. The account was not too specific about the people who had experienced something unusual at the house, but it did mention mysterious footsteps, cold drafts, unseen presences staring over one's shoulder and the scent of perfume where no such odor could logically be—the gamut of uncanny phenomena, in short. My appetite was whetted. Evidently the curators, Mr. and Mrs. James Redding, were making some alterations in the building when the haunting began.

I marked the case as a possibility when in the area, and turned to other matters. Then fate took a hand in bringing me closer to San Diego.

I had appeared on Regis Philbin's network television show and a close friendship had developed between us. When Regis moved to San Diego and started his own program there, he asked me to be his guest.

We had already talked of a house he knew in San Diego that he wanted me to investigate with him; it turned out to be the same Whaley House. Finally we agreed on June 25th as the night we would go to the haunted house and film a trance session with Sybil Leek, then talk about it the following day on Regis' show.

Sybil Leek came over from England a few years ago, after a successful career as a producer and writer of television documentaries and author of a number of books on animal life and antiques. At one time she ran an antique shop in her beloved New Forest area of southern England, but her name came to the attention of Americans primarily because of her religious convictions: she happened to be a witch. Not a Hallowe'en type witch, to be sure, but a follower of "the Old Religion," the pre-Christian Druidic cult which is still being practiced in many parts of the world. Her personal involvement with witchcraft was of less interest to me than her great abilities as a trance medium. I tested her and found her capable of total"dissociation of personality," which is the necessary requirement for good trance work. She can get "out of her own body" under my prodding, and lend it to whatever personality might be present in the atmosphere of our quest. Afterwards, she will remember nothing and merely continue pleasantly where we left off in conversation prior to trance—even if it is two hours later! Sybil Leek lends her ESP powers exclusively to my research and confines her "normal" activities to a career in writing and business.

We arrived in sunny San Diego ahead of Regis Philbin, and spent the day loafing at the Half Moon Inn, a romantic luxury motel on a peninsula stretching out into San Diego harbor. Regis could not have picked a better place for us—it was almost like being in Hawaii. We dined with Kay Sterner, president and chief sensitive of the local California Parapsychology Foundation, a charming and knowledgeable woman who had been to the haunted Whaley House, but of course she did not talk about it in Sybil's presence. In deference to my policy, she waited until Sybil left us. Then she told me of her forays into Whaley House, where she had felt several presences. I thanked her and decided to do my own investigating from scratch.

My first step was to contact June Reading, who was not only the director of the house but also its historian. She asked me to treat confidentially whatever I might find in the house through psychic means. This I could not promise, but I offered to treat the material with respect and without undue sensationalism, and I trust I have not disappointed Mrs. Reading too much. My readers are entitled to all the facts as I find them.

Mrs. Reading herself is the author of a booklet about the historic house, and a brief summary of its development also appears in a brochure given to visitors, who keep coming all week long from every part of the country. I quote from the brochure.

"The Whaley House, in the heart of Old Town, San Diego—restored, refurnished and opened for public viewing—represents one of the finest examples extant of early California buildings.

"Original construction of the two-story mansion was begun on May 6, 1856, by Thomas Whaley, San Diego pioneer. The building was completed on May 10, 1857. Bricks used in the structure came from a clay-bed and kiln—the first brick-yard in San Diego—which Thomas Whaley established 300 yards to the southwest of his projected home.

"Much of 'old San Diego's' social life centered around this impressive home. Later the house was used as a theater for a traveling company, 'The Tanner Troupe,' and at one time served as the San Diego County Court House.

"The Whaley House was erected on what is now the corner of San Diego Avenue and Harney Street, on a 150-by-217-foot lot, which was part of an 8½-acre parcel purchased by Whaley on September 25, 1855. The North room originally was a granary without flooring, but was remodeled when it became the County Court House on August 12, 1869.

"Downstairs rooms include a tastefully furnished parlor, a music room, a library and the annex, which served as the County Court House. There are four bedrooms upstairs, two of which were leased to "The Tanner Troupe' for theatricals.

"Perhaps the most significant historical event involving the Whaley House was the surreptitious transfer of the county court records from it to 'New Town,' present site of downtown San Diego, on the night of March 31, 1871.

"Despite threats to forcibly prevent even legal transfer of the court house to 'New Town,' Col. Chalmers Scott, then county clerk and recorder, and his henchmen removed the county records under cover of darkness and transported them to a 'New Town' building at 6th and G Streets.

"The Whaley House would be gone today but for a group of San Diegans who prevented its demolition in 1956 by forming the Historical Shrine Foundation of San Diego County and buying the land and the building.

"Later, the group convinced the County of San Diego that the house should be preserved as an historical museum, and restored to its early-day splendor. This was done under the supervision and guidance of an advisory committee including members of the Foundation, which today maintains the Whaley House as an historical museum.

"Most of the furnishings, authenticated as in use in Whaley's time, are from other early-day San Diego County homes and were donated by interested citizens.

"The last Whaley to live in the house was Corinne Lillian Whaley, youngest of Whaley's six children. She died at the age of 89 in 1953. Whaley himself died December 14, 1890, at the age of 67. He is buried in San Diego in Mount Hope Cemetery, as is his wife, Anna, who lived until February 24, 1913."

When it became apparent that a thorough investigation of the haunting would be made, and that all of San Diego would be able to learn of it through television and newspapers, excitement mounted to a high pitch.

Mrs. Reading kept in close touch with Regis Philbin and me, because ghosts have a way of "sensing" an impending attempt to oust them—and this was not long in coming. On May 24th the "activities" inside the house had already increased to a marked degree; they were of the same general nature as previously noticed sounds.

Was the ghost getting restless?

I had asked Mrs. Reading to prepare an exact account of all occurrences within the house, from the very first moment on, and to assemble as many of the witnesses as possible for further interrogation.

Most of these people had worked part time as guides in the house during the five years since its restoration. The phenomena thus far had occurred, or at any rate been observed, mainly between 10 a.m. and 5:30 p.m., when the house closes to visitors. There is no one there at night, but an effective burglar alarm system is in operation to prevent flesh-and-blood intruders from breaking in unnoticed. Ineffective with the ghostly kind, as we were soon to learn!

I shall now quote the director's own report. It vouches for the accuracy and calibre of witnesses.

PHENOMENA OBSERVED AT WHALEY HOUSE
By Visitors

Oct. 9, 1960—Dr. & Mrs. Kirbey, of New Westminster, B.C., Canada. 1:30–2:30 P.M. (He was then Director of the Medical Association of New Westminster.)

While Dr. Kirbey and his wife were in the house, he became interested in an exhibit in one of the display cases and she asked if she might go through by herself, because she was familiar with the Victorian era, and felt very much at home in these surroundings. Accordingly, I remained downstairs with the Doctor, discussing early physicians and medical practices.

When Mrs. Kirbey returned to the display room, she asked me in a hesitating fashion if I had ever noticed anything unusual about the upstairs. I asked her what she had noticed. She reported that when she started upstairs, she felt a breeze over her head, and though she saw nothing, felt a pressure against her, that seemed to make it hard for her to go up. When she looked into the rooms, she had the feeling that someone was standing behind her, in fact so close to her that she turned around several times to look. She said she expected someone would tap her on the shoulder. When she joined us downstairs, we all walked toward the courtroom. As we entered, again Mrs. Kirbey turned to me and asked if I knew that someone inhabited the court-room. She pointed to the bailiff's table, saying as she did, "Right over there." I asked her if the person was clear enough for her to describe, and she said:

"I see a small figure of a woman who has a swarthy complexion. She is wearing a long full skirt, reaching to the floor. The skirt appears to be of calico or gingham, small print. She has a kind of cap on her head, dark hair and eyes and she is wearing gold hoops in her pierced ears. She seems to stay in this room, lives here, I gather, and I get the impression we are sort of invading her privacy."

Mrs. Kirbey finished her description by asking me if any of the Whaley family were swarthy, to which I replied, "No."

This was, to my knowledge, the only description given to an apparition by a visitor, and Mrs. Kirbey the only person who brought up the fact in connection with the courtroom. Many of the visitors have commented upon the atmosphere in this room, however, and some people attempting to work in the room mentioned upon the difficulty they have in trying to con-centrate here.

The Whaley House Ghosts

By Persons Employed at Whaley House

April, 1960. 10:00 A.M. By myself, June A. Reading, 3447 Kite St. Sound of Footsteps—in the Upstairs.

This sound of someone walking across the floor, I first heard in the morning, a week before the museum opened to the public. County workmen were still painting some shelving in the hall, and during this week often arrived before I did, so it was not unusual to find them already at work when I arrived.

This morning, however, I was planning to furnish the downstairs rooms, and so hurried in and down the hall to open the back door awaiting the arrival of the trucks with the furnishings. Two men followed me down the hall; they were going to help with the furniture arrangement. As I reached up to unbolt the back door, I heard the sound of what seemed to be someone walking across the bedroom floor. I paid no attention, thinking it was one of the workmen. But the men, who heard the sounds at the time I did, insisted I go upstairs and find out who was in the house. So, calling out, I started to mount the stairs. Halfway up, I could see no lights, and that the outside shutters to the windows were still closed. I made some comment to the men who had followed me, and turned around to descend the stairs. One of the men joked with me about the spirits coming in to look things over, and we promptly forgot the matter.

However, the sound of walking continued. And for the next six months I found myself going upstairs to see if someone was actually upstairs. This would happen during the day, sometimes when visitors were in other parts of the house, other times when I was busy at my desk trying to catch up on correspondence or bookwork. At times it would sound as though someone were descending the stairs, but would fade away before reaching the first floor. In September, 1962, the house was the subject of a news article in the *San Diego Evening Tribune*, and this same story was reprinted in the September 1962 issue of *Fate* magazine.

347

Oct. & Nov. 1962 We began to have windows in the upper part of the house open unaccountably. We installed horizontal bolts on three windows in the front bedroom, thinking this would end the matter. However, the really disturbing part of this came when it set off our burglar alarm in the night, and we were called by the Police and San Diego Burglar Alarm Co. to come down and see if the house had been broken into. Usually, we would find nothing disturbed. (One exception to this was when the house was broken into by vandals, about 1963, and items from the kitchen display stolen.)

In the fall of 1962, early October, while engaged in giving a talk to some school children, class of 25 pupils, I heard a sound of someone walking, which seemed to come from the roof. One of the children interrupted me, asking what that noise was, and excusing myself from them, I went outside the building, down on the street to see if workmen from the County were repairing the roof. Satisfied that there was no one on the roof of the building, I went in and resumed the tour.

Residents of Old Town are familiar with this sound, and tell me that it has been evident for years. Miss Whaley, who lived in the house for 85 years, was aware of it. She passed away in 1953.

Mrs. Grace Bourquin, 2938 Beech St. Sat. Dec. 14, 1963, noon—Was seated in the hall downstairs having lunch, when she heard walking sound in upstairs.

Sat. Jan. 10, 1964, 1:30 P.M.—Walked down the hall and looked up the staircase. On the upper landing she saw an apparition—the figure of a man, clad in frock coat and pantaloons, the face turned away from her, so she could not make it out. Suddenly it faded away.

Lawrence Riveroll, resides on Jefferson St., Old Town. Jan. 5, 1963, 12:30 noon—Was alone in the house. No visitors present at the time. While seated at the desk in the front hall, heard sounds of music and singing, described as a woman's voice. Song "Home Again." Lasted about 30 seconds.

Jan. 7, 1963, 1:30 P.M.—Visitors in upstairs. Downstairs, he heard organ music, which seemed to come from the courtroom, where there is an organ. Walked into the room to see if someone was attempting to play it. Cover on organ was closed. He saw no one in the room.

Jan. 19, 1963, 5:15 P.M.—Museum was closed for the day. Engaged in closing shutters downstairs. Heard footsteps in upper part of house in the same area as described. Went up to check, saw nothing.

Sept. 10–12, 1964—at dusk, about 5:15 P.M.—Engaged in closing house, together with another worker. Finally went into the music room, began playing the piano. Suddenly felt a distinct pressure on his hands, as though someone had their hands on his. He turned to look toward the front hall, in the direction of the desk, hoping to get the attention of the person seated there, when he saw the apparition of a slight woman dressed in a hoop skirt. In the dim light was unable to see clearly the face. Suddenly the figure vanished.

J. Milton Keller, 4114 Middlesex Dr. Sept. 22, 1964, 2:00 P.M.—Engaged in tour with visitors at the parlor, when suddenly he, together with people assembled at balustrade, noticed crystal drops hanging from lamp on parlor table begin to swing back and forth. This occurred only on one side of the lamp. The other drops did not move. This continued about two minutes.

Dec. 15, 1964, 5:15 P.M.—Engaged in closing house along with others. Returned from securing restrooms, walked down hall, turned to me with the key, while I stepped into the hall closet to reach for the master switch which turns off all lights. I pulled the switch, started to turn around to step out, when he said, "Stop, don't move, you'll step on the dog!" He put his hands out, in a gesture for me to stay still. Meantime, I turned just in time to see what resembled a flash of light between us, and what appeared to be the back of a dog, scurry down the hall and turn into the dining room. I decided to resume a normal attitude, so I kidded him a little about trying to scare me. Other people were present in the front hall at the time, waiting for us at the door, so he turned to them and said in a rather hurt voice that I did not believe him. I realized then that he had witnessed an apparition, so I asked him to see if he could describe it. *He said he saw a spotted dog, like a fox terrier, that ran with his ears flapping, down the hall and into the dining room.*

May 29, 1965, 2:30 P.M. —Escorting visitors through house, upstairs. Called to me, asking me to come up. Upon going up, he, I and visitors all witnessed a black rocking chair, moving back and forth as if occupied by a person. It had started moving unaccountably, went on about three minutes. Caused quite a stir among visitors.

Dec. 27, 1964, 5:00 P.M. —Late afternoon, prior to closing, *saw the apparition of a woman dressed in a green plaid gingham dress.* She had long dark hair, coiled up in a bun at neck, was seated on a settee in bedroom.

Feb. 1965, 2:00 P.M. —Engaged in giving a tour with visitors, when two elderly ladies called and asked him to come upstairs, and step over to the door of the nursery. These ladies, visitors, called his attention to a sound that was like the cry of a baby, about 16 months old. All three reported the sound.

March 24, 1965, 1:00 P.M. —He, together with Mrs. Bourquin and his parents, Mr. and Mrs. Keller, engaged in touring the visitors, when for some reason his attention was directed to the foot of the staircase. He walked back to it, and heard the sound of someone in the upper part of the house whistling. No one was in the upstairs at the time.

The Whaley House Ghosts

Mrs. Suzanne Pere, 106 Albatross, El Cajon. April 8, 1963, 4:30 P.M. —Was engaged in typing in courtroom, working on manuscript. Suddenly she called to me, calling my attention to a noise in the upstairs. We both stopped work, walked up the stairs together, to see if anyone could possibly be there. As it was near closing time, we decided to secure the windows. Mrs. Pere kept noticing a chilly breeze at the back of her head, had the distinct feeling that someone, though invisible, was present and kept following her from one window to another.

Oct. 14, 21; Nov. 18, 1964— During the morning and afternoon on these days, called my attention to the smell of cigar smoke, and the fragrance of perfume or cologne. This occurred in the parlor, the upstairs hall and a bedroom. In another bedroom she called my attention to something resembling dusting powder.

Nov. 28, 196, 2:30 P.M. —Reported seeing an apparition in the study. A group of men there, dressed in frock coats, some with plain vests, others figured material. One of this group had a large gold watch chain across vest. Seemed to be a kind of meeting; all figures were animated, some pacing the floor, others conversing; all serious and agitated, but oblivious to everything else. One figure in this group seemed to be an official, and stood off by himself. This person was of medium stocky build, light brown hair, and mustache which was quite full and long. He had very piercing light blue eyes, penetrating gaze. Mrs. Pere sensed that he was some kind of official, a person of importance. He seemed about to speak. Mrs. Pere seemed quite exhausted by her experience witnessing this scene, yet was quite curious about the man with the penetrating gaze. I remember her asking me if I knew of anyone answering this description, because it remained with her for some time..

Oct. 7, 1963, 10:30 A.M. —Reported unaccountable sounds issuing from kitchen, as though someone were at work there. Same day, she reported smelling the odor of something baking.

Nov. 27, 1964, 10:15 A.M.—Heard a distinct noise from kitchen area, as though something had dropped to the floor. I was present when this occurred. She called to me and asked what I was doing there, thinking I had been rearranging exhibit. At this time I was at work in courtroom, laying out work. Both of us reached the kitchen, to find one of the utensils on the shelf rack had disengaged itself, fallen to the floor, and had struck a copper boiler directly below. No one else was in the house at the time, and we were at a loss to explain this.

Mrs. T.R. Allen, 3447 Kite Street—Was present Jan. 7, 1963, 1:30 P.M. Heard organ music issue from courtroom, when Lawrence Riveroll heard the same (see his statement).

Was present Sept. 10–12, 1964, at dusk, with Lawrence Riveroll, when he witnessed apparition. Mrs. Allen went upstairs to close shutters, and as she ascended them, described a chill breeze that seemed to come over her head. Upstairs, she walked into the bedroom and toward the windows. Suddenly she heard a sound behind her, as though something had dropped to the floor. She turned to look, saw nothing, but again experienced the feeling of having someone, invisible, hovering near her. She had a feeling of fear. Completed her task as quickly as possible, and left the upstairs hastily. Upon my return, both persons seemed anxious to leave the house.

May, 1965 (the last Friday), 1:30 P.M.—Was seated in the downstairs front hall, when she heard the sound of footsteps.

Regis Philbin himself had been to the house before. With him on that occasion was Mrs. Philbin, who is highly sensitive to psychic emanations, and a teacher-friend of theirs considered an amateur medium.

The Whaley House Ghosts

They observed, during their vigil, what appeared to be a white figure of a person, but when Regis challenged it, unfortunately with his flashlight, it disappeared immediately. Mrs. Philbin felt extremely uncomfortable on that occasion and had no desire to return to the house.

By now I knew that the house had three ghosts, a man, a woman and a baby—and a spotted dog. The scene observed in one of the rooms sounded more like a psychic impression of a past event to me than a bona fide ghost.

I later discovered that still another part-time guide at the house, William H. Richardson, of 470 Silvery Lane, El Cajon, had not only experienced something out of the ordinary at the house, but had taken part in a kind of séance with interesting results. Here is his statement, given to me in September of 1965, several months *after* our own trance session had taken place.

In the summer of 1963 I worked in Whaley House as a guide.

One morning before the house was open to the public, several of us employees were seated in the music room downstairs, and the sound of someone in heavy boots walking across the upstairs was heard by us all. When we went to investigate the noise, we found all the windows locked and shuttered, and the only door to the outside from upstairs was locked. This experience first sparked my interest in ghosts.

I asked June Reading, the director, to allow several of my friends from Starlight Opera, a local summer musical theatre, to spend the night in the house.

At midnight, on Friday, August 13, we met at the house. Carolyn Whyte, a member of the parapsychology group in San Diego and a member of the Starlight Chorus, gave an introductory talk on what to expect, and we all went into the parlor to wait for something to happen.

The first experience was that of a cool breeze blowing

through the room, which was felt by several of us despite the fact that all doors and windows were locked and shuttered.

The next thing that happened was that a light appeared over a boy's head. This traveled from his head across the wall, where it disappeared. Upon later investigation it was found to have disappeared at the portrait of Thomas Whaley, the original owner of the house. Footsteps were also heard several times in the room upstairs.

At this point we broke into groups and dispersed to different parts of the house. One group went into the study which is adjacent to the parlor, and there witnessed a shadow on the wall surrounded by a pale light which moved up and down the wall and changed shape as it did so. There was no source of light into the room and one could pass in front of the shadow without disturbing it.

Another group was upstairs when their attention was directed simultaneously to the chandelier which began to swing around as if someone were holding the bottom and twisting the sides. One boy was tapped on the leg several times by some unseen force while seated there.

Meanwhile, downstairs in the parlor, an old-fashioned lamp with prisms hanging on the edges began to act strangely. As we watched, several prisms began to swing by themselves. These would stop and others would start, but they never swung simultaneously. There was no breeze in the room.

At this time we all met in the courtroom. Carolyn then suggested that we try to lift the large table in the room.

We sat around the table and placed our fingertips on it. A short while later it began to creak and then slid across the floor approximately eight inches, and finally lifted completely off the floor on the corner where I was seated.

Later on we brought a small table from the music room into the courtroom and tried to get it to tip, which it did. With just our fingertips on it, it tilted until it was approximately one inch from the floor, then fell. We righted the table and put our

The Whaley House Ghosts

fingertips back on it, and almost immediately it began to rock. Since we knew the code for yes, no and doubtful, we began to converse with the table. Incidentally, while this was going on, a chain across the doorway in the courtroom was almost continually swinging back and forth and then up and down.

Through the system of knocking, we discovered that the ghost was that of a little girl, seven years old. She did not tell us her name, but she did tell us that she had red hair, freckles, and hazel eyes. She also related that there were four other ghosts in the house besides herself, including that of a baby boy. We conversed with her spirit for nearly an hour.

At one time the table stopped rocking and started moving across the floor of the courtroom, into the dining room, through the pantry, and into the kitchen. This led us to believe that the kitchen was her usual abode. The table then stopped and several antique kitchen utensils on the wall began to swing violently. Incidentally, the kitchen utensils sung for the rest of the evening at different intervals.

The table then retraced its path back to the courtroom and answered more questions.

At 5:00 a.m. we decided to call it a night—a most interesting night. When we arrived our group of 15 had had in it a couple of real believers, several who half believed, and quite a few who didn't believe at all. After the phenomena we had experienced, there was not one among us who was even very doubtful in the belief of some form of existence after life.

It was Friday evening, and time to meet the ghosts. Sybil Leek knew nothing whatever about the house, and when Regis Philbin picked us up the conversation remained polite and non-ghostly.

When we arrived at the house, word of mouth had preceded us despite the fact that our plans had not been announced publicly; certainly it had not been advertised that we would attempt a séance that evening. Nevertheless, a sizable crowd had assembled at the house and only Regis' polite insistence that their presence might harm whatever results we could obtain made them move on.

It was quite dark now, and I followed Sybil into the house, allowing her to get her clairvoyant bearings first, prior to the trance session we were to do with the cameras rolling. My wife Catherine trailed right behind me carrying the tape equipment. Mrs. Reading received us cordially. The witnesses had assembled but were temporarily out of reach, so that Sybil could not gather any sensory impressions from them. They patiently waited through our clairvoyant tour. All in all, about a dozen people awaited us. The house was lit throughout and the excitement in the atmosphere was bound to stir up any ghost present!

And so it was that on June 25, 1965, the Ghost Hunter came to close quarters with the specters at Whaley House, San Diego. While Sybil meandered about the house by herself, I quickly went over to the Court House part of the house and went over their experiences with the witnesses. Although I already had their statements, I wanted to make sure no detail had escaped me.

From June Reading I learned, for instance, that the Court house section of the building, erected around 1855, had originally served as a granary, later becoming a town hall and Court House in turn. It was the only two-story brick house in the entire area at the time.

Not only did Mrs. Reading hear what sounded to her like human voices, but on one occasion, when she was tape recording some music in this room, the tape also contained some human voices—sounds she had not herself heard while playing the music!

"When was the last time you yourself heard anything unusual?" I asked Mrs. Reading.

"As recently as a week ago," the pert curator replied, "during the day I heard the definite sound of someone opening the front door. Because we have had many visitors here recently, we are very much alerted to this. I happened to be in the Court Room with one of the people from the Historical Society engaged in research in the Whaley papers, and w both heard it. I went to check to see who had come in, and there was no one there, nor was there any sound of footsteps on the porch outside. The woman who works here also heard it and was just as puzzled about it as I was."

I discovered that the Mrs. Allen in the curator's report to me of uncanny experiences at the house was Lillian Allen, her own mother, a lively lady who remembered her brush with the uncanny only too vividly.

"I've heard the noises overhead," she recalled. "Someone in heavy boots seemed to be walking across, turning to come down the stairway—and when I first came out here they would tell me these things and I would not believe them—but I was sitting at the desk one night, downstairs, waiting for my daughter to lock up in the back. I heard this noise overhead and I was rushing to see if we were locking someone in the house, and as I got to almost the top, a big rush of wind blew over my head and made my hair stand up. I thought the windows had blown open but I looked all around and everything was secured."

"Just how did this wind feel?" I asked. Tales of cold winds are standard with traditional hauntings, but here we had a precise witness to testify.

"It was cold and I was chilly all over. And another thing, when I lock the shutters upstairs at night, I feel like someone is breathing down the back of my neck, like they're going to touch me—at the shoulder—that happened often. Why, only a month ago."

A Mrs. Frederick Bear now stepped forward. I could not find her name in Mrs. Reading's brief report. Evidently she was an additional witness to the uncanny goings-on at this house.

"One evening I came here—it was after five o'clock; another lady was here also—and June Reading was coming down the stairs, and we were talking. I distinctly heard something move upstairs, as if someone were moving a table. There was no one there—we checked. That only happened a month ago."

Grace Bourquin, another volunteer worker at the house, had been touched upon in Mrs. Reading's report. She emphasized that the sounds were those of a heavy man wearing boots—no mistake about it. When I questioned her about the apparition of a man she had seen, about six weeks ago, wearing a frock coat, she insisted that he had looked like a real person to her, standing at the top of the stairs one moment, and completely gone the next.

"He did not move. I saw him clearly, then turned my head for a second to call out to Mrs. Reading, and when I looked again, he had disappeared."

I had been fascinated by Mrs. Suzanne Pere's account of her experiences, which seemed to indicate a large degree of mediumship in her makeup. I questioned her about anything she had not yet told us. "On one occasion June Reading and I were in the back study and working with the table. We had our hands on the table to see if we could get any reaction."

"You mean you were trying to do some table-tipping."

"Yes. At this point I had only had some feelings in the house, and smelled some cologne. This was about a year ago, and we were working with some papers concerning the Indian uprising in San Diego, and all of a sudden the table started to rock violently! All of the pulses in my body became throbbing, and in my mind's eye the room was filled with men, all of them extremely excited, and though I could not hear any sound, I knew they were talking, and one gentleman was striding up and down the center of the room, puffing on his cigar, and from my description of him June Reading later identified him as Sheriff McCoy, who was here in the 1850's. When it was finished I could not talk for a few minutes. I was completely disturbed for a moment."

McCoy, I found, was the leader of one of the factions during the "battle" between Old Town and New Town San Diego for the county seat.

Evidently, Mrs. Bourquin had psychically relived that emotion-laden event which did indeed transpire in the very room she saw it in!

"Was the Court House ever used to execute anyone?" I interjected.

Mrs. Reading was not sure; the records were all there but the Historical Society had not gone over them as yet for lack of staff. The Court functioned in this house for two years, however, and sentences certainly were meted out in it. The prison itself was a bit farther up the street.

A lady in a red coat caught my attention. She identified herself as Bernice Kennedy.

"I'm a guide here Sundays," the lady began, "and one Sunday recently, I was alone in the house and sitting in the dining room reading, and I heard the front door open and close. There was no one there. I went back to continue my reading. Then I heard it the second time. Again I checked, and there was absolutely no one there. I heard it a third time and this time I took my book and sat outside at the desk. From then onward, people started to come in and I had no further unusual experience. But one other Sunday, there was a young woman upstairs who came down suddenly very pale, and she said the little rocking chair upstairs was rocking. I followed the visitor up and I could not see the chair move, but there was a clicking sound, very rhythmic, and I haven't heard it before or since."

The chair, it came out, once belonged to a family related to the Whaleys.

"I'm Charles Keller, father of Milton Keller," a booming voice said behind me, and an imposing gentleman in his middle years stepped forward.

"I once conducted a tour through the Whaley House. I

noticed a lady who had never been here act as if she were being pushed out of one of the bedrooms!"

"Did you see it?" I said, somewhat taken aback.

"Yes," Mr. Keller nodded, "I saw her move, as if someone were pushing her out of the room."

"Did you interrogate her about it?"

"Yes, I did. It was only in the first bedroom, where we started the tour, that it happened. Not in any of the other rooms. We went back to that room and again I saw her being pushed out of it!"

Mrs. Keller then spoke to me about the ice-cold draft she felt, and just before that, three knocks at the back door! Her son, whose testimony Mrs. Reading had already obtained for me, then went to the back door and found no one there who could have knocked. This had happened only six months before our visit.

I then turned to James Reading, the head of the Association responsible for the upkeep of the museum and house, and asked for his own encounters with the ghosts. Mr. Reading, in a cautious tone, explained that he did not really cotton to ghosts, but—

"The house was opened to the public in April 1960. In the fall of that year, October or November, the police called me at two o'clock in the morning, and asked me to please go down and shut off the burglar alarm, because they were being flooded with complaints, it was waking up everybody in the neighborhood. I came down and found two officers waiting for me. I shut off the alarm. They had meantime checked the house and every door and shutter was tight."

"How could the alarm have gone off by itself then?"

"I don't know. I unlocked the door, and we searched the entire house. When we finally got upstairs, we found one of the upstairs front bedroom windows open. We closed and bolted

360

the window, and came down and tested the alarm. It was in order again. No one could have gotten in or out. The shutters outside that window were closed and hooked on the inside. The opening of the window had set off the alarm, but it would have been impossible for anyone to open that window and get either into or out of the house. Impossible. This happened *four times.* The second time, about four months later, again at two in the morning, again that same window was standing open. The other two times it was always that same window."

"What did you finally do about it?"

"After the fourth incident we added a second bolt at right angles to the first one, and that seemed to help. There were no further calls."

Was the ghost getting tired of pushing *two* bolts out of the way?

I had been so fascinated with all this additional testimony that I had let my attention wander away from my favorite medium, Sybil Leek. But now I started to look for her and found to my amazement that she had seated herself in one of the old chairs in what used to be the kitchen, downstairs in back of the living room. When I entered the room she seemed deep in thought, although not in trance by any means, and yet it took me a while to make her realize where we were.

Had anything unusual transpired while I was in the Court Room interviewing?

"I was standing in the entrance hall, looking at the postcards," Sybil recollected, "when I felt I just had to go to the kitchen, but I didn't go there at first, but went halfway up the stairs, and a child came down the stairs and into the kitchen and I followed her."

"A child?" I asked. I was quite sure there were no children among our party.

"I thought it was Regis' little girl and the next thing I

361

recall I was in the rocking chair and you were saying something to me."

Needless to say, Regis Philbin's daughter had *not* been on the stairs. I asked for a detailed description of the child.

"It was a long-haired girl," Sybil said. "She was very quick, you know, in a longish dress. She went to the table in this room and I went to the chair. That's all I remember."

I decided to continue to question Sybil about any psychic impressions she might now gather in the house.

"There is a great deal of confusion in this house," she began. "Some of it is associated with another room upstairs, which has been structurally altered. There are two centers of activity."

Sybil, of course, could not have known that the house consisted of two separate units.

"Any ghosts in the house?"

"Several," Sybil assured me. "At least four!"

Had not William Richardson's group made contact with a little girl ghost who had claimed that she knew of four other ghosts in the house? The report of that séance did not reach me until September, several months after our visit, so Sybil could not possibly have "read our minds" about it, since our minds had no such knowledge at that time.

"This room where you found me sitting," Sybil continued, "I found myself drawn to it; the impressions are very strong here. Especially that child—she died young."

We went about the house now, seeking further contacts.

"I have a date now," Sybil suddenly said, "1872."

The Readings exchanged significant glances. It was just after the greatest bitterness of the struggle between Old Town and New Town, when the removal of the Court records from Whaley House by force occurred.

"There are two sides to the house," Sybil continued. "One side I like, but not the other."

The Whaley House Ghosts

Rather than have Sybil use up her energies in clairvoyance, I felt it best to try for a trance in the Court Room itself. This was arranged for quickly, with candles taking the place of electric lights except for what light was necessary for the motion picture cameras in the rear of the large room.

Regis Philbin and I sat at Sybil's sides as she slumped forward in a chair that may well have held a merciless judge in bygone years.

But the first communicator was neither the little girl nor the man in the frock coat. A feeble, plaintive voice was suddenly heard from Sybil's lips, quite unlike her own, a voice evidently parched with thirst.

"Bad . . . fever . . . everybody had the fever . . ."

"What year is this?"

"Forty-six."

I suggested that the fever had passed, and generally calmed the personality who did not respond to my request for identification.

"Send me . . . some water. . . ." Sybil was still in trance, but herself now. Immediately she complained about there being a lot of confusion.

"This isn't the room where we're needed . . . the child . . . she is the one. . . ."

What is her name?"

"Anna . . . Bell . . . she died very suddenly with something, when she was thirteen . . . chest. . . ."

"Are her parents here too?"

"They come . . . the lady comes."

"What is this house used for?"

"Trade . . . selling things, buying and selling."

"Is there anyone other than the child in this house?"

"Child is the main one, because she doesn't understand anything at all. But there is something more vicious. Child would not hurt anyone. There's someone else. A man. He knows some-thing about this house . . . about thirty-two, unusual name, C . . . Calstrop . . . five feet ten, wearing a green coat, darkish, mustache and side whiskers, he goes up to the bedroom on the left. He has business here. His business is with things that come from the sea. But it is the papers that worry him."

"What papers?" I demanded.

"The papers . . . 1872. About the house. Dividing the house was wrong. Two owners, he says."

"What is the house being used for, now, in 1872?"

"To live in. Two places . . . I get confused for I go one place and then I have to go to another."

"Did this man you see die here?"

"He died here. Unhappy because of the place . . . about the other place. Two buildings. Some people quarrelled about the spot. He is laughing. He wants all this house for himself."

"Does he know he is dead?" I asked the question that often brings forth much resistance to my quest for facts from those who cannot conceive of their status as "ghosts."

Sybil listened for a moment.

"He does as he wants in this house because he is going to live here," she finally said. "*It's his house.*"

"Why is he laughing?"

A laughing ghost, indeed!

"He laughs because of people coming here thinking it's *their* house! When he know the truth."

"What is his name?" I asked again.

"Cal . . . Caltrop . . . very difficult as he does not speak very clearly . . . he writes and writes . . . he makes a noise . . . he says he will make even more noise unless you go away."

"Let him," I said, cheerfully hoping I could tape-record the ghost's outbursts.

The Whaley House Ghosts

"Tell him he has passed over and the matter is no longer important," I told Sybil.

"He is upstairs."

I asked that he walk upstairs so we could all hear him. There was nobody upstairs at this moment—everybody was watching the proceedings in the Court Room downstairs.

We kept our breath, waiting for the manifestations, but our ghost wouldn't play the game. I continued with my questions.

"What does he want?"

"He is just walking around, he can do as he likes," Sybil said. "He does not like new things . . . he does not like any noise . . . except when he makes it. . . ."

"Who plays the organ in this house?"

"He says his mother plays."

"What is her name?"

"Ann Lassay . . . that's wrong, it's Lann—he speaks so badly . . . Lannay . . . his throat is bad or something. . . ."

I later was able to check on this unusual name. Anna Lannay was Thomas Whaley's wife!

At the moment, however, I was not aware of this fact and pressed on with my interrogation. How did the ghost die? How long ago?

"'89 . . . he does not want to speak; he only wants to roam around. . . ."

Actually, Whaley died in 1890. Had the long interval confused his sense of time? So many ghosts cannot recall exact dates but will remember circumstances and emotional experiences well.

"He worries about the house . . . he wants the whole house . . . for himself . . . he says he will leave them . . . papers . . . hide the papers . . . he wants the other papers about the house . . . they're four miles from here . . . several people have these papers and you'll have to get them back or he'll never settle . . . never . . . and if he doesn't get the whole house back, he will

365

be much worse . . . and then, the police will come . . . he will make the lights come and the noise . . . and the bell . . . make the police come and see him, the master . . . of the house, he hears bells upstairs . . . he doesn't know what it is . . . he goes upstairs and opens the windows, wooden windows . . . and looks out . . . and then he pulls the . . . no, it's not a bell . . . he'll do it again . . . when he wants someone to know that he really is the master of the house . . . people today come and say he is not, but he is!"

I was surprised. Sybil had no knowledge of the disturbances, the alarm bell, the footsteps, the open window . . . and yet it was all perfectly true. Surely, her communicator was our man!

"When did he do this the last time?" I inquired.

"This year . . . not long. . . ."

"Has he done anything else in this house?"

"He said he moved the lights. In the parlor."

Later I thought of the Richardson séance and the lights they had observed, but of course I had no idea of this when we were at the house ourselves.

"What about the front door?"

"If people come, he goes into the garden . . . walks around . . . because he meets mother there."

"What is in the kitchen?"

"Child goes to the kitchen. I have to leave him, and he doesn't want to be left . . . it was an injustice, anyway, don't like it . . . the child is twelve . . . chest trouble . . . something from the kitchen . . . bad affair. . . ."

"Anyone's fault?"

"Yes. Not chest . . . from the cupboard, took something . . . it was an acid like salt, and she ate it . . . she did not know . . . there is something strange about this child, someone had control of her, you see, she was in the way . . . family . . . one

The Whaley House Ghosts

girl . . . those boys were not too good . . . the other boys who came down . . . she is like two people . . . someone controlled her . . . made her do strange things and then . . . could she do that."

"Was she the daughter of the man?"

"Strange man, he doesn't care so much about the girl as he does about the house. He is disturbed."

"Is there a woman in this house?"

"Of course. There is a woman in the garden."

"Who is she?"

"Mother. Grandmother of the girl."

"Is he aware of the fact he has no physical body?"

"No."

"Doesn't he see all the people who come here?"

"They have to be fought off, sent away."

"Tell him it is now seventy years later."

"He says seventy years when the house was built."

"Another seventy years have gone by," I insisted.

"Only part of you is in the house."

"No, part of the house . . . you're making the mistake," he replied.

I tried hard to convince him of the real circumstances. Finally, I assured him that the entire house was, in effect, his.

Would this help?

"He is vicious," Sybil explains. "He will have his revenge on the house."

I explained that his enemies were all dead.

"He says it was an injustice, and the Court was wrong and you have to tell everyone this is his house and land and home."

I promised to do so and intoned the usual formula for the release of earthbound people who have passed over and don't realize it. Then I recalled Sybil to her own self, and within a few moments she was indeed in full control.

367

I then turned to the director of the museum, Mrs. Reading, and asked for her comments on the truth of the material just heard.

"There was a litigation," she said. "The injustice could perhaps refer to the County's occupancy of this portion of the house from 1869 to 1871. Whaley's contract, which we have, shows that this portion of the house was leased to the County, and he was to supply the furniture and set it up as a Court Room. He also put in the two windows to provide light. It was a valid agreement. They adhered to the contract as long as the Court continued to function here, but when Alonzo Horton came and developed New Town, a hot contest began between the two communities for the possession of the county seat. When the records were forcefully removed from here, Whaley felt it was quite an injustice, and we have letters he addressed to the Board of Supervisors, referring to the fact that his lease had been broken. The Clerk notified him that they were no longer responsible for the use of this house—after all the work he had put in to remodel it for their use. He would bring the matter up periodically with the Board of Supervisors, but it was tabled by them each time it came up."

"In other words, this is the injustice referred to by the ghost?"

"In 1872 he was bitterly engaged in asking redress from the County over this matter, which troubled him some since he did not believe a government official would act in this manner. It was never settled, however, and Whaley was left holding the bag."

"Was there a child in the room upstairs?"

"In the nursery? There were several children there. One child died here. But this was a boy."

Again, later, I saw that the Richardson séance spoke of a boy ghost in the house.

The Whaley House Ghosts

At the very beginning of trance, before I began taping the utterances from Sybil's lips, I took some handwritten notes. The personality, I now saw, who had died of a bad fever had given the faintly pronounced name of Fedor and spoke of a mill where he worked. Was there any sense to this?

"Yes," Mrs. Reading confirmed, "this room we are in now served as a granary at one time. About 1855 to 1867."

"Were there ever any Russians in this area?"

"There was a considerable otter trade here prior to the American occupation of the area. We have found evidence that the Russians established wells in this area. They came into these waters then to trade otters."

"Amazing," I conceded. How could Sybil, even if she wanted to, have known of such an obscure fact?

"This would have been in the 1800's," Mrs. Reading continued. "Before then there were Spaniards here, of course."

"Anything else you wish to comment upon in the trance session you have just witnessed?" I asked.

Mrs. Reading expressed what we all felt.

"The references to the windows opening upstairs, and the ringing of these bells. . . ."

How could Sybil have known all that? Nobody told her and she had not had a chance to acquaint herself with the details of the disturbances.

What remained were the puzzling statements about "the other house." They, too, were soon to be explained. We were walking through the garden now and inspected the rear portion of the Whaley house. In back of it, we discovered to our surprise still another wooden house standing in the garden. I questioned Mrs. Reading about this second house.

"The Pendington House, in order to save it, had to be moved out of the path of the freeway . . . it never belonged to

369

the Whaleys although Thomas Whaley once tried to rent it. But it was always rented to someone else."

No wonder the ghost was angry about "the other house." It had been moved and put on *his* land . . . without his consent!

The name *Cal . . . trop* still did not fall into place. It was too far removed from Whaley and yet everything else that had come through Sybil clearly fitted Thomas Whaley. Then the light began to dawn, thanks to Mrs. Reading's detailed knowledge of the house.

"It was interesting to hear Mrs. Leek say there was a store here once . . ." she explained. "This is correct, there was a store here at one time, but it was not Mr. Whaley's."

"Whose was it?"

"It belonged to a man named Wallack . . . Hal Wallack . . . that was in the seventies."

Close enough to Sybil's tentative pronunciation of a name she caught connected with the house.

"He rented it to Wallack for six months, then Wallack sold out," Mrs. Reading explained.

I also discovered, in discussing the case with Mrs. Reading, that the disturbances really began after the second house had been placed on the grounds. Was that the straw that broke the ghost's patience?

Later, we followed Sybil to a wall adjoining the garden, a wall, I should add, where there was no visible door. But Sybil insisted there had been a French window there, and indeed there was at one time. In a straight line from this spot, we wound up at a huge tree. It was here, Sybil explained, that Whaley and his mother often met—or are meeting, as the case may be.

I was not sure that Mr. Whaley had taken my advice to heart and moved out of what was, after all, his house. Why should he? The County had not seen fit to undo an old wrong.

The Whaley House Ghosts

We left the next morning, hoping that at the very least we had let the restless one know someone cared.

A week later Regis Philbin checked with the folks at Whaley House. Everything was lively—chandelier swinging, rocker rocking; and June Reading herself brought me up to date on July 27th, 1965, with a brief report on activities—other than flesh-and-blood—at the house.

Evidently the child ghost was also still around, for utensils in the kitchen had moved that week, especially a cleaver which swings back and forth on its own. Surely that must be the playful little girl, for what would so important a man as Thomas Whaley have to do in the kitchen? Surely he was much too preoccupied with the larger aspects of his realm, the ancient wrong done him, and the many intrusions from the world of reality. For the Whaley House is a busy place, ghosts or not.

On replaying my tapes, I noticed a curious confusion between the initial appearance of a ghost who called himself Fedor in my notes, and a man who said he had a bad fever. It was just that the man with the fever did not have a foreign accent, but I distinctly recalled "fedor" as sounding odd.

Were they perhaps two separate entities?

My suspicions were confirmed when a letter written May 23, 1966—almost a year later—reached me. A Mrs. Carol DeJuhasz wanted me to know about a ghost at Whaley House . . . no, not Thomas Whaley or a twelve-year-old girl with long hair. Mrs. DeJuhasz was concerned with an historical play written by a friend of hers, dealing with the unjust execution of a man who tried to steal a harbor boat in the 1800's and was caught. Make no mistake about it, nobody had observed this ghost at Whaley House. Mrs. DeJuhasz merely thought he ought to be there, having been hanged in the backyard of the house.

Many people tell me of tragic spots where men have died unhappily but rarely do I discover ghosts on such spots just because of it. I was therefore not too interested in Mrs. DeJuhasz' account of a possible ghost. But she thought that there ought to be present at Whaley House the ghost of this man, called Yankee Jim Robinson. When captured, he fought a sabre duel and received a critical wound in the head. Although alive, he became delirious and was tried without representation, *sick of the fever*. Sentenced to death, he was subsequently hanged in the yard behind the Court House.

Was his the ghostly voice that spoke through Sybil, complaining of the fever and then quickly fading away? Again it was William Richardson who was able to provide a further clue or set of clues to this puzzle. In December of 1966 he contacted me again to report some further experiences at the Whaley House.

"This series of events began in March of this year. Our group was helping to restore an historic old house which had been moved onto the Whaley property to save it from destruction. During our lunch break one Saturday, several of us were in Whaley House. I was downstairs when Jim Stein, one of the group, rushed down the stairs to tell me that the cradle in the nursery was rocking by itself. I hurried upstairs but it wasn't rocking. I was just about to chide Jim for having an overactive imagination when it began again and rocked a little longer before it stopped. The cradle is at least ten feet from the doorway, and a metal barricade is across it to prevent tourists from entering the room. No amount of walking or jumping had any effect on the cradle. While it rocked, I remembered that it had made no sound. Going into the room, I rocked the cradle. I was surprised that it made quite a bit of noise. The old floorboards were somewhat uneven and this in combination with the wooden rockers on the cradle made a very audible sound.

"As a matter of fact, when the Whaleys were furnishing carpeting for the house, the entire upstairs portion was carpeted. This might explain the absence of the noise.

The Whaley House Ghosts

"In June, Whaley House became the setting for an historical play. The play concerned the trial and hanging of a local bad man named Yankee Jim Robinson. It was presented in the Court Room and on the grounds of the mansion. The actual trial and execution had taken place in August of 1852. This was five years before Whaley House was built, but the execution took place on the grounds.

"Yankee Jim was hanged from a scaffold which stood approximately between the present music room and front parlor.

"Soon after the play went into rehearsal, things began to happen. I was involved with the production as an actor and therefore had the opportunity to spend many hours in the house between June and August. The usual footsteps kept up and they were heard by most of the members of the cast at one time or another. There was a group of us within the cast who were especially interested in the phenomenon: myself, Barry Bunker, George Carroll, and his fiancée, Toni Manista. As we were all dressed in period costumes most of the time, the ghosts should have felt right at home. Toni was playing the part of Anna, Thomas Whaley's wife. She said she often felt as if she were being followed around the house (as did we all).

"I was sitting in the kitchen with my back to the wall one night, When I felt a hand run through my hair. I quickly turned around but there was nothing to be seen. I have always felt that it was Anna Whaley who touched me. It was my first such experience and I felt honored that she had chosen me to touch. There is a chair in the kitchen which is made of rawhide and wood. The seat is made of thin strips of rawhide crisscrossed on the wooden frame. When someone sits on it, it sounds like the leather in a saddle. On the same night I was touched, the chair made sounds as if someone were sitting in it, not once but several times. There always seems to be a change in the temperature of a room when a presence enters. The kitchen is no exception. It really got cold in there!

"Later in the run of the show, the apparitions began to appear. The cast had purchased a chair which had belonged to Thomas Whaley and placed it in the front parlor. Soon after, a mist was occasionally seen in the chair or near it. In other parts of the house, especially upstairs, inexplicable shadows and mists began to appear. George Carroll swears that he saw a man standing at the top of the stairs. He walked up the stairs and through the man. The man was still there when George turned around but faded and disappeared almost immediately.

"During the summer, we often smelled cigar smoke when we opened the house in the morning or at times when no one was around. Whaley was very fond of cigars and was seldom without them.

"The footsteps became varied. The heavy steps of the man continued as usual, but the click-click of high heels was heard on occasion. Once, the sound of a small child running in the upstairs hall was heard. Another time, I was alone with the woman who took ticket reservations for *Yankee Jim.*. We had locked the doors and decided to check the upstairs before we left. We had no sooner gotten up the stairs than we both heard footfalls in the hall below. We listened for a moment and then went back down the stairs and looked. No one. We searched the entire house, not really expecting to find anyone. We didn't. Not a living soul.

"Well, this just about brings you up to date. I've been back a number of times since September but there's nothing to report except the usual footfalls, creaks, etc.

"I think that the play had much to do with the summer's phenomena. Costumes, characters, and situations which were known to the Whaleys were reenacted nightly. Yankee Jim Robinson certainly has reason enough to haunt. Many people, myself included, think that he got a bad deal. He was wounded during his capture and was unconscious during most of the trial. To top it off, the judge was a drunk and the jury and townspeople wanted blood. Jim was just unlucky enough to bear their combined wrath.

"His crime? He had borrowed (?) a boat. Hardly a hanging offense. He was found guilty and condemned. He was unprepared to die and thought it was a joke up to the minute they pulled the wagon out from under him. The scaffold wasn't high enough and the fall didn't break his neck. Instead, he slowly strangled for more than fifteen minutes before he died. I think I'd haunt under the same circumstances myself.

"Two other points: another of the guides heard a voice directly in front of her as she walked down the hall. It said, 'Hello, hello.' There was no one else in the house at the time. A dog fitting the description of one of the Whaley dogs has been seen to run into the house, but it can never be found."

Usually, ghosts of different periods do not "run into" one another, unless they are tied together by a mutual problem or common tragedy. The executed man, the proud owner, the little girl, the lady of the house—they form a lively ghost population even for so roomy a house as the Whaley House is.

Mrs. Reading doesn't mind. Except that it does get confusing now and again when you see someone walking about the house and aren't sure if he has bought an admission ticket.

Surely, Thomas Whaley wouldn't dream of buying one. And he is not likely to leave unless and until some action is taken publicly to rectify the ancient wrong. If the County were to reopen the matter and acknowledge the mistake made way back, I am sure the ghostly Mr. Whaley would be pleased and let matters rest. The little girl ghost has been told by Sybil Leek what has happened to her, and the lady goes where Mr. Whaley goes. Which brings us down to Jim, who would have to be tried again and found innocent of stealing the boat.

There is that splendid courtroom there at the house to do

it in. Maybe some ghost-conscious county administration will see fit to do just that.

I'll be glad to serve as counsel for the accused, at no charge.